6/6/97

Dear Wilson,

Hope you enjoy the
book and it helps you
in your work

motivating clients in therapy

motivating clients in therapy:

values, love, and the real relationship

Richard L. Rappaport, Ph.D.

Published in 1997 by
Routledge
29 West 35th Street
New York, NY 10001

Published in Great Britain by
Routledge
11 New Fetter Lane
London EC4P 4EE

Library of Congress Cataloging-in-Publication Data is available
from the Library of Congress.

contents

dedication

To my students in the Washington, D.C., training program, for inspiring and challenging me to formally develop the ideas presented in this book.

The greatest gift as a teacher is to have students who are open without being naive, questioning without being cynical, and above all committed to learning.

I'm especially grateful to Jane Carey, Glyn Ford, Jim and Judy Hall, Gretchen Miller, and Ann and Bill Newland.

I'd also like to acknowledge Rita Hurley-Chiles, Mary Keenan, Michael Morbitzer and Cynthia Treuhitt.

acknowledgments

I'd like to acknowledge the contribution of my wife and colleague, Judy Rappaport, MSN, for her brilliant editing and cogent suggestions on the manuscript. To my son, Max Jacob, whose realness continues to provide living proof. Special thanks to Elaine Burns for her detailed devotion to the technical production of the manuscript.

I'd also like to acknowledge Drs. Sam and Diana Kirschner, who served as extraordinary teachers and mentors in the early phase of my career and who are now respected colleagues and good friends. I'd like to also extend a special note of gratitude to Herb and Miriam Cohen, Allan Goldberg, Howard and Bonnie Horwitz, Judy and Warren Kurnick, Christina and Jeffrey Lurie, and Jim Sharp and Nora Sweeney. They have all been very supportive to me and my family while I was writing this book. Thanks as well to Dr. Nedra Fetterman for her feedback on an earlier draft of the manuscript. Thanks also to Jim Hall for his energy in driving the first few years of the Washington, D.C. training program.

I'd also like to acknowledge my clients, who continue to be a source of great energy for me. I'd especially like to acknowledge my gay and HIV-positive clients, for whom being real may be a matter of survival.

And finally, a special note of appreciation to Bruce Springsteen for providing the soundtrack and musical inspiration for so many of these ideas.

a word about words

I've had the great fortune of being trained as an integrative psychotherapist. As such, I carry few theoretical allegiances. Therefore, I borrow, and prefer to use, terminology from a multitude of sources. The reader may be surprised to see me employ terminology that is normally embedded in a particular theory of psychotherapy. I acknowledge that removing concepts from the context in which they derived poses some risks, but I strongly believe that these risks are outweighed by the benefit of having a common language for psychotherapy (see also Beitman, 1994). In the past, many models of psychotherapy have reinvented the wheel, so to speak, by utilizing existing concepts but giving theirs a different name. I realize, however, that the subtlety of the concepts may be lost or muted when removed from their original theoretical home.

I do offer several original constructs that I name. These include the default regression, therapeutic penetration, the four phases of motivation (primitive, external, internal, and spiritual), the primitive subphase typology (AA, A, B, BB type), etc. Wherever possible, I attempt to use words that do not introduce new jargon to a field that is already inundated with jargon. The future of psychotherapy is, I believe, in commonality and refined synthesis (Wachtel, 1991). I hope this work is a step in that direction.

Moreover, since I tend to favor generic terminology, some readers may be troubled by my lack of specificity regarding what psychotherapy is. I am aware of Kiesler's (1966) and now Fischer's (1995) uniformity myths, but my intention is to reach the broadest audience possible. As such, this work should not be interpreted as a how-to therapy manual since each psychotherapy case presents unique challenges. I offer case illustrations and transcribed material to illustrate and enliven the concepts I discuss.

Finally, model building and alteration are best served by dialogue with others, particularly those who operate from different therapeutic systems. I therefore invite the interested reader to contact me either by mail or telephone.

Dr. Richard L. Rappaport
137 North 21st Street
Philadelphia, PA 19103
(215) 977-8334

chapter 1

motivation and psychotherapy:
an introduction

We are now into the second century of psychotherapy. Several notable pundits have argued quite compellingly that psychotherapy remains an endeavor of questionable utility. There has been a line of investigation and critique dating back to Eysenck (1952) through Hillman and Ventura (1992) which concludes that psychotherapy in general, and depth psychological approaches in particular, despite their consistent popularity, at least among practitioners, have failed to fulfill even the most basic of expectations, symptom amelioration.

A more research-influenced viewpoint also exists. Well-crafted studies and meta-analysis of several studies (Andrews and Harvey, 1981; Garfield, 1992a; Gurman, Kriskern and Pinsoff, 1986; Lambert, Shapiro and Bergin, 1986; Piercy and Sprenkle, 1990; Smith, Glass and Miller, 1980), including a reworking of Eysenck's original data [see McNeilly and Howard (1991)], have led to the well-documented conclusion that psychotherapies of various orientations, using many measures of change, lead to statistically significant results in roughly two-thirds of all cases. Moreover, the so-called Dodo bird verdict reached during and after a spate of outcome studies in the 1970s has, despite some revision (cf. Luborsky, 1995; Norcross, 1995), withstood the cogent observation that "all therapies have won and all must have prizes" (Luborsky, Singer and Luborsky, 1975). There appear to be slight advantages to behavior and cognitively oriented treatments (Antonuccio, 1995; Bellack and Henson, 1993) or to certain combinations of treatments (e.g., cognitive therapy and pharmacotherapy) for particular conditions (e.g., depression) but in all, there is at least moderate empirical support for the generic practice of psychotherapy (Seligman, 1996).

I would like to offer a companion, albeit more optimistic, viewpoint in my interpretation of the extant psychotherapy literature. Simply put, considering the vast array and complexity of life problems that psychotherapists have been called upon to ameliorate, from drug and alcohol addictions, eating disorders, dysfunctional marital relationships, recovery from traumatic life experiences, depression, to conduct disorders, anxiety disorders, psychosomatic conditions, grief reactions, parent-child dysfunctions, and so forth, psychotherapy *works* — in fact, psychotherapy works quite well.

The one caveat to this optimistic view is the assumption of a motivated client. When clients are committed to their own treatment, psychotherapy has the potential of effecting significant change. This simple notion is based on the arguable observation that the great majority of psychotherapy clients are *not* committed to their own treatments; indeed, most clients are resistant to change. The concept of psychotherapeutic resistance has received a good deal of attention in the literature (Allen, 1991; Strean, 1990, 1996; Wachtel, 1982) and has been redefined in several quarters (Anderson and Stewart, 1983). Beyond the literature on paradoxical approaches to therapy (Ascher, 1989) which has received criticism even from its own advocates (Seltzer, 1986), the overwhelmingly popular view of resistance among theoreticians is that it is largely a problem of therapist perception or countertransference (Langs, 1981).

In other words, client resistance is posited to be a construction (Watzlawick, Weakland and Fisch, 1974) of the therapist who is frustrated by the client's refusal to engage in behavior or activities that the *practitioner* deems appropriate but that the client may not. In this viewpoint, there exists at least an image of an overeager, boundary-less, directive, or omnipotent therapist who "knows what's best" and a client who has his or her own ideas about change (or non-change).

Still, for all the philosophical and sociopolitical appeal of such concepts of resistance, with their accompanying buzz-phrases like "respecting the client's resistance," everyday practitioners struggle mightily with clients who come to therapy requesting help, yet sabotage and undermine our, as well as their own, best efforts. This is not surprising; in fact, addressing self-and-other sabotage may be at the heart of psychotherapeutic work.

As practitioners, we are not short on our collective ability to offer support; to listen empathetically; to give advice; to direct clients into a fruitful area of dialogue, exchange, and emotional experience; to help them discover lost aspects of themselves; to help them listen to significant others; to help them be more assertive and self-affirming; to guide them through difficult life transitions; to help them overcome fears and worries that block them from full self-expression, and so forth. We have in our collective arsenals a plethora of techniques and approaches to a wide and varied assortment of client problems. What we lack, we may find by consulting with a community of practitioners and experts directly or indirectly, through workshops, books, and journals. The psychotherapy and mental health literature is burgeoning with more concepts, ideas, and treatments than one could possibly consume, let alone utilize.

We know how to treat mental disorders from a variety of perspectives. Sometimes competing models confuse us and sometimes the treatments (e.g., psychoanalytically oriented therapies, self-psychological approaches) require a long-term commitment on the part of the client; but the treatment *is* available. Sometimes, the treatments call for the client to be willing to take various kinds of risks (e.g., confronting family-of-origin members, expressing real feelings of despair, engaging in difficult behaviors) but again, the treatment *is* available. Simply put, we have the treatments, and for the most part these treatments work (Lipsey and Wilson, 1993). The skill and talent of the therapist and the potency of the therapist's approach are factors here as well, of course. Yet there are many capable and talented therapists employing an enormous number of approaches that, given the motivational level of the client, will effect change.

More specifically, systematic desensitization *works* at alleviating many phobic conditions (Barlow and Waddell, 1985). Behaviorally-oriented sex therapy techniques *work* at alleviating premature ejaculation and disorders of desire (Kaplan, 1979). Cognitive-behavioral therapies *work* in the treatment of depression (Antonuccio, 1995). Structural family therapy (Minuchin and Fishman, 1981) *works* in the treatment of adolescent anorexia (Sergant, Liebman, and Silver, 1985). Various forms of marital therapy are effective in treating distressed marital relationships (Dunn and Schwelsel, 1995). There are plenty of good-enough treatments, techniques, and theories of psychotherapy, and we keep getting better at refining these treatments.

The fields of cognitive therapy, behavior therapy, psychodynamic therapy, experiential therapy, object relations, marital and family therapy at the level of theory and technical intervention continue to develop and shape increasingly refined methods (e.g., Robins, 1993; Scaturo, 1994). The treatment approaches as we approach the millennium are, despite protests to the contrary, state-of-the-art. We've had a hundred years of psychotherapy (cf. Freedheim, 1992; Zeig, 1987) and theoretically, scientifically, and technically we've made great advancements in the treatment of an array of mental disorders.

The condition I set, that of a committed client, is no small one, however. Much, if not most, of the time therapists do not work with clients who are motivated to change. The average course of psychotherapy is between five and six sessions (Phillips, 1988). Sometimes clients lose motivation to change from the period of time between making telephone contact with a mental health professional and the time of the scheduled first appointment (Saunders, 1993; Weiss and Schaie, 1958). Some, perhaps those in the greatest need for it, never even seriously consider treatment (Kazdin, Mazurice and Siegel, 1994; Vessey and Howard, 1993). The no-show and cancellation rates at community mental health centers are discouragingly high (Beck et al., 1987; Sartorius et al., 1993; Sue, McKinney and Allen, 1976). Therapists in private practice, with clients less concerned with daily survival questions (as in community settings) also report high rates of therapy drop-outs and premature terminations (Koss, 1979). Among families who begin treatment 40 to 60 percent terminate prematurely (Kazdin, Stolar and L'Marciano, 1995). The advent and popularity of brief therapies (Binder, 1993) and even single-session therapy (Rosenbaum, 1994; Talmon, 1990) reflect not only shifting third-party-payer mentalities but the reality that precious few clients remain for a full course of treatment (Wierzbicki and Pekarik, 1993).

Even the most motivated of clients may lose their commitment to change. Relapse rates for many disorders are high (Barlow, 1993). Nowhere is this more evident than in addictions treatment where clients may remain sober, motivated, and treatment-responsive for a period of time and then relapse in three, six, or twelve months (Helzer et al., 1985; Horvath, 1993; Institute of Medicine, 1990; Simpson and Joe, 1993).

What we often discover is that underlying many disorders (defined here as syndromes of various symptoms) are dysfunctional personality structures (such as clients displaying borderline, narcissistic, or schizoidal tendencies); interlocking systemic forces (such as dysfunctional family-of-origin or marital relationships); and traumatic life-events, usually in childhood (such as sexual, physical, and emotional abuse and abandonment).

As well, there are more clients entering psychotherapy with various diffuse complaints of general malaise or specifically interested in addressing their problematic way of relating to others or working through a contemporary life event. This is the level of psychotherapeutic work where presenting complaints tend to recede and all clients tend to resemble one another and ourselves. Problems in living, choosing a more satisfying and rewarding career, rearing psychologically healthier children, or developing a more intimate and satisfying marriage, are often core issues that exist for virtually all psychotherapy clients, whether presented as such or not. Here is where therapists become the secular ministers that London (1964), Frank (1973), and Schofield (1964) first hinted at in the 1960s.

We may call these the common-factors problems of therapy in that all clients have issues in these areas to varying degrees. Again, many clients come to treatment unaware that more salient problems exist in an area other than the one in which they are requesting help. A woman may come to us because she is feeling depressed and unfulfilled. We may find that six to eight sessions of cognitive work or a combination of cognitive therapy and the common-factors provision of therapeutic attentiveness or empathy provides enough of a positive impact to ameliorate the presenting symptomatology. Moreover, the woman may, after a period of some improvement, come to her eighth session highly agitated, complaining now more forcefully of her husband's lack of support or subtle or overt abusiveness. Alternatively and perhaps more typically, she may have terminated therapy after the sixth session, thanking the therapist for all his or her help.

When the therapist suggests she bring her husband into a session or makes a recommendation for a course of couples therapy, the woman may or may not be motivated to do so. If she is interested, she may lose her motivation by the ninth session when she reports that her husband refuses to participate in any therapy. Or she may cancel the session, leaving a message on the therapist's answering machine saying financial obligations have arisen which make it impossible for her to continue therapy at this time. Similarly, she may lose motivation by the tenth session, after her husband has offered up a series of complaints and criticism of *her* which she prefers not to address, in the couple's ninth session.

Or the husband and wife may get into a prototypical argument—this one about whether to see her therapist or his therapist, or a neutral therapist, should it turn out that he, too, is in individual therapy. Our client may terminate treatment altogether at this point and reexperience the same depression that she did when first entering therapy. She may or may not get further professional help to resolve it.

This is by no means meant to be an argument for partners to be involved in the therapy of their spouses (a viewpoint I am sympathetic with) since other similar dilemmas may occur even if the partner has been included (Rappaport, 1991a). Nor do I mean to suggest that interlocking systemic forces are the only, or are always, ones associated with individual psychopathology, although I would contend that much of the time they are. Rather, I mean to suggest that we have good-enough treatments, whether it be cognitive therapy for certain kinds of depression, marital therapy for certain kinds of couples difficulties, or for that matter, integrated cognitive-couples therapy.

We may or may not, of course, be good at recommending, implementing, or referring clients into those treatments systematically (Beutler, 1986, 1989). Yet, even if we could get the client into those good-enough treatments systematically, we may be faced with a resistant, frightened, or overwhelmed, unmotivated client.

In our hypothetical case example, the cognitive therapy worked, as it often does in the reality of daily practice. Couples therapy of some sort would likely bring some benefit as well. Do we need to get increasingly better at assessing Paul's (1967) advocacy of what treatment for whom, when? Absolutely. Do our theoretical and technical models of cognitive and couples therapies need more fine tuning in terms of providing better treatments for varied populations of clients? Yes. Are all psychotherapeutic models equally valid, or for that matter even reliable, among practitioners? No. Are all models equally applicable and appropriate for the assortment of problems they purport to account for? No. But all in all, I am less worried about progress in better treatments for more people. In my view, we are consistently approaching this telos.

What I do worry about is our lack of understanding and insight into the problem of client resistance. I am similarly worried about therapist anemia toward the notion of motivating clients to change. Our focus continues to be on theory, model building, epistemology—essentially anything *but* the messy, nitty-gritty, in-your-face problem of client motivation. *This*, I contend, is our greatest failure.

Yet practitioners sit in peer groups, seek out supervision, and go to workshops, generally to deal with these very problems. Distinguished and seasoned psychotherapeutic veterans wax eloquent about the "art" of therapy or the need for experience in dealing with problematic non-textbook cases.

But this is wholly inadequate. I have never seen a client who is a "textbook" example of anything. The *essence* of therapy resides as much within the vicissitudes of the therapeutic relationship as in our theories and techniques. We tend to give lip service to this idea or treat the therapy relationship as a function of our treatment model with roles prescribed by the theoretical orientation or approach. The conceptualization that theoretical orientation controls the variable, therapist relationship behavior, is unsupported empirically (Rappaport, 1988). Theoretical orientation is in any case a weak predictor of therapist behavior, particularly the operations associated with relationship factors (Lazarus, 1989; 1993). The problem remains, however, that therapist relationship behavior, for all its hypothetical and confirmed potency (Lambert, 1989), is one of the least understood variables when removed from the context of specific treatment approaches or orientations (Norcross, 1993).

Therapist relational behavior, or as I prefer to call it, therapist relational posture, is less a function of theoretical orientation than of therapist values and personality (Rappaport, 1991b; Rappaport and Kirschner, 1991). While observers and researchers note that most psychoanalysts do not and (perhaps dating back even as far as Freud [see Roazen, 1995 and Vogel, 1994]) never did operate on the principle of a blank screen or anything even closely approximating it, the mythology surrounding these relational roles persists. How many Rogerian therapists enact the prescribed role of empathic kindred spirit (Weinrach, 1990, 1995)? And, what of eclectic and integrative therapists, who, depending upon the survey, make up from 30 to 70 percent of all therapists (Norcross, Alford and DeMichele, 1992). Indeed, orientation tells us little about clinical operations (Buckley et al., 1979).

How important is the relational posture variable? It tells us about the therapist's view and, more important, operations, in terms of the scope and level of therapeutic directiveness, responsibility-taking, the degree of intimacy allowed for, the distribution of power in the therapeutic relationship, the activity level of the therapist, the therapist's position on client dependency, etc. Yet in the field we continue to act *as if* theoretical orientation alone controls the role behavior of the therapist.

What models *are* therapists operating on as they take these various value positions? Beyond a few well-intentioned suggestions, (e.g., Abroms, 1978; Aponte, 1986) we lack established, well-conceived models. What we have instead largely are private and idiosyncratic to individual clinicians, a problematic state of affairs at best (Rappaport, 1993a).

To the extent that we apply pristine theoretical models to each client, the clinician is never forced to make many value-based postural decisions. Unfortunately, this is rarely, if ever, the case. Therapists are bombarded with a host of hour-by-hour decisions to make, generally without a model to guide them. For example: if a client wishes to terminate therapy prematurely, how does the therapist manage this situation? What is the therapist's viewpoint on how much change is possible for each client? How does the therapist encourage the client? Or, is it the therapist's view that the client will search out their own solutions? What these questions have in common is that they address the motivation-resistance dimension that in my view is at the heart of psychotherapeutic practice. Our theoretical models do not adequately handle these dilemmas.

In fact, what treatment models tend to do is to label as "resistant" any client who does not fit or improve in one's preferred theoretical model. I call this phenomenon the "not-ifying" of clients. In other words, there is one model of treatment for clients who fit, stay in therapy, or get better, and then there is a corresponding "not" model of treatment for clients who prematurely terminate or do not get better— for whom the model does not work.

These clients tend to be accounted for in one of two ways. Sometimes the resistant client is labeled as "not ready for treatment" or given puzzling assessments such as being in some form of "pre-therapy" to gain "ego-strength." Potential analytic patients who are resistant to "getting on the couch" are labeled as "not ready" for psychoanalysis. The obvious idea that the model cannot or does not account for what's happening and more significantly, that another model accounts better for the same phenomenon appears to go unrecognized. A contemporary example of this is the Imago Relationship model of couples therapy (Hendrix, 1990). It purports to account for virtually all kinds of couples and presenting complaints (an admirable quality in a model, I believe). Yet, since I first learned of the model I have questioned how it was possible to engage regressed couples with individual personality dysfunction in intimate dialogue with each other, with the therapist solely in the role of facilitator.

While I agree with Hendrix's supporting theory of the therapist's facilitating the natural process of couples reparenting each other, I have repeatedly found (as have others, in work that predated Hendrix; see Kirschner and Kirschner, 1986) that there was a significant minority of couples who required a combination of individual work and carefully orchestrated couples work with the therapist in a more active reparental role. Recently, I heard that some of Hendrix's adherents now call these couples "pre-dialogic," meaning that they presumably require more active input and individual work with the therapist, which many Imago therapists now do.

We thus have many treatment models continuously reinventing the wheel. To label one group of clients "dialogic" and "ready" for your model, and another "pre-dialogic" and hence "not ready" for your model, and then suggest that the "not-ready" groups get "something else" is problematic. This "something else" is an already available, more sophisticated treatment approach. What is "pre-dialogic therapy" and do we really need to discover it?

Let's briefly explore another example of this. Family therapy and theory represented a paradigmatic shift when it was developed in the 1950s and 1960s (Hoffman, 1981). By the late 1970s, however, many theorists and practitioners found that the pure systemic models did not adequately handle or explain all phenomena, just like individually oriented models before them (Lebow, 1984). Similarly, I once asked a leading structural family theorist how Structural Family Therapy (SFT) explains individual behavior if actual family members are deceased, since the model only addresses the influence of contemporary family members on an individual's behavior. Indeed, how would one offer treatment in such cases? I am certain that I was not the first to ask such an obvious question and be given what seemed to be the standard reply that the individual family member would tend to find another social system that in some way mimicked (*sic*, my word) the family-of-origin, essentially enacting a similar familial role.

What the SFT therapist was clearly talking about, I had to assume, presupposed the concept of parental or familial introjection, a phenomenon explained rather well by object-relations theory (Fairbairn, 1952) and in the family therapy field by Framo (1970). Now if people tend to do this when family members are deceased, how can one not integrate object relations concepts into the SFT model when family members are alive? I am not raising this issue to stress the need for integrative models, although I support such efforts, but rather to point out that in virtually every model of therapy that purports to account for virtually all client behaviors (e.g., psychoanalysis, behavior therapy, cognitive therapy, Bowen family-systems therapy), resistance tends to be explained as any aspect of client behavior that does not fit the preferred model. The fact that another model may explain the behavior more efficiently or thoroughly is generally not considered.

Another prototypical theory-bound model for explaining client resistance arises when the theoretical model does *not* purport to explain everything. Certain models hold themselves out as a treatment for a particular kind of client with a particular kind of problem. These specific models tend to be offshoots of large theoretical approaches. There is an established model of treating acting-out (or conduct disordered, for those who prefer DSM-IV terminology) adolescents within the context of family therapy. If families are motivated such a highly specified treatment program will tend to work. Just as with motivated sex therapy clients, teaching the Seamons technique or reciprocal inhibition for premature ejaculation and disorders of desire respectively, will tend to work (Kaplan, 1979, 1992). Systematic desensitization tends to work with most phobic clients (Barlow, 1993). And if we return to the Imago-therapy example, if we have a motivated couple who are committed to remain together, and develop their marriage, the approach is a sound one and the techniques tend to work.

Another related phenomenon among practitioners in attempting to deal with client resistance is what I call model-hopping. In other words, if SFT doesn't produce the expected result, the clinician decides to see the adolescent in individual reality therapy (Glasser, 1965) or sends the client for a psychiatric medication consult, "suspecting organicity." Therapists will sometimes contend that a certain client is appropriate for a particular type of therapy, presumably because the presenting nosology "fits" a particular model.

This kind of thinking is at best a sloppy eclecticism. The worst aspect of model-hopping, though, rests with its inability to understand problems of client resistance as being more of a function of the therapist's *relational* failure to motivate the client versus a deficiency in the theoretical precepts and technical aspects of the approach. Model-hopping leads to premature *model*-blaming, which can be as destructive as the *client*-blaming phenomenon of explaining resistance problems. The inadequacies of the therapist's relational abilities is a potentially more fruitful source of exploration.

Directing reasonably motivated clients into appropriate specific treatments with a competent and committed practitioner is one problem I am hopeful about the field's ability to eventually resolve. Systematic eclecticism (Beutler, 1986; Beutler and Clarkson, 1990; Beutler and Consoli, 1993; Lazarus, Beutler and Norcross, 1992) is one suggested model. The problem that I am *less* hopeful about and which is the subject of this book, is a client's motivation to enter and successfully remain in these treatments. I am convinced that given a motivated client, we have successful treatments available, and if we direct the motivated client into the appropriate treatment with the appropriate practitioner, with the time, resources, and training, we will reach this end.

The field is in a primitive state of affairs on the issue of motivating clients. I continue to speak of unmotivated and resistant clients, not to engage in the clandestine therapeutic sport of client-blaming. Virtually all clients lose motivation to change at one point or another in treatment. Most, in fact, come to therapy hopeless and despairing (Frank and Frank, 1991). We should not be surprised by this; indeed, that is why most clients are there. Generally speaking, people who are motivated to solve their problems can do so without the help of a therapist, using existing social structures and institutions and therapeutically oriented relationships, like friends, family, and spouses. Self-help methodologies that predate the popularizing of psychotherapy, like Alcoholics Anonymous, are thriving, and for *motivated* people, tend to be very successful.

Psychotherapy, in my view, must address the hopelessness and despair that form the core of resistance to change. Our ability to motivate clients to grow and change is our greatest challenge. Yet beyond the theory-specific ideas about resistance I mentioned previously, therapists do not understand motivation well, nor do they even see their role as needing to motivate clients. Generally, motivation has been conceptualized as a client-factor that is solely within the realm and locus of control of the client (Beckman, 1980; Miller, 1985; Horvath, 1993). While, of course, the client is *ultimately* responsible for changing or not changing, the influence of the therapist is paramount in altering the client's level of motivation at any given time. Yet our field has no generic models of motivation to speak of, and the few notable exceptions emanate from the addictions literature (Horvath, 1993; Prochaska and DiClemente, 1982; Prochaska, DiClemente and Norcross, 1992).

Why this is so has more to do with a series of continuing sociopolitical forces that tend to pull in the direction of minimizing or diminishing overt therapist influence. I highlight the word *overt* here because covertly therapists engage in many operations that are unaccounted for by theory (see Rappaport, 1991b).

Since the field's origins are in the realm of psychoanalysis, where overt psychotherapist influence was taboo, the blank-screen therapeutic role paradigm thrives in various forms, approximations, and variations. The influence of psychoanalysis has been so great that it was until the 1970s virtually synonymous with psychotherapy (and in some insulated quarters still is). Any therapist who *claimed* to enact a posture (e.g., offering advice) other than the blank screen was viewed as a non-therapist; that is, a counselor.

Continuing on through Rogers (1951), even the more active therapies such as behavioral, cognitive, experiential, and family therapies generally prescribed a relational posture, such as "facilitator," "consultant," or "tactician," which tended to diminish the direct influence of the therapist, albeit only in theory. By the 1980s, ethical concerns about gender and power took hold, further preventing the field from developing explicit models of therapist influence and motivation. Again, these issues tended not to affect everyday considerations in practice (Lazarus, 1993), as common knowledge strongly suggests therapists continue to enact roles and engage in behaviors designed to directly influence the client. The clandestine nature of such operations, however, keeps innovation stagnant, and puts too much power in the hands of the individual practitioner, with no model to offer direction and feedback (Held, 1995; Rappaport, 1991c).

Heretofore, motivation has been posited as a client-factor outside the therapist's purview, let alone influence. Clients are seen as motivated or not to varying degrees, and this is what the client brings into the treatment situation; it's part of the client's raw materials, so to speak. Many experienced therapists *intuitively* understand motivation to be a core issue in therapy and have ideas about how to manage it, work around it, bypass it, ignore it, or play with it. A few have written what one could call the seasoned-practitioner genre of psychotherapy books, which talk about difficult cases and the like. But if indeed client motivation is a factor separate and distinct from the therapist's standardized operations, that is, the therapy itself, then we need to understand what contributes to client motivation and how practitioners of various orientations can harness it therapeutically.

To briefly summarize, our current approaches to motivation-resistance are largely reactive. For instance, we offer Treatment A. Should the client resist Treatment A we say the client is "not ready" for treatment (the "not-ifying" phenomenon) or decide Treatment A is inappropriate and determine that Treatment B, C, or D would be better (the model-hopping phenomenon). What are needed are meta-models that cut across therapeutic modalities. This book will offer one such model.

How do we increase the motivation level of the unmotivated client? How do we explain why a client comes to us extremely motivated to change and then three months later, on the brink of growth, terminates therapy? How do we maintain the motivation level of an already motivated client? What factors contribute to client resistance?

This book will attempt to address these questions by offering a comprehensive and synthesized model of motivation and resistance. The model has its roots in a therapeutic approach, Comprehensive Family Therapy (CFT). Most recently referred to as Comprehensive Therapy (CT), developed originally by Arthur Stein (1980) and formalized by Sam and Diana Kirschner [see Kirschner and Kirschner (1986) Kirschner and Kirschner (1990) and Kirschner, Kirschner and Rappaport (1993) and Kirschner and Kirschner (in press)] and their associates at the Institute for Comprehensive Family Therapy during the 1980s, CT integrates potent elements of psychodynamic, systems, and behavioral theory into a treatment model encompassing individual, couple, and family therapies.

My approach here, however, is to extract the elements of CT that are not treatment specific. In other words, this book is not meant as a how-to-model of doing therapy, although the model offers certain prescriptions. Rather, the book is offered as a means of explaining client motivation and resistance that in principle can be applied by practitioners of virtually any school of therapy. The model is metatheoretical in that it provides a framework or a way of choosing among types of treatments, techniques, but most significantly, therapist relational postures (TRP). I see TRP as a therapist-factor largely separate from theoretical orientation (see also Arnkoff, 1995 and Poznanski, 1995).

TRP is hence defined as the way in which the practitioner chooses to relate to his or her clients, based more on the therapist's values, philosophy, and personality. TRP is further defined as the collection of beliefs and behaviors that represent the therapist's basic attitude and stance vis-à-vis his or her clients, himself or herself as a therapeutic agent, and the therapy itself. TRP is a reflection of the clinician's values regarding his or her role as a therapist and the nature of therapeutic change. Therapist posture is best thought of as a clinician's basic concept toward the therapeutic endeavor, more reflective of a system of values than theoretical orientation.[1]

---

1. I am applying English and English's (1958) definition, in which 'value' is defined as the degree of worth assigned to an idea or an activity and where value system is defined as the more or less coherent set of values that regulates a person's conduct, often without awareness.

I am specifically interested in the beliefs, decisions, and thoughts that clinicians of varied schools, disciplines, and settings routinely make in the generic practice of psychotherapy. For example, if a client does not show up for a scheduled appointment, whether the therapist should contact the client and in what manner is not an issue addressed in the theoretical models of therapy, but rather reflects the clinician's values about the appropriate limits of therapeutic responsibility. Similarly, the issue of whether therapists should physically touch their clients (Kertay and Reviere, 1993) may reflect the clinician's values about appropriate interpersonal or therapeutic distance (Schwartz, 1993), or how the therapist responds to the client's direct questions (Clickauf-Hughes and Chance, 1995) is another example of the kinds of issues and questions that may seem minor, but in the context of the client's experience, are not (Sugarman and Martin, 1995). If one asks a client who has a positive relationship with his or her therapist about their treatment, they will not talk about the superior techniques or approach of the therapist, but will generally talk about the therapist as a person *within* the therapeutic approach: "She's tough on me—she doesn't let me get away with anything." Or, "He's always there when I need him." Or, "She's a real person—she doesn't hide behind a facade."

In my view, one that I will reiterate throughout this book, therapy occurs around the so-called edges, when the therapist and client together and separately take interpersonal risks. The therapist's willingness not to be role-bound, when appropriate, often leads to interpersonal risk-taking behavior which forms the core of corrective emotional and transactional experiences (Weinberger, 1993).

These experiences tend to modify transferential distortions and allow the client to abate or overcome the foundational fears of engulfment, annihilation, and most significantly, abandonment. The abatement of these powerfully dysfunctional fears frees the client to risk changes in whatever areas there is a deficiency. In other words, to the extent the client abates these fears, s/he will be more motivated to enter a phase of therapy that is potentially growthful. To the extent that these foundational fears remain untouched in therapy, the client will be resistant to enter new phases of growth.

TRP, then, may be broken down into two components. First, there is the relational posture that is generic, in other words, the therapist's essential model and view of the therapeutic relationship regardless of who the client is. This includes the therapist's basic attitude toward client dependency, therapeutic directiveness, power, and intimacy, etc. Specific TRP is referred to here as the therapist's stance, or the particular posture a therapist enacts in response to individual client(s). For example, a therapist may choose to be more or less directive with a particular client, based on the characteristics of that client. In contrast, generic TRP may be thought of as the basic tendency or potential of the therapist. In other words, a therapist may have a core belief that, in general, therapeutic directiveness is a valid approach (or stated differently, as valid as nondirectiveness) or that client dependency is an acceptable albeit temporary, course of events in treatment. Yet, specifically, s/he may choose to discourage dependency in particular situations or with particular clients. This book will address both forms of TRP.

Despite the significance of the motivation issue for the everyday psychotherapy practitioner, theoreticians and researchers have avoided explicating motivational phenomena. The reasons for this are closely related to therapeutic anathema toward what Wiesskopf-Joelson (1982) calls the *enfant terrible* of psychotherapy, values.

why motivation is an ignored construct in psychotherapy:
the myth of client motivation

the myth of value neutrality lives on

Constructs in the psychotherapy field are subject to fashion and aesthetic preference (Ryle, 1995). Certain constructs have inherent appeal; others connote negative images. While the aesthetic preference of therapists has changed over the last fifty or so years, the appeal-ing constructions, whether philosophically, scientifically, or practically sound, continue to survive and often thrive, albeit in different forms and embedded in other theories.

An example of this is the concept of therapeutic neutrality and that therapy is a valueless or value-neutral enterprise. Therapists, for some time now, have recognized that therapy is *not* a valueless endeavor (Glad, 1959; Kessel and McBrearty, 1967; Samler, 1960; Weisskopf-Joleson, 1953). And while I'm certain the practice of most therapists would reflect that, the implication of that notion is rarely explicated (Rappaport, 1994).

If therapy is not value-free, then it follows that therapists should feel comfortable, if not ethically bound, to express their values openly in their writings, at conferences, with colleagues, and, most importantly, to their clients. Their ideas about how people *should* live their lives, what's healthy and not healthy would guide them in their therapeutic role and be openly examined in the therapeutic community (Patterson, 1989; Schwartz, 1990). Such statements of desirable operations are sparse in a literature dominated instead by psychopathology and assessments of what's wrong with people, that is, what to move clients away *from*. The idea of assisting people to move *toward* something of the therapist's choosing usually afforded the label of values imposition. Imposing a value is viewed as undesirable.

Yet the term, *imposing*, despite our intuitive dislike of its implications is methodologically correct and philosophically unavoidable (Tjeltveit, 1986). Values are always imposed (Beutler, 1979). However, when we conceive of the word "imposed" we unnecessarily associate it with the idea of forcing someone to follow something. Mythical notions of the great power of the therapist to the contrary, therapists are by definition wholly incapable of *forcing* anyone to do anything except perhaps in court-ordered treatment, a concept I oppose. The client holds the power by the inalienable right to end treatment at any time. As a matter of fact, clients exercise this option quite often to the dismay of their therapists, on a disturbingly routine basis. Between 20 percent and 60 percent of all clients who initiate treatment in a clinic setting do not return after a single visit (Baekland and Lundwall, 1975). Wierzbicki and Pekarik's (1993) meta-analysis cited a 47 percent dropout rate for psychotherapy. A mean course of psychotherapy is a mere six sessions, regardless of type of therapy or presenting problem (Phillips, 1988). As the number of sessions increases, the number of clients continuing treatment decreases greatly (Pollack, Mordecai and Gumpert, 1992). Indeed, few clients complete psychotherapies that are moderate to long-term in duration (Baekeland and Lundwall, 1975). Clients often cancel or do not show for psychotherapy appointments (Beck, et al. 1987). When they do, the rate of noncompliance with treatment procedures and goals is great.

Lest my intention be misunderstood, I do not mean this as a criticism of psychotherapy clients.[1] I am merely stating, as most everyday practitioners will attest, some facts of therapeutic life. It is this way because psychotherapy is a noncompulsory activity that one may enter and exit at any time. The freedom to exit is one mechanism by which clients may reject the values of the therapist and/or the therapy. One may argue that the freedom to exit is an insufficient safeguard against potential abuses of therapeutic power since clients, perhaps by definition, tend to be weak and dependent, hence inordinately subject to inappropriate therapeutic manipulation.[2] But again, if clients are so passive, weak, and dependent, then why do so few complete therapy to the satisfaction of their therapists? The influence of the 50-minute-per-week psychotherapy session is, I'm afraid, minimal at best. Moreover,

---

1. Quite often these statistics are cited as empirical support for briefer treatment models (see Rosenbaum, 1994). Implied in these arguments is the suggestion that longer term therapies are unnecessary or inappropriate. While I agree that this set of data supports a continued emphasis on brief therapies, we cannot escape the conclusion that psychotherapists largely fail at engaging clients in treatment that is longer than one to six sessions.

2. I use the word inappropriate here to qualify since I contend therapy is always manipulative, whether obviously, such as in the case of paradoxical techniques, or less overtly and more subtly in the case of psychoanalysis.

most therapists as you may have noted, are not exactly the quintessence of power.

Having said that, is there a small subset of particularly vulnerable clients who would not be inclined to exit deleterious treatment by a self-serving therapist whose tendency to exploit clients for their own gain, whether that be monetary or as fodder for his or her own narcissism (see Clickauf-Hughes and Mehlman, 1995 for a discussion of therapist narcissism)? Absolutely. Yet this does not accurately portray the vast majority of clients or therapists for that matter. Most clients are not dependent upon their therapists and most therapists tend to resist clients being dependent upon them. Indeed, clients have little problem rejecting therapeutic directions, suggestion, or advice. They disagree with interpretative insights. They refuse, for example, to bring their spouse to session should the therapist suggest it.

So the values of the therapist are always imposed. Therapists have the freedom to impose them and clients have the freedom to reject them. I state this as unidirectional simply to make the point that clients have ultimate control over the process of therapy. They decide when to start it, with whom, and how often to attend. The therapist, on the other hand, has minimal power in the process. S/he can terminate the treatment as well, yet there are ethical principles concerning the abandonment of clients in need to counteract that. Clients are not bound to any such principle and routinely "abandon" their therapists. To comprehend the power imbalance simply compare the vast number of clients who end their therapies with the number of therapies ended by the therapist. Also, therapists can be easily replaced. Clients, on the other hand, are a valued commodity (as the consumer) to the therapist and less easily replaced for most practitioners.

Yes, there are clients who feel abandoned, feel helpless and victimized, and *believe* they have no power in the therapy relationship. But let us not confuse the psychic life of that client with the reality of the therapy situation. There are some clients who are terrorized at the thought of losing their therapist, of being abandoned by an authority figure at a time of needfulness. Unless this is actually enacted by the therapist, we call such phenomenon negative transference. As further irony, many clients terminate treatment prematurely as a kind of pre-emptive strike because they anticipate this feeling of need, helplessness, or impending dependency. But we need not take steps to counter the therapists' excessive power to influence clients who feel this way, since this would represent a reaction to phenomena that is not real in the first place. If we do then we are essentially *enacting* the client's transference. In other words, the therapist is being cautious about imposing values upon a client who fears a kind of dependency that is truly not possible since the client is free to end the relationship at any time. Furthermore, to alter psychotherapeutic philosophy in the direction of being less influential because some clients may experience this essentially intrapsychic phenomenon is unnecessarily restrictive.

I do not mean to suggest that dependency is not possible in the therapy situation. In fact, I see dependency as a desirable event, assuming it is in the best interest of the client and it functions in the service of the client's growth. But such a dependency is mutually agreed upon and entered into with the client holding the option to end the dependent relationship at any time by any variety of means up to and including termination of the relationship.

Do people enter dependent relationships which they can realistically exit, but have difficulty exiting? Yes. People may develop (negatively) dependent relationships with alcohol, drugs, and people. By people we would certainly include psychotherapists. But, as is pointed out to addicts as a matter of course, there is choice. One may pose biological and sociological challenges to such an argument, for example, how much choice does an African-American physically addicted user of heroin living in a culture of racism, classism, and economic despair truly hold?

But we cannot lose sight of the fact that at the heart of it, and indeed its beauty, psychotherapy is a process that involves affective, cognitive, behavioral, or contextual change. The essence of change lies in a philosophy of choice and free will. Clients who come to therapy who are more environmentally and constitutionally privileged have more choices available to them, no doubt, but therapy even for the most disadvantaged cannot be determined.

Whatever percentage of the variance in the hands of the disadvantaged and their change agents (or "fate" for that matter), even if only 20 percent, then that is the 20 percent we need to address as therapists. It is this 20 percent that present possibilities and hope. The 80 percent that is biologically or socioeconomically determined is out of the control of therapists and better attended by scientists, academicians, and politicians. Furthermore, we must always remember that biological or sociological determinism may provide useful predictions for large numbers of subgroups but cannot predict for any one person.

As therapists we need only concern ourselves with the ideography of single cases such as the person who sits across from us on our couch. We must believe that our client has the freedom to make choices, among them entering or exiting, any kind of relationship the therapist offers.

Yet there exists an atmosphere of suspicion toward any therapist or therapeutic theory that explicitly imposes values, even though as I've stated, clients may, and do, reject those values, at any time. Therapists are enjoined to be careful, to pay close attention to countertransference, and the like. Hence, the myth of value neutrality lives on. One cannot be careful *not* to impose their viewpoint. One can only be careful about what those values are and the appropriateness of those values for their specific client situation. Finally, we must examine how those values are transmitted during treatment (Rappaport, 1994).

Even therapeutic silence can reflect a values position. A male client who behaves abusively, whether physically or emotionally, toward his wife, who is met with silence or benign questions and interpretations has the value of nonintrusiveness in the face of emotional or physical violence imposed upon him. While I do not wish to debate the clinical utility of such an intervention, I point out that the intervention is rooted in a values position and embedded within, an intention.

The therapist evaluates and judges the behavior and the actor as even the most benign question (e.g., "What were you feeling before you hit her?") implies the intent of questioner. In this case, the implicit value is, if the client understands the pattern and range of his feelings, it might help him restrain his impulses in the future. If the client responds, "I don't care, she deserved it [maltreatment]," the therapist is then confronted with another value-based decision. The therapist makes a determined response of one sort or another. This response is not countertransferential in nature, it is based rather on the practitioner's ideas about what a healthy marital relationship looks like, and even more significantly, the limits of therapeutic responsibility.

In my own clinical practice, I have responded very strongly and explicitly by using value-based words in an attempt to impact the client in such situations. And, as I have stated previously, the client retains the freedom to exit if he believes my response to be nontherapeutic or simply not to his liking. Much more often than not, the client chooses not to exit (although it is not my intention here to point out the clinical efficacy of such an approach). Rather, I simply point out what my view of therapeutic responsibility is, and that it is my role to help this client change problematic behaviors within the safe frame of the professional 50-minute relationship.

Another therapist may disagree and never use value-based language with the client, possibly believing that by doing so, s/he would be extricating the client from responsibility-taking. I am aware that my client may cease the noxious behavior and change "for me" because I made an issue of it. As you'll see later in the book, this externalized motivation is to be expected at this point. I do not have a problem that he may be motivated to change his behavior, let's say, to maintain our relationship or my respect for him.

The client of the practitioner who chooses not to use value-based language may cease the behavior and change for the very same reason, however, since clients are capable of interpreting the intention of the practitioner from any number of verbal and nonverbal cues. In other words, if the therapist believes it is wrong to physically hit or, to make our example, less extreme or more ambiguous, emotionally abuse one's spouse, the client may interpret a value judgment from the actions or nonactions of the therapist.[3]

Some therapist's "true" judgment may be "that's not for me to decide, that's for the client to decide, it's my job to help him understand why or clarify his feelings about it, etc." Even if this was the case, the client may possibly misinterpret the nonaction as tacit approval since the cultural expectation generally is that others, including therapists, will and do make judgments. Moreover, the decision not to make a judgment in response to a behavior, particularly a behavior that most people in the culture would consider noxious, is a value-based decision. The credo from the 1960s seems apropos here—if you're not part of the solution, you're part of the problem. Thus, despite an overwhelming amount of evidence debunking the notion of value-neutrality, the concept lives on in ordinary theoretizing and even more so in ordinary practice within various reincarnations (Greben and Lesser, 1983).

The prejudice and even rancor against the active/directive cluster of therapeutic relational postures is evidenced by Weinberg (1996), who offers a not atypical view on the subject: "Giving advice is nine times out of ten a *substitute* for psychotherapy." (Italics mine, p. 208).

---

3. My use of value-laden terminology, such as "right" or "wrong" and "good" or "bad" is not only purposeful but philosophically, although perhaps not politically, correct. Therapists make value *judgments*, whether consciously or unconsciously, overtly or covertly.

The centrist position is reified such that legitimate differences in approach are regarded as heresay and not really psychotherapy.[4] Curiously, Weinberg goes on to acknowledge quite accurately that "even if (the therapist says) nothing and kept a poker face, the patient in such a case would almost assuredly (be) able to infer his preference. It is false to imagine that the therapist can ever fully delete his preferences on all matters in the patient's life" (p. 212). But Weinberg's solution to the dilemma is the approximation of the unattainable ideal of value neutrality: "All we can do is to try to avoid giving endorsements as much as possible" (p. 213).

The concern around the active/directive cluster of relational postures is primarily one of client dependency. Weinberg and others err by assuming that by *not* giving advice the therapist avoids inappropriate dependency. This is not accurate as the client may continue to return to the practitioner, repetitiously searching for the concealed advice or go signals. Moreover, giving advice does not automatically discharge the client of responsibility. In fact, if the advice is well formulated, it will have the effect of *increasing* the responsibility demands upon the client (see Chapters 8 and 9 for a discussion of progressive movements prescribed by the therapist).[5] The client's continuous struggling to make meaning for themselves and to find their own solutions may be the client's way of avoiding responsibility taking where it matters—outside the 50-minute hour and in their lives.

the myth of client motivation

Another construct that has been de-emphasized in ordinary theorizing but perhaps not in ordinary practice for a number of sociopolitical, as well as aesthetic preference reasons, is client motivation. For most therapists, the motivation for the client to change is considered to exist within the purview of the client. The client is said to be ready for change or not. Clients' motivation is something that seems to belong to them; one in the package of client factors presented to the therapist

---

4. Claims such as Weinberg's are akin to a cognitive therapist saying that the therapist's offering interpretations is not *actual* psychotherapy. The field's acceptance of points of view such as this with regard to relational paradigms and appropriate role of the therapist belies our continuous calls for theoretical pluralism.

5. Again I point out that I am merely arguing for the use of either TRP cluster. There are a host of therapeutic situations I could identify where it's inappropriate to offer advice, for example. I am calling for relational flexibility.

(Horvath, 1993). The client is viewed by the therapist as either motivated to change or not, to varying degrees. If the client begins treatment motivated and then over time becomes less motivated, we do not adequately account for this phenomenon in our theorizing.

Rarely, if ever, do you hear therapists saying things like, "I failed to keep this client motivated to grow" or "I failed to adequately catalyze this motivated client." Or, "I failed to provide motivation to this very unmotivated client." The reasons for this, I believe, relate to an almost implicit rejection of a particular cluster of values, a value orientation, so to speak. These values include responsibility taking for treatment success or failure on the part of the therapist, the willingness of the therapist to take charge of the change process when necessary and beneficial, the extent to which intimacy and dependency is allowed for, and attitudes about the distribution of power in the therapy relationship.

Taken together, we may consider these values the boundary issues of therapy, questions of how far the therapist can go in his or her relationship with the client. The frame of therapy then, which is different for each therapist-client dyad, defines these boundaries. This frame helps define the role of the therapist as well.

Conventional therapeutic role boundaries have evolved over the course of the history of therapy. Although there have been outlayers and exceptions to the generic pattern, the paradigmatic role of the therapist remains remarkably unchanged since the time of Freud and the advent of psychoanalysis. Despite the proliferation of literally hundreds, if not thousands of schools of therapy, the traditional role of the therapist remains a minimalistic, if not an exceptionally conservative one (Cecchin, 1987; Cherry and Gold, 1989; Dewald, 1992).

This is not surprising since psychotherapy has become institutionalized. Educational entities have been created to credential therapists, licensing boards have been formed, standards and ethics have been established and re-established (Danish and Smyer, 1981; Phillips, 1982). Institutions, whether the Catholic Church or marriage, are by nature centrist, slow-moving, and resistant to change.

Liberalization only occurs via a cooptation of more radical ideas and concepts. A relevant parallel may be found in Western medicine, for example. The very way in which illness and disease were defined blinded the medical profession to more holistic approaches and the notion of preventive medicine until the 1960s. Once considered a radical concept and a paradigm shift, disease prevention has been so coopted into the mainstream medical establishment, that ideas about nutrition or the relationship between psychological stress and physical disease tend to be given lip service while being misunderstood and virtually unrecognizable when presented in mainstream practice.

The same phenomenon can be seen in the mental health field. In attempts to be more comprehensive, integrative, and eclectic, mainstream therapy practice has suffered from the same kind of cooptation of valuable constructs. Hospital treatment programs, for example, often offer an all-encompassing range of services. The patient receives a little individual therapy, psychopharmacology, some family therapy, a touch of group therapy, etc. This has happened because there is a legitimate recognition of the validity of each approach. However, the family therapy that may occur in such programs would be hardly recognizable to the family therapists and theoreticians who heralded systems theory as a paradigmatic shift in the 1950s, 1960s, and 1970s. This occurs largely because of the tendency toward the cooptation of radical concepts once they are recognized as valid by the mainstream.

Virtually every student in professional psychology, psychiatry, or social work is exposed to a course or two in "Family Therapy." A certain level of expertise and/or knowledge in the concepts is required for graduation, credentials, or licensure. No self-respecting inpatient hospital program would not claim to offer "Family Therapy" as part of a comprehensive treatment package. As "Family Therapy" has become standardized and institutionalized, it has become theoretically less vital and in practice, less potent.

I do not mean this as an indictment of the popularization of radical constructs since there is a great positive benefit to the process of cooptation which is that the excesses, extraneous, or nonessential aspects of the model can be discarded. I am merely suggesting that cooptation occurs and we need to examine its effects. As psychotherapy has become legitimized, standardized, and accepted on a broader scale, radical ideas about the therapy relationship that have gained popularity have been coopted into mainstream practice in a form that is almost unrecognizable. The origins of any field when it first becomes legitimized become the foundation and the center of future alterations.

For psychotherapy, that center is psychoanalysis, in particular pre-1920 ego-psychology psychoanalysis (reference unknown). Thus the centrist institutionalized position on what's appropriate or inappropriate, what's good, what's bad, what works, what doesn't work in the therapeutic relationship is based on early psychoanalytic modes and methods (see Greeson, 1967). I outlined how the value-neutral therapy viewpoint continues to exist in the face of conflicting evidence.[6] The same may be said for therapeutic approaches that allow for more activity, involvement, or direction on the part of the therapist. Such approaches are suspect according to the established centrist position of the therapy relationship. So despite the accepted and intuited importance of motivation as a factor in treatment success, irrespective of model, the notion of the therapist being seen as the *motivator* in the therapy process has been virtually nonexistent in the literature.

motives and the intersection of values and motivation

Interestingly, and not coincidentally, the root of the word "motivate" is "motive." For one to have a motive has a negative connotation. It is seen as bad, that is, that one should not have a motive. It is acceptable that the client have a motive in the centrist viewpoint, but not the therapist (Walsh, 1995). If the therapist does have a motive, it is acceptable (sometimes) to direct a client *away* from pathology as opposed to *toward* some desired end. If the therapist has a motive, then s/he has an agenda. It is assumed that if the therapist has an agenda then s/he will not be open to the agenda of the client. "It is up to the client to decide to change or not change (and in what areas)" is the standard refrain heard when a therapist is frustrated by the client's resistance or lack of motivation.

This continuous call to arms is much ado about nothing. My position, and perhaps shared on an intuitive level by many practicing therapists (as opposed to therapist/theoreticians), is that there are values that can never be imposed in the sense of real (versus agreed upon) compliance. The responsibility to motivate is 100 percent for the therapist as well as 100 percent for the client. The therapist's responsibility to motivate is that to the extent that the client is not self-motivating, the therapist must attempt to motivate the person which is accomplished via the therapeutic relationship. As the client becomes more self-motivating, the therapist becomes less motivating. This is the dialectic that is at the heart of this model.

---

6. For a good explication of this one may look at current cultural attitudes or norms toward psychotherapy. Despite the debunking of the value-neutrality concept, many clients are influenced by the filtering down of the centrist position. For example, some clients have said things to me like, "Oh, I can't expect that you'll tell me your opinion or tell me what you think about X or Y." Some naive therapists may say, "you're not allowed to tell the client what you think," as if there were some accepted agreed-upon list of normative behaviors for therapists.

Some may suggest that to the extent that the therapist is motivating the client, then the client will tend to be less motivated as a consequence. This would indeed occur if the therapist was not sensitive to the readiness cues from the client, which will be discussed in detail in this book. These readiness cues are not new to practitioners of therapy on an intuitive level; they are part and parcel of the artistry of good clinical practice, I believe. It is my intention to specify and put names to this artistry to make the art of knowing what to do when more teachable and transferable.

This is not meant as a new model of therapy, although some therapists may find some of the constructs to be new. I am not an originator; I am not even an integrator; I am a synthesizer. I attempt here to synthesize crucial elements of the therapy relationship and the factor of client motivation into a framework that may be useful to therapists of virtually all orientations.

seeing client motivation as a nonnormative event

When we think of a motivator, we may think of a football coach, like Vince Lombardi, perhaps, or a motivational speaker who is a consultant to business. The task of the coach or manager is to motivate his or her employees to work more productively and efficiently. We rarely think of a therapist as a motivator. The ideal state of affairs would be if the therapist did not need to motivate the client. Certainly, therapists speak fondly of their motivated (as distinguished from inappropriately compliant) clients.

In many ways, therapy theory is rested upon the notion of this ideally motivated client. It is a basic assumption of virtually every model of therapy. When I am presented with a new approach or model, my tendency is not to challenge the model itself, as I find most models of therapy sensible, well-conceived, and useful. My customary response when I'm presented with a new approach to psychotherapy is, what do you do when the client does not comply with the model's aims, objectives, or rules? As I stated in Chapter 1, most models of therapy work to some degree or another in some therapeutic situations or with certain clients. Conversely, most models do not work to some degree or another, some of the time, with certain clients.

New approaches to existing complex phenomena (e.g., how to treat depressed people) are important but too much emphasis has been placed on developing newer and better approaches (in the face of consistent evidence that no single approach is *vastly* superior to any other) rather than on the common phenomena of what to do when that approach is not working.

For example, Harville Hendrix claims to have developed a superior model of couples therapy. I agree it is a highly effective form of couples therapy, and let's say we could prove its superiority to other models. My best clinical guess is that it is indeed superior to other models of couples therapy that I have studied. But so what? We now have a better model of couples therapy than we had before. But what about when clients do not comply with the aims, objectives, and rules of the model?

For example, one of the rules of Hendrix's model is that both partners agree to commit to actively participate in a set number of sessions.[7] It is a necessary condition for the model to work. I would imagine that when this condition is met the model works very well. That's great and if it does a better job than other models of couples therapy for these committed couples, that's even better.

However, the assumption of a committed couple is akin to requiring that a client of therapy be motivated. The majority of distressed couples seeking therapy are *not* committed and *not* motivated. The motivated and committed clients will receive benefit from most forms of well conceived couples therapy. If motivated and committed, let's say, clients receive significantly more benefit from Imago therapy than other therapies. But I'm not worried about the motivated clients of psychotherapy. The motivated will find the help they need, since by definition, they are quite resilient.

The precondition of having a motivated client is the hidden a priori assumption of therapy. I am more interested in the distressed couples that are not motivated to grow or change. Our theories of therapy must address *these* (potential) clients.

Many clients come to therapy presenting unsatisfactory and distressed marriages. Some of these clients will talk about it; some will not. Some may be aware of it; some will not. For example, an abused woman who is an incest survivor may not even be aware of how dysfunctional her marriage really is. If the therapist recommends marital therapy, this unmotivated client would likely resist, or, if the client agrees, is unlikely to comply with the demands of marital therapy, or her partner will be unlikely to comply with the demands of marital

---

7. Participation in therapy is contrasted with *commitment* to therapy. Many clients choose to participate, but not necessarily commit.

therapy. The couple's resistance may be acted out in a host of ways at virtually any point in the process.

The question of how to help clients in these situations is of much more utility since most clients arrive in therapy undermotivated and those who don't, soon become undermotivated. We should not be surprised by this since demotivation may lie at the heart of problems in living.

I am also interested in the people who are so unmotivated that they do not seek therapy. Often these are the significant others (e.g., family members, bosses, coworkers, spouses) who get talked about in therapy (the standing client joke of "he *really* needs to be here"). I am interested in these people because they help us understand the demotivation phenomenon of therapy clients. There is nothing more emblematic of demotivation than a distressed person *not* seeking help.

Unfortunately we tend to treat, in some cases, *overtreat*, the persons who perhaps are just as unhealthy but more motivated to change than other members of given systems. Our offices are filled with identified patients, scapegoats, and black sheep. How many wives seek treatment for what are not only individual but also marital difficulties while the husband chooses not to? How to get the resistant spouse to come to therapy is a question reserved for the Q&A portion of a couples therapy presentation, whereas the dilemma needs to be central to the model itself. What you do when a client wants to drop out of treatment after three sessions for any number of reasons is not tangential to the given model, but essential. Our models of therapy do not address these kinds of routine dilemmas. This gives a particularly skewed impression of the therapist's relational posture since the role of the therapist in any model must include *all* relevant therapeutic dilemmas.

In this sense, therapy is like parenting. You can have the knowledge and the preparation about what to do, and how and when to do it, until your child is born. Do we need more child rearing theories or yet another baby care book? No. What we need are models to explain how, why, and what happens when (good) theory no longer adequately explains this phenomenon. What the field of pedagogy needs are more models that are nonnormative, as well as nonpathogenic, that account for wider ranges of variance.

In therapy, what are considered to be nonnormative events are relegated to either nonspecific factors, the art of therapy, therapist "style" or even more obliquely, aspects of the therapeutic relationship. Nonnormative events are typically handled in the aged apprentice/

supervisor/mentor model of teaching. There are several problems with this model of teaching psychotherapy, not the least of which is that much of what occurs in therapy *is* nonnormative; indeed, the most salient aspects of therapy are nontechnical and unrelated to questions of theoretical orientation (Rappaport and Delpino, 1990). We need our models of therapy to take account of these nonnormative events.

The question of the client's motivation level affects and predominates the process, course, and outcome of therapy. This motivation affects the very initiation of therapy, the continuance in therapy, compliance with treatment procedures, willingness to bear the psychic pain and anxiety inherent in most depth-oriented approaches, the will to accept what are often ambiguous and uneven treatment results, and the willingness to expose aspects of the self that are considered shameful. Therefore, if we treat motivation as a nonnormative event, psychotherapy theory and technique recede to ground and values and motivation become figure in an emerging Gestalt, while the client remains undermotivated.

In Chapter 6, we will discuss the relationship between motivational phenomenon and our more conventional explanations and treatments for various psychopathologies. But before we do that, I will outline in Chapter 3 the theoretical and philosophical foundation for the therapy model we present in Chapters 7, 8, 9, and 10.

an evolutionary model of psychological health and motivation:
toward individuation

In the history of human civilization, the notion of the self is a relatively recent construction. Before the Industrial Revolution people were defined by their connections and affiliations (and still are today in less-developed cultures), with their loyalties almost exclusively to their families-of-origin. Individuation from the family-of-origin is also quite recent. The notion of marrying someone because of romantic feelings versus family arrangements or reasons of financial survival has been a common artifact of only the last century or so. All of this has occurred in the context of increasingly democratic political cultures in which individual and personal freedoms are more valued. Loyalty is now given not to predetermined monarchy but rather to a chosen and changeable leader. Just as changes in global physical climates create new biological adaptations and new species, this revolutionary change in the sociopolitical climate has led to the emergence of a psychological evolutionary adaptation—the individuated person.

The Industrial Revolution, urbanization, a more equitable distribution of resources and wealth, increased mobility of the population, and vast arrays of communication networks continue to spur this adaptation. There are increasingly more possibilities for the self to survive apart from its family-of-origin and from the religious and cultural communities the family created, in part, to aid them in survival. The concept of the individuated self has come about as the possibility of interacting with those other than family members and family-like members of their religious and cultural community has increased. For the growing child, the idea that there may be something "out there" more, better, or different from what it knows in its family/community was once, and in some cultures and families still is, nothing short of an act of rebellion, foolishness, or craziness.

Contemporary culture allows children to experience noncritically what's "out there" much more easily, quickly, and with an absence of moral commentary. A middle-class American child, with an act as simple as turning on the television, can experience a vast array of attitudes and ideas foreign to its home life. The child, or adult, too, for that matter, may incorporate, redefine, or reject these attitudes, ideas, and values.

But even with this bombardment of extrafamilial "other" ideas in the culture, a child may still grow up relatively sheltered and believe that what is learned in the family-of-origin and the local church, for example, is the only set of legitimate ideas and values. Just last week, a sexually inhibited client was startled when I suggested as a homework assignment that she masturbate herself to orgasm. "Masturbation is a sin, isn't it?" she asked me. When I asked her who had taught her this, she said it was her father. Her father, incidentally, had sexually abused her from the time she was five until she was 15.*

Without my having to say it, she realized the hypocrisy of her father and could make her own choices about which values make the most sense to her, as well as which are more pragmatic. The "isn't it?" added at the end of the sentence was a request to experience a different "out-there" notion about masturbation. If she had said to me flatly, "Masturbation is a sin," I likely would not have made the intervention in the first place, since I would not have experienced an adequate invitation from her to do so. One of the many issues she brought to therapy was sexual inhibition and difficulty in achieving orgasm. The idea of masturbation as a sin based in her familial and religious value system was not a particularly useful one in helping her overcome her sexual difficulties.[1] The intervention that I proposed was based on a *different* system of values, among them that sexual pleasuring is important to self-development, no act is in and of itself sinful, and that the context in which an act occurs is decisive in determining what is good or bad and right or wrong.

Indeed this client would not have sought therapy at all if not for her experience, however ambivalent, of identifying to some extent with a growing subculture espousing some of the values I was trying to impart. It was perhaps her unspoken but implicit acknowledgment of her father's hypocrisy, and that of her church, that led her to seek

---

* Names and any identifying details have been changed in all cases presented in this book. In cases using transcripted material, permission of the client has been obtained.

1. At age 12 she told a nun in Catholic school about the sexual abuse in an attempt to have someone "out there" help her grow. All that she remembers of this incident was that when she got home from school, her father beat her with a belt because she was "spreading lies." Her mother, she said, did nothing to stop him.

another "out there" to help her, first through books, magazines, articles, television talk shows, and then by seeking therapy herself. Her knowledge of some other unambiguous idea "out there," such as "A father should not sexually abuse his daughter," created the possibility of reframing her own psychic pain (shame, betrayal) and a recognition that these painful feelings may have resulted from maltreatment.[2]

Trying to implement familial values that one experiences as not working will lead a person to seek another viewpoint "out there." Since these alternative viewpoints are now so readily available "out there," along with a reasonable freedom to act on them, the individual has the relatively new option of choice.

For older children and adults, familial values take the form of psychological introjects. In my client's case, "I am a bad person" was introjected from her father's projection of his "badness" onto her. Such values may be reinforced in adult attachments and relationships. In my client's case, she married a man who would essentially rape her as her father had (before which she would numb herself with alcohol) as well as physically abuse her.

Her choice of husband was based on an attachment to someone psychologically familiar to her, but also on a possibility of change. He ceased the physical and sexual abuse after two years of therapy, which she had originally sought for herself and her children, who had been acting out in the community.

I had insisted that she bring her husband to the first family session. He very reluctantly came, which was much more than her father would have done if some other "out there" got involved (as shown in the father's behavior after the telephone call from the nun). He reluctantly but slowly bonded with me so that after two years of therapy, he had ceased many of his abusive behaviors, largely, I would say, because of my direct influence, a result of confrontation and education.

At some apex in the treatment, though, he decided that this other "out there" could not be fully trusted since the viewpoint I was espousing was so different from what he had learned in his own, not surprisingly, abusive, background. He had a difficult time facing the reality of the disparity between me and his family since it forced him to make at the very least a psychological choice: if I accept what Rick is

---

2. I say unambiguous here because her family and certainly the Church have an explicit taboo of incest. It is just that other principles of the Church may take precedence in the actual operations of life. Presumably, the nun chose the value "Honor thy father" over the incest taboo because she did not believe my client.

espousing, that being physically abusive is unacceptable, it is a good thing, not a weak thing, to be nurturing to my wife, I must then reject most of my parental introjects. This became his unspoken and unconscious but real dilemma.

He also found it disquieting that his wife was espousing many of the values of the therapist and the therapy. She was also, for the first time ever, openly acknowledging the pain of her past, which was threatening to him. She, for example, recognized that her alcoholism was largely related to the sexual abuse she experienced. But he could not recognize, for example, that her drinking would remind him of his mother's abusive alcoholic behavior and would trigger a contemporary marital dance—she drinks so she can have sex with him (something she wanted that had been taken from her—a normal sexual life) and her drinking reminds him of his unresolved and unrecognized rage toward his mother. He would end up abusing his wife.

To emotionally remember or experience the pain he felt as a child when his mother would drink proved too difficult for him, and he chose to drop out of treatment. After one particularly violent interchange with his wife, he ultimately lost the marriage. Interestingly, and not coincidentally, he moved out of the marital home and in with his mother, where he remains. He ultimately chose to remain loyal to his family-of-origin. For a time he chose to do both, maintain loyalty to his family-of-origin introjects and apply some of the values of the therapist, but he was unable to take the necessary leap of faith.

Since the family-of-origin exists not only in the form of psychological introjects but is also a real and functioning contemporary unit, he also faced a dilemma. How do I continue to have a relationship, and of what kind, with my mother if I acknowledge the pain she caused me? His wife, of course, faced the same dilemma, and she attempted to come to some resolution with her family members about her experience growing up. As a child, she had been alternately labeled "bad" and "crazy" for bringing such issues to the surface. Her family's denial reached absurd heights when one of the client's sisters said in a family-of-origin session that was boycotted by the parents, "She (my client) was their father's favorite, his little princess who would get special treatment from him." It was after this session that my client decided to break off contact with her family "for my own sanity and healing. It's hard enough for me to deal with all the fucked-up messages I have in my head about myself. . . . I cannot be around people who refuse to acknowledge the truth. . . . I can't pretend anymore. . . ."

She openly chose to accept more and more of the therapist's ideas and views about her. I saw her as very intelligent, but her family had always laughed at her for reading so much. I suggested that she get a college degree. She showed me some of her paintings and I encouraged her to work on it. I told her when I thought that she was being mistreated, whether by her teenage son, by a dentist who touched her inappropriately, or by a friend who would take advantage of her. I taught her how to be assertive in such situations. I confronted her about her tendency to be uncommunicative, which tended to feed her self-obsessive view of things. Her family accused me of brainwashing her. She followed through on much of what we had worked on in therapy and her life changed dramatically, as one would imagine.

It is not my intention here to discuss the efficacy of this approach, especially since the cost of her success in this case included a temporary cut-off from some family members and loss of her marriage, no matter how positively or necessary she or others may view this. Certainly, my approach was largely unsuccessful with her husband.[3] Rather, I wish to point out the dilemmas that one confronts when one ventures outside the family-of-origin and its contemporary representatives (e.g., spouse, internal familial introjects, the client's own family) for a different viewpoint or set of values. Conflict and tension is created, although in most cases not nearly as dramatically as this one.

In most cases, the adult who is able to individuate can go out and find extrafamilial others (I might point out, since adult parents can grow, too, extrafamilial influences in the form of a healthier parent) in order to heal aspects of oneself and to fill the gaps and deficiencies from the family-of-origin that remain incomplete.

We call this tendency to grow morphogenesis, one parallel to that of homeostasis, which is the tendency to keep things as they are and in balance. The dialectical tension between the two is at the heart of the change process. When one finds another "out there" with whom one bonds or trusts, we call this person the therapeutic other or reparental agent.

Reparental agents begin to appear in the life of a child as early as three or four, but generally later, and include extended family members, teachers, and coaches. Early nonfamilial caretakers essentially act

---

3. I sometimes like to say, however inaccurately, that good work in therapy skips a generation. Their four children are sober, working productively, and are in committed relationships. None are, to the best of my knowledge, engaged in overtly abusive relationships.

in the role of parents since the very young child makes few significant interpersonal distinctions. Therapeutic others may also be represented in the culture at large, for example in the form of a talk-show host who, during a show on incest, tells her audience she is a survivor of incest, and that it is okay to talk about it. People can then introject these "others" in the same way one introjects the values of the family-of-origin.

I do not mean to suggest that the values of the family tend to be bad and the values of extrafamilial persons tend to be good (often the reverse is true), but this book will reflect a bias toward a parent-responsibility model. The basic assumption I operate from is that beyond biochemical, and temperamental factors, the family is the prime source of the psychological health and well-being or difficulties of the children. I in no way mean to minimize individual differences or the role of biology in psychopathology. Rather, I am suggesting that the parent is responsible for maximizing the potential of each *unique* child, which may include biochemical imbalances and great individual differences.

Just as the role of a parent for a child with a physical disorder like juvenile diabetes, is to maximize the potential of the child given the disorder, the role of the parent for a child with attention-deficit disorder, for instance, is to help that child succeed to the best of their abilities, taking into account their limitations. It is not for a parent to say something like, "Oh, well, the kid's hyperactive; it's not my fault," or "He got involved with a bad peer group and that's why he dropped out of school and is doing drugs."

I am not suggesting a model that emphasizes blame, but rather taking 100 percent responsibility for the behavior under one's own control, for what one can do differently. Holding individuals responsible for what they do, good as well as bad, I point out, is not blaming them when it is "bad" or praising them when it's "good." Rather we must attempt to evaluate them honestly for their merits and faults. Also, since this is a book about therapy, I am emphasizing situations where parenting has gone awry or when the tasks of adulthood prove greater than the ability of the parents to provide.

This parent-responsibility assumption is not a minor one, but rather in my view is a key element as it sets the stage for evolutionary development of the self. The parents are responsible for the personal growth of their children and for providing what each child uniquely requires to grow. Each parent, of course, is limited by their own psychological deficiencies and gaps. How can a parent give what they themselves did not receive from their own parents or are incapable of providing, however one defines that? In the parent-responsible model this is a reason, not an excuse. In other words, if the parent is deficient in some way that has a negative impact upon their children, then it is up to the parent to make up these deficiencies through whatever means available when they become, or *could* become, sufficiently aware of this deficiency. This kind of "buck-stops-here" (always with the parent) approach may be read as a moral imperative. Rather, it is also meant as a psychological imperative to increase the parenting capabilities of successive generations, leading to increased opportunities for evolution of self and other. As a result, one may create a more psychologically developed "species" with increased opportunities for survival in a tumultuous postmodern climate.

In many cultures, individuation clearly is *not* a valued endeavor; in those cultures psychotherapy (which has never been value-free with regard to its advocation of individuality) is correspondingly devalued. One observes, though, that as family members of virtually any cultural group gain economic freedom and mobility, there is a tendency for succeeding generations toward increased individual expression and individuation, either through selection of mates (or friends and associates) who are not members of the same cultural group, differentiation from the religious community that surrounds the family group, or through geographic relocation. This is based on the innate tendency of the human species toward completion, adaptation, and evolution.

This has not occurred without cultural instabilities like increased rates of divorce and of single-parent-headed and blended families (Bray and Hertherington, 1993) but these are often attempts of individuals, albeit often wrongheaded ones, to evolve and grow. The acceptance and indeed popularization, of divorce is essentially a progressive cultural movement in that it provides married individuals, particularly women, with an opportunity to express themselves more powerfully (i.e., if you don't meet my needs or treat me better, I may leave). Of course, with this increased freedom comes increased responsibility. Freedom exercised irresponsibly is, of course, *not* a progressive cultural movement. Interestingly, in the last ten years or so, the culture has begun adapting to this development through the infusion of new ideas about the nature of marital life and the advent of marital therapies (e.g., Hendrix, 1990; Weiner-Davis, 1993; see also Lee, Picard and Blain, 1994 for a review of divorce therapy).

At the same time, there have been what I deem regressive movements away from individuation. Cultural critics consider individuation to be a white/male/Western/American construct and antithetical to the aims of many minority culture groups. Certain religious and conservative political figures have decried the disintegration of "the family" and call for "family values." Even within the therapeutic community, particularly among family therapists, the concept of the family is often reified. The originators of family therapy emphasized individuation and differentiation. In the 1980s, culturally sensitive family therapists criticized therapists' implicit and explicit attempts to lead minority families in the direction of white majority goals like individuation. The appeal of constructivist epistemologies and approaches to therapy led to the idea that all world-views are equally valid. [See Held, 1995, for a cogent and overdue critique of the relativist antirealist movement in psychotherapy.] These subtle and not so subtle movements toward a reification of the family and family values romanticize the family-of-origin and the "old" ways of that family. The family-of-creation or the family-of-choice is viewed with skepticism by many cultural critics, since loyalty to the family-of-choice over the family-of-origin is a very recent phenomenon.

We must remember that individuation is essentially a radical concept. Any psychotherapy that supports individuation is revolutionary, in that it seeks to question the prevailing social order. Psychotherapy is a potentially radical endeavor. The values implicit and explicit in the kind of psychotherapy I propose support the individual and the choices of that individual. With that comes a concomitant responsibility for these choices and experiences.[4] The psychotherapy I propose encourages responsible individual expression which usually turns out to be, to some extent or another, against established culture and the institutions that represent it. Cultural institutions are naturally regressive and homeostatic in that they tend to support the status quo. As agents of *change*, psychotherapists must, at a minimum, pose the possibility for disruption of the status quo. I must vehemently point out that I am referring to psychotherapy voluntarily entered and exited that is designed for the individual client(s), and not for some larger social purpose or cause.

---

4. A frequent outcome of successful individually oriented depth psychotherapy for married individuals, as has been recognized since Hurvitz (1967), is a break-up of relationships and dissolution of the family. This is an excellent example of individual choice-making in the absence of responsibility. Therapists participate in this by not involving, or at times, insisting that the partner be included in the growth process.

I favor psychotherapeutic values that disrespect the existing social order and conventions since it is one of the few sanctioned endeavors that exist for the purposes of disrupting social order and power imbalances.[5] Psychotherapy is one of the few activities that offers people an opportunity to upend the rules and old ways of doing things. Again, my only proviso is that this be accomplished by concomitant and increasing levels of responsibility-taking.

Individuation is both a concept and an act that disrupts the social order of the family-of-origin, which is a good thing in that it increases the possibility of evolution for the next generation and leaves behind a better place (culture, world, planet) than the one we inherited. To accomplish this one must be willing to discard what does not work from the previous generation and to forge new territory, maps, and belief systems. It is this willingness to discard the extraneous, the pathogenic, and the negative that allows for individual growth and development.

Undue loyalty to the family-of-origin and its related institutions will virtually ensure that the succeeding generation will have yet more work to do if *they* wish to discard old maps, scripts, and programs (the baggage of the past generation) and achieve evolutionary growth. One changes ultimately not for oneself but for the next generation, so as to not pass down the negative introjects of the family. The ultimate goal of parenting is to provide good-enough input so that one's child may leave, then outdo, the parent with regard to these inputs. The child receiving good-enough inputs is in a more advantageous position to offer more to the world (e.g., their own children, their spouse, their work) than the giver (parent), and so on with succeeding generations.

It is the adult child's undue loyalty to the ways of the family-of-origin that inhibits the growth process since the family represents only one way or correct path, no matter how good or appropriate that path may be (or in the case of the counterdependent adult child, one correct *antipath*.) Continued growth requires equal consideration of many paths and alternative paradigms. The fact that the family-of-origin presents one path is neither good nor bad; it just is. I am therefore not in favor of liberal or permissive or democratic parenting models that attempt to offer an assortment of equally valid paths for the child.

---

5. Other culturally sanctioned endeavors that tend to disrupt existing social order include noninstitutionalized education and marriages entered into on the basis of romantic love.

Rather, I favor a parenting model that is explicitly value-based but promotes values that are growth- and process-oriented rather than content-specific. For example, the parent models and infuses the child with a notion of intimacy (*process* value: intimacy is good or beneficial) versus a particular kind of intimacy (*content* value: intimacy with a woman of your own kind is good; intimacy with a woman we don't approve of, is bad). It is hard for me to imagine my son, for instance, living a life devoid of intimacy (although perhaps we're due for some other kind of psychological revolution) but I certainly expect and hope it's easier for him to achieve intimacy with his spouse than it has been for me. And if that is so it may leave a psychological vacuum to create something evolutionary and unpredictably new, different, and better.

The same expectation and hope exist for my clients as well. The therapist offers as much as possible (in our model, reparenting) and then the client leaves the therapist, and hopefully as the receiver of presumably better inputs may outdo the therapist. It is this cycle of transcendence of parental/therapist needs for the needs of the other (child/client) that forms the, for lack of a better word, spiritual basis of this model.

I'd like to point out two major comparisons with other models of therapy at this point. First, I do not believe I am saying anything that isn't an intrinsic part of many therapies and in the unconscious minds of many therapists. Stated in such value-explicit form, it may strike the reader as different. Secondly, the role of therapist in this model is more active, more intensive, and more directive in nature than many other approaches.

In this way the client will be much less likely to reject the pathogenic ways of the family-of-origin without a new "parent-like" figure to be there for them, to activate and structure while they are still engaged in the individuation process (what I call the Primitive Phase). The role of the therapist is to provide *external* motivation while the client is letting go of old ways and developing new ones that are co-created with the therapist and sensitive to the unique temperament, needs, and personality of that client. This enables the client to proceed forward toward goals they establish with the help of the therapist and away from the family-of-origin, in what I call the External Phase.

Moreover, the client will not be able to make a leap toward independence without an adequate enough experience of dependency upon the therapist to whatever extent necessary. If we believed that they could, they would not need the therapist, and would not enter, or would soon exit, therapy. And again, the values of the therapist must be growth-oriented; that is, they must lead the client away from the therapist toward independence, in what I call the Internal Phase. Finally, the person individuates from the therapy and may provide the same, but hopefully even better, parenting to their children and reparenting to spouse, and others in the world, in what I call the Spiritual Phase.

Obviously, the goals of this model go beyond symptom amelioration or restoration of functioning. The movement toward health as opposed to away from pathology is, again, not unique in the realm of psychotherapeutic practice, but is usually not explicit in theorizing. When the co-creation of healthy functioning is theorized, as in the humanistic-experiential psychotherapy traditions, the relationship between constructs of health and actual practice tends to be vague and often irrelevant to the practice of therapy. Moreover, the preferred model of change in these orientations is generally nondirective, relationally noneclectic, and implicitly presupposes an adequately motivated client.

Undermotivated clients generally require therapeutic flexibility, activity, and direction. Some may argue that aiding clients toward "health" is not within the purview of the therapy process, that is, it is more appropriate to religious or spiritual movements. But a therapist cannot operate without some kind of model of health, albeit unconscious and covert, any more than someone cannot hold an opinion. Value judgments, both positive and negative, are constantly being formulated. Thus, we ought to make these judgments and models as explicit as possible, so that they may be evaluated and configured for applicability and usefulness. This book offers one such model.

motivation in everyday life

primitive motivation in the infant and very young child

The desire or motivation to change or grow may be understood developmentally. Young children have no intrinsic motivation from within. As infants, toddlers, and very young children, we are basically instinctual; our behavior is guided by the desire to satisfy needs, to seek pleasure, and to avoid pain.

Children, from birth until ages five or six, are almost completely dependent upon their families for survival. The dependency is both physical and emotional; the infant, toddler, and very young child require adequate nutrition, shelter, safety from harm, and emotional support to thrive and survive. The family unit—caretakers or parents—are the sole source of nurturance for the child. A child's motivation is not to *please* the parents, per se; rather, there exists an unconscious instinctual mechanism designed to maintain psychological proximity. The child makes no real choices regarding "rightness" or "wrongness" for him or herself. The child is unduly influenced by the roles and structure of the family. His or her motivation is to survive; survival occurs via loyalty to the caretakers.

The child does not make decisions regarding activity and the like as much as decisions are made for him or her. If the child is left to make his or her own decisions regarding caretaking, no matter what the constitution of the child, s/he would assuredly self-destruct. At these ages, the child cannot adequately request help from extrafamilial sources even in the worst cases of abuse and neglect, due to their obvious lack of interpersonal skills. To the child, it does not matter who the parents are—children do not have ideas about good parenting or bad parenting, and if they do, these notions have no particular consequences. There is a loyalty to parents, family, and caretakers. It is not until later that the child begins to experience their parents as psychologically separate entities, or as people about whom they can make decisions regarding rightness or wrongness.

The child essentially is narcissistic. The parents are experienced as a psychological extension of the child, which is why there is no questioning and no separate independent decision-making. There is not even the kind of choice-making that is related to pleasing the parent. Young children do not please their parents to get their needs met; they simply have the instinctual expectation that their needs will be met. The desire to please, we may say, is biologically instinctual, and when the parent is "pleased" the infant coos and smiles to ensure continuity of care and nurturance. They care little about who feeds them as long as they are fed. I do not mean to suggest that infants do not bond with their particular caretakers. Rather, I make the point that the child will not lose motivation to eat, sleep, or play based on the loss of mother. Their behavior and affect may be altered in some significant negative fashion, of course, but their instinct to survive and to grow remains intact. Thus, the very young child is imprinted with the experiences of their family and caretakers.

Object relationists would refer to this mechanism as introjection, but, for purposes of this model, I wish to distinguish between the instinctual and biologically based introjection of very early childhood and the more relational and emotionally based introjection of ensuing years. This early introjection process represents a bonding for essentially physical and then emotional survival; while an older child chooses aspects of others to introject based on a motivation toward a psychological end. Therefore, early introjection may be best conceived of as a more primitive and instinctual process, hence the term imprinting. I call this first period of motivation, the "primitive phase."

Later when the child matures, s/he begins to view the parents as psychologically separate beings, not only from him or herself but from each other and others in their environment (e.g., mom is different than me, from dad, and from my babysitter). When this occurs, children begin to make choices about who to input, who to listen to, who not to listen to, whose direction to follow, and who makes more "sense." These "choices" indicate an emerging sense of identity that is no longer narcissistic but instead includes others as real people, not objects. In the primitive phase, however, others are psychologically indistinguishable. To the very young child, if others in the environment meet the needs for adequate food, shelter, safety, and emotional comfort, the instinct to grow remains essentially intact. To the extent that others in the environment do not meet these needs, a child's instinct to thrive is thwarted.

When these needs go unmet, this represents a loss to the child which we may refer to as an abandonment. The infant who cries through the night for milk or for the physical/emotional contact of the caretakers and whose needs are not responded to adequately will experience this loss. Over time, this loss becomes an imprinted experience. Children vary in their response to loss: some will manifest a quiet withdrawal and despair that may mimic depression in early years and perhaps in adult years if there is not intervention either by the family itself or others (e.g., mentors, therapists, teachers, coaches.), while others may act out by developing protective and/or false modes of relating.

In all children, though, the optimal object relations process is affected. The expectation for gratification is an internal imprint of "my self is okay, as long as my needs are met." As the child expects his or her needs to be fulfilled, s/he develops a healthy expectation or imprint that others in their environment are fulfilling. This imprint prepares the staging for healthy object relations in the future.

When the child's expectation for the fulfillment of various needs is more haphazard, random, or unpredictable, s/he develops an inadequate sense of others in his or her environment. Since, in the earliest years, these "others" represent the self, the imprint may become "when I need something, I may not receive it." The very young child, however, is not as capable of reasoning as to why this may be as they are in succeeding years. Again, this is why I refer to the introjection of "others" as imprinting; it exists as it is in the absence of communicating cognition.

The imprint is experienced by the young child, and later the older child and adult, as a sensation (or an intuition) of okayness or not-okayness to varying degrees. This sense of self may be reinterpreted by the older child as a state of being ("I am good," "I am bad") or as a feeling ("I feel good," "I feel bad"), and in the adult who has access to a library of communicating cognitions, as a mood state ("I feel empty," "I feel fulfilled"), or even a diagnosis and category ("I am depressed").

This imprint is best thought of as the rudimentary and foundational sense of self-esteem and self-worthiness. The *expectation* of object loss, or that others cannot be counted upon is internalized as, "I cannot or will not get my needs met", or "*I* cannot be counted upon" since the psychological separation of I and others is incomplete at these ages.

To briefly review, in the primitive phase, while there is a natural wiring for growth, this wiring must be catalyzed through the parent-child relationship. A child left to his or her own devices without a parent or substitute parent figure will lose motivation and will ultimately fail to thrive. This motivation to change or grow may therefore be termed primitive or predependent.

external motivation in the young child

If attachment is sufficiently built, the child is free to identify with *the* parent, as opposed to *a* parent, in that a healthy dependency develops between child and parent. This occurs because the child no longer fears losing the parent's love, which again, is the child's only life-line of support. This represents the first kind of psychological working through for the child associated with the fear of abandonment, the idea that one can be loved unconditionally. The child feels that he or she can be loved for who they are and not whether they enacted a particular role or set(s) of behaviors for that parent.

If the parent, who presumably because of his or her own background is not capable of offering unconditional love, does not allow the child to complete the separation process and work through his or her fear-of-loss, the child will not have formed a secure attachment. There may be an insecure attachment or an enmeshment but this serves to keep the child on a repetitive, transactional search for completion and for the missing elements of unconditional love. The child may grow in other ways, but at a foundational level of ego, s/he maintains the fear-of-loss. The child who fears abandonment may in time develop associated fears of engulfment, and to a lesser extent, annihilation.

The child who remains in this stage, is enmeshed not only to the family system, but ultimately to the values and ways of their parents.[1] He or she has two choices, to enact those values, that is, to be dependent, or to enact the opposite of those values in *reaction*, that is, to be counterdependent. The child cannot truly *be* safely different because that involves the making of independent choices, which risks losing the contemporary family system or the role that s/he has become.

This same young child, as an *adult*, will likely choose a partner who is characteristically similar to the parents and who functions at the same level of object relating (defined as the ability to healthily interpret and manage one's own emotions and the emotions of others) because that spouse is at once familiar. To the extent that the partner is similar to the parents, the adult child remains loyal to the original family system and the enacted role.

---

1. By values, I am referring here to *process* values of living. Process-oriented values are, for example, notions about intimacy and distance regulation in relationships. A *content* value, such as an opinion about abortion, is of no relevance to this model. A child and a parent may have very different content values, and hence, *appear* very different but *psychologically* may be quite similar.

Of course, life provides new experiences to grow, and a child may psychologically outgrow their parents. In fact, how this occurs is the crux of this model. The only way in which a child can accomplish this is to risk losing the parents by enacting new values and *being* different than the role prescribed to them by the family. The child must overcome this elemental fear-of-loss. Again, the fear of abandonment is present because the parents' provision of love is conditional. The child feels that if s/he acts in ways that are unacceptable (i.e., not role-bound) s/he will be abandoned. Likewise, the attachment needs of the child will go unmet. The real self cannot fully develop in the absence of that original holding environment since the child will simply behave in ways that promote proximity, even though that may involve enacting false modes of relating.[2]

The potentially growthful experiences that the child may come in contact with are the influences of significant others or parent-like figures who can provide an alternative mirror to the child; they may provide the child with a more congruent and empathic view of themselves. These significant others include teachers, coaches, extended family members, mentors, spouses, and significantly for our model, therapists. Generally speaking, friends cannot provide corrective experiences since the power differential is minimal, and therefore lacking in transferential meaning.[3]

These significant others may take a special interest in the child and provide needed doses of nurturance, discipline, and guidance. The problem remains, however, that these significant others will expectedly have a difficult time penetrating the psychological space of the child since the child feels essentially unlovable. The child who has not developed an attachment to the parent will transfer the same set of expectations onto the significant others, primary among them, "we will not form a meaningful attachment, or if we do, in the process of doing

---

2. It is important to note at this point in the discussion, that unconditional love, contrary to some definitions, does not exclude appropriate discipline and limit-setting. An all nurturing, all accepting parent does not provide the necessary boundaries for the child and can have a paradoxical effect of making the child feel the same fear-of-loss as if there was a lack of nurturance. This is so because the parent who does not set limits communicates to the child an undercurrent message of, "I'm afraid of disciplining you because it makes *me* feel like I may stop loving you," which will tend to create an insecure attachment.

3. Power here is defined, consistent with the model, to be the significant other's potential for healthily distancing from the attachment relationship with the person. The significant basis of a friendship is mutual need and reciprocity.

so, I will experience the same hurt that I did with my parents." This is called negative transference or the unconscious expectation that significant others will treat the child similarly to his or her parents. The child will organize significant others to enact this, partially in attempts to have it turn out differently or to change the ending of the repetitive dance.

For a period of time, positive transference may exist creating a feeling of hopefulness, but as soon as there is a disappointment, the negative transference emerges swiftly, and the child disengages. This process may occur and recur. Typically, the significant other grows weary of this, and out of good sense, may disconnect partially or fully from the child. The child then has his or her transferentially distorted view of parent-like others reconfirmed, that in the end they will abandon the child.

This can be broken, however, through the significant other's steadfast refusal to own or enact the negative transference projected onto him or her. This requires a great deal of genuine caring, patience, toughness, and reassurance. It does not require a Ph.D. in psychology, but it may require the *frame* and *context* of therapy to allow a special relationship to emerge and to allow the penetration of the healthier object to occur. For this attachment to occur, the child must, by necessity, separate from the parental introject, begin the process of individuation from the family system, and see the reality of the parents' limitations.

Again, the critical caveat in all this is that the new significant other, or the therapist, must represent a healthier set of principles for being, otherwise the child has merely found an embodiment of the parental introjects. This occurs all the time in the form of "attachment" to spouses, bosses, cult leaders, gurus, and therapists, who are functioning at the same level of object relations and who offer little, if anything, new to the child. I have, for example, seen people stay with therapists who are not helping them grow, yet they remain unhealthily dependent upon their therapists. Healthy attachment is a dependency that is in the service of growth or ultimate independence of the client.

However, it is important to point out that significant others by definition will retain some, if not many, aspects of the original parents. In other words, they cannot be too different or unfamiliar, lest the adult child be put off by the psychological or relational differences. In fact, I recommend that therapists mimic certain aspects and characteristics of the parents as part of the selection of a specific therapist relational posture early in the treatment. These are the kinds of inert substances that assist in the client's acceptance of the more potent substances necessary for growth.

A person who does not let the significant other penetrate them because of this fear-of-loss, may find it is safer to maintain distance. This distance may be obvious through the person's façade where the offered *appearance* of closeness is not genuine. Likewise, distance may be maintained by a superficial merging with others or via an emotional cut-off.

In this sense, relational health is viewed as the development of an intimate attachment to the significant other. Interestingly, another pathway of health is for the person to go back to their family system and forge a new attachment to their parents who may, out of their own experiences of growth or newfound capabilities, see that the child is now at a different age or stage of development. However, negative transference may develop with the now *external* parent.[4] If the person is willing to confront the fear-of-loss of the *introjected* parent, an attachment to the now healthier parent or therapeutic other may develop. A person may only be willing to take this step if the new figure has something to offer to the person and is capable, i.e., s/he is unafraid of penetrating the psychological space of the person.

Many therapists, however, operate out of a fear of their own power or a fear of engulfment and do not offer themselves fully as an alternative reparental figure. A client will not give up an unhealthy attachment to say, aspects of the family-of-origin, an abusive spouse, or even alcohol or drugs, unless they have something to attach *to* as a replacement. Again, that "something" must be a healthier alternative; that is, offer missing, needed inputs which have a transforming effect on the person.

If the person can make this psychological stretch and develop an attachment to a healthier parent-like figure, we say s/he has moved from the primitive stage of motivation to the external or *dependent* stage of motivation. Here the person is motivated to change and grow because

---

4. This is a quite curious notion, that of a person developing negative transference to their own parents based on historical experiences, but one that may explain the commonly observed phenomenon of seemingly good-enough parent(s) being unable to reach their troubled child. The child often acts *as if* their parent(s) are behaving destructively. When this occurs in therapy, we may need to work to convert these contemporary distortions (Framo, 1976).

they identify with and wish to please the parent-figure. In healthy child development, this person is, ideally but not necessarily, the same-sex parent. A young boy begins to identify with his father, because of who the father is. Previously, "any father will do" is the moniker of the primitive phase's survival-by-loyalty. At this stage of motivational development, one thrives, versus survives, by subscribing to a healthy set of values or principles.

If the very young child was allowed to separate and return, thus developing a secure attachment, then that child is now free to introject the parent, which simply translates into taking on aspects of the parent(s) such as their healthy values. A child or adult stuck in the primitive stage of development is incapable of introjection because s/he does not have the psychological capacity to have a separate relationship with others. Others are viewed as objects to manipulate, to create pleasure, and to avoid pain, a philosophy of living that is successful for an infant or toddler but disastrous for the adult attempting to handle individual and interpersonal responsibilities.

The primitive person's energies are tied to the maintenance of proximity to others. Others are their lifeline, if they get too far away from an other, there is an internal experience of abandonment and the person will act to bring the other, or *any* other, closer. If an other gets closer, not in a familiar and nonintimate way, but in a genuine attempt to achieve intimacy, the person will very likely experience this as engulfing because it is so unfamiliar. In the primitive stage of motivation, the person is motivated by this fear-of-loss of the familiar. The person is not motivated by what's healthy, but rather by what will keep them attached to the familiar other.

growth and motivational difficulties in later life transactions

In the primitive phase of development, the family's values and modes of living strongly influence the person. For the adult person, the family-of-origin may be represented by some combination of parental/familial introjects from their childhood or the family-of-origin functioning presently in the person's life. This family within (the introjected family-of-origin) the person, and the family outside (the contemporary family-of-origin) have a powerful impact on behavior, self-concept, role definition, outlook on life, and approach to living.

Quite often, the introjected family-of-origin gets reenacted in the person's family-of-creation. To the extent the person denies the existence of these most negative aspects, the person's spouse will tend to, for example, enact some of the most negative introjects in the form of projective identification.[5] This process seems to maintain an intrapsychic, as well as interpersonal, homeostasis.

There is an almost unswerving loyalty to these introjects and the ways of the family-of-origin. This loyalty may manifest itself in either a dependent or counterdependent fashion. In other words, the person may follow the messages and prescribed roles of the family directly (a kind of my-family-right-or-wrong mode), or indirectly by rebelling. The person's rebellious stance, while in apparent opposition to the values of the family-of-origin is problematic since this person is not following a positive course of life; rather they are enacting an anti-negative pattern of response. In general, the person attempting to enact the opposite of their familial influences may serve to replicate those negative introjects, albeit in a disguised form. Adults retain loyalty to familial introjects, though possibly painful and unproductive, because they are familiar.

However, there is a natural process of evolution and growth as well. The dialectical tension between homeostasis and morphogenesis forms the most fundamental and basic of life's struggles. We are wired from birth to evolve, to seek out new experiences, to try out new modes of behavior and living. If, however, the wiring for growth is not catalyzed in early childhood, the natural morphogenic process becomes thwarted. The early childhood experiences that matter most in the development of this growth instinct are the attachment and rapprochment experiences of the child. Specifically, the balance between the parents' expectations of correct or appropriate behavior (the experience of conditional love), and the parents' bestowing of unconditional love in the form of empathy, trust, as well as a psychological claiming of the child, form the set of experiences that becomes the child's template for growth.

We call these expectations of appropriate or correct behavior, where there is an increased expectation from the child, *progressions*. For

---

5. Projective identification is defined here as the process whereby one denies a significant aspect of the self, and "sees" (i.e., projects) it in the other. That other, because of their own denial of certain aspects of themselves and their unique relational history, will have a tendency to enact the projection, thereby completing the projective identification process.

example, parents may not expect a two-week-old baby to sleep through the night, but parents would expect an eight-month-old baby to sleep through the night. Since children have unique temperaments, biochemestries, and hence, different timing and readiness points, certain expectations such as the aforementioned example, may or may not be appropriate.

If the parent is tuned into their child's albeit subtle sense of timing, s/he will raise the progressive expectation at the age, stage, and task-appropriate time. Even in the best of circumstances, these changes can be difficult due to the pulls of homeostasis and the behaviorial reinforcement contingencies of habit. In the face of each progression, the child naturally regresses.

The parents must balance the progressive and regressive needs of the child; for instance, in our sleep example, perhaps soothing the child through the transition period of change is necessary. Here the child introjects a sense of okayness from the parent for their present feelings of stress thus causing a positive reapproachment experience. The child internalizes a sense of okayness about growth and developmental changes—that is, change may take one into unfamiliar territory and that can be somewhat frightening—but s/he is not abandoned. Rather, the child is supported through this time of intrapsychic upheaval. If the child is not soothed, is not supported, and to some degree or another, *abandoned* through this process, progression becomes a skewed event.

Likewise, if the progressive expectation is not developmentally appropriate, there are many ways for the process of growth to become warped. For example, the child may enact the desired behavior but at a cost to self-esteem in the form of a self-hating introject (e.g., "I am abandoned because I am unworthy of love or support") that may resemble masochism in adulthood. Because of the lack of support, the child may resist change and become progression-averse, either passively, in the form of adult passive-aggressiveness, or actively, in the form of counterdependency and rebellion. In all cases, the child may become untrusting of caretakers and others who expect too much, too little, or nothing at all.

In the case of too little or too late progressive expectation, the parent may infantilize the child such that the child gets the message of incapability, that s/he cannot trust himself to handle forward movement. The parent who is so inclined will tend to create a similar dependency as in the case of the parent who offers too many and/or too early inappropriate developmental expectations, and therefore resulting in the development of similar abandonment fears. The parent, here, gives the message to the child that s/he cannot handle separation, thereby denying the child positive experiences of separation and individuation.

It is this oscillation between progressive and regressive phenomena that lies at the heart of the motivation to develop and grow. There exists a natural human drive toward completion, to make whole, to heal, to utilize resources, to increase skills, and to function more efficiently. Virtually every significant theory of personality and most recently of psychology generically is rooted in the notion of human beings as evolving beings (see Buss, 1995, for a relevant discussion of evolutionary psychology). The completion of one stage of growth signals morphogenesis, a seemingly prewired tendency to approach the next. In other words, we are born with a motivation to grow and to explore. While each person's unique temperament and biological makeup sets the tone and rhythm for this evolvement, there is uniformly an innate desire to do so.

All children who are biologically capable will crawl, then walk, run, and then jump. All children who are biologically capable will smile, then coo, then babble, emit sounds, utterances, and say words, and then sentences. These are natural developmental drives toward motoric movement and communication. With time, these drives become more sophisticated, as in the case of cognitive skills, such as abstract thinking. How these innate drives are catalyzed is essentially an environmental phenomenon, remaining largely a function of the input of family, specifically parents and caretakers. We know that even the most fundamental of all instinctual drives, to eat, may be skewed in infants who are not provided with adequate nurturance by their caretakers, will suffer a disorder known as failure to thrive. Thus, the natural morphogenic drive, while strong, is susceptible to variance in the familial environment. It is the effect of these variations and the reversal of the ill effects of these childhood experiences in adult psychotherapy that we are concerned with here.

Until quite recently developmental psychologists had not concerned themselves with the unique tasks and challenges of adulthood and have tended to focus on cognitive rather than emotional functioning (Simmerman and Schwartz, 1986). Explication of the emotional challenges of adulthood have been left to the fields of psychopathology and psychotherapy which have unfortunately tended to focus on the *absence* of mental health. Many theorists have assumed that the removal of psychopathology is synonymous with good mental health although there have certainly been theories that offer sets of generic dynamics that attempt to explain healthy functioning, such as many humanistic and object-relations formulations.

The central tasks of adulthood are primarily *emotional* and *spiritual* in nature. The exploration, finding, initiation, and maintenance of a committed intimate love relationship; the creation of a healthy familial/parenting unit; and the fulfillment and satisfaction derived from work and career form the basis of adult development. Though, I strongly point out that the form and content of these relationships (whether heterosexual or homosexual, monogamous or non-monogamous), the *kind* of parenting provided, or the *type* of work one engages in is not of significance here.

It is not my intention to offer specific prescriptions of the development of adult intimacy or what the ideal family should look like—there are an infinite number of healthy combinations and permutations from a *content* perspective—I am concerned with, however, the generic structural components of love and work. This is by no means value free, but the values I am interested in explicating are larger, process-oriented ones, such as valuing committed love relationships that have a goal of continuing increased intimacy. I am much less interested in the particular subtext for a kind of relationship, although I will highlight how the application of certain subtexts by certain people may be more or less growth inhibiting.

Another generic value is that transcendence of the self is a developmental task of adulthood via the separation from material and self-interests either through work, love relationships, and contributions to partner, child, and community. How one achieves this transcendental state, whether through some form of solo- or group-spiritual, religious, or psychotherapeutic experience is of little consequence here. I merely state that transcendence of the self is a more evolved state of being than not, and is central to adult development. So the question becomes, why are some of us more or less successful in this quest for love and work, increased intimacy, commitment, and transcendence? Why are some of us more or less motivated to grow than others?

The groundwork for motivation is laid in early childhood and repeated throughout the life cycle. Holding biological predilections equal, the key mechanism associated with this cycle is what has been referred to as the process of rapprochement, which has been posited to continue throughout the life cycle. Progressive growth moves one forward into new territory thus creating a natural tendency to become fearful and anxious. In this state of anxiety and sometimes panic (again, dependent upon the temperament of the person), the child looks to the caretaker/parent for feedback. The feedback the child looks for is in the nature of—"is it okay for me to proceed forward?" and "will you still be there for me?" Mahler (1980) described this rapprochement dance elegantly, and attachment theorists have researched the various attachment styles of children and of child-caretaker dyads. Object-relationists have described the attachment patterns of adults as well.

My purpose at this point is to avoid the specifics of these formulations and extract a basic principle that Stein (1980) and Kirschner and Kirschner (1986) have described, a process called progressive-abre-active-regression (PAR). PAR is seen as the normal growth process of life. Growth involves progressive movements forward, followed by what we may call normal fears, associated with varying degrees of loss of attachment and fear of abandonment. We see this process quite easily in children. The toddler first takes a few steps away from the parent and then seeing s/he is present, available, and approving; takes further steps, thereby acquiring new independent skills through adventure and practice. This rapprochement occurs and recurs forming a basic imprint upon the child.

The same can be said for events that are more psychological in nature such as when the child exhibits emotional behavior that is representative of real and emerging aspects of the child's unique temperament and personality. The child may receive varying degrees of praise, support, nurturance, guidance, and positive discipline in the face of these behaviors, which will tend to create a positive and loving (rapprochement) introject. Likewise, the child may internalize varying degrees of shame, pity, abuse, aloofness, and indifference which will tend to create a negative (rapprochement) introject.

In other words, exhibition of the real self of the child may lead to external disapproval or indifference which later forms the basis for the older child and adult's introjected parent(s) in the form of internalized maps, programs, and messages. That older child and adult "consults" with this introjected mentor when naturally fearful in the face of progressive movement forward. This consultant/rapprochement figure may indicate "it's okay to proceed, it's safe" or reinforce fearful messages that one may get annihilated, engulfed, or abandoned by going forward. The adult may find others in their contemporary lives to enact these introjects actively as well.

reparenting in everyday life

At the same time, though, other opportunities for healing are present throughout the life cycle because the child exists in the extraparental world of siblings, extended family members, friends, neighbors, teachers, coaches, and therapists. The child (and adult) will naturally seek out others in an attempt to replace the gaps and deficiencies from the parental experience. Others may provide needed doses of nurturance, discipline, and guidance.

We call this process reparenting, and the quite natural tendency to seek out reparental agents is one's search for psychological completion. This process begins in early childhood and repeats throughout the life cycle. To illustrate the malleable nature of this enterprise, I contend one's own parents can also serve as reparental agents by correcting past errors in relating. We have seen this phenomenon in adulthood in integrational family therapy (Bosznormenyi-Nagy and Spark, 1973; Bowen, 1978).

Furthermore, the person carries their template of object expectancy into new relational situations such that, even when there is not an inclination from the other to behave in the expected, usually negative way. The person may, however, at the slightest hint of the negative-expected behavior, react in a negative fashion. This may occur with a child and his own parents who essentially may be behaving differently in reality than the introject. When this phenomenon occurs in therapy, we call this negative object expectancy or negative transference.

But as previously indicated, there exists the possibility for healing. The basis for this healing is *positive* object expectancy, the hopefulness that the gaps and deficiencies from the family-of-origin may be provided by an other. When this phenomena occurs in therapy, we call this positive transference.

Transference, as we know, is not limited to the psychotherapy experience, but is an everyday occurrence. The tendency to organize others who may resemble aspects of prior relational experiences is common. Therefore, the possibility of changing the negative introjects to a more positive, self-loving one is always, at least theoretically, possible. It is on that basic assumption that the tenets and principles of this book's model rest.

Growth, then, may be seen as a series of successful PAR-experiences. This is the work of the externalized phase of motivation where the reparental-other, for us, the therapist, takes advantage of the natural positive expectancy or transference to assist the client in progressing forward in the various transactions of adulthood (intimate coupling, work, and rearing children). At the same time, the therapist works through the inevitable negative transference that develops and is triggered as well.

Unfortunately, most clients do not come to therapy in this (the PAR-) state of motivation because most people are in what we refer to as the "primitive phase" of motivation. In the primitive or predependent (to a therapeutic other) phase of motivation, the person relies on the maps and programs of childhood to guide decision-making, regarding kinds and degrees of intimacy allowed for in relationships, dependency upon others, as well as the assumption of power in the world, and the like. The primitive state is created when the PAR-process breaks down in childhood resulting in an avoidance of progressive movements forward, because proximity to the rapprochement object dominates the intrapsychic and interpersonal life of the person. Successful PAR-experiences are predicated on the notion of an available object/rapprochement figure either in reality in the form of a reparental other, or in the psychic reality of introjected parent. Continued failures in early and then later childhood PAR-experiences will tend to create this negative-object expectancy that we spoke of previously, perhaps better defined intrapsychically as an inner sense of object loss. This inner-object loss occurs when the progressive expectation of the parent or caretaker is inappropriate for the child.

An example of this may be in the case of timed feedings for infants. Perhaps an artifact of infant development theory, there was an era in the not-so-distant past that suggested parents only feed infants every four hours on a regular schedule of feedings versus the now and prior to the 1950s, more accepted practice of on-demand feedings which makes intuitive sense to most parents who themselves can get very cranky when they are hungry, and who tend not to conform to regular eating schedules. Babies communicate their hunger between feedings in the only fashion we can interpret—they cry. Indeed, their crying may or may not be related to hunger.

The effect of not providing this nurturance, the same as the archaic child-rearing practice of not picking up a crying baby for fear of "spoiling it," continues to guide some parents, since the infant has no object-relations skills and presumably no reparental agents readily available. A sense of object loss develops which we define as the gap between the appropriate expectation for that child and what is ultimately expected.

I do not mean to suggest that a few occasions of this kind of parenting will damage a child, nor that this kind of transaction cannot be overridden by future positive experiences of nurturance with these very same parents. I do mean to suggest, though, that persistent and consistent object loss is a demotivating force in the development of good-enough object relations. In this circumstance, the person's primary motivation is not necessarily to grow but rather to maintain object proximity with either the parents or themselves, the introjected parents, and/or those in the life of the person who enact aspects of the introjected parents. These relational values and messages to the child from the parents are introjected and the person remains loyal to these, however dysfunctional, for fear of losing the only object connection s/he knows. Fulfilling this sense of object loss becomes the focus of the person's quest to quell their omnipresent foundational fear of abandonment.

I call this experience the *default regression,* a regressive experience of fear, anxiety, and dysphoria that appears unrelated to the presence of a progressive expectation. The default regression is a demotivated state of demoralization, hopelessness, and despair. The default regression may be acted-out in the form of addictive disorders, or acted-in in the form of depression and anxiety. Again, reparental others (including the very same parents) can quell this fear of abandonment by impinging upon the default regression process.

The default regression becomes the intrapsychic systems' shut-down mode when the object loss is triggered. It is preferable to the hopefulness and ensuing feelings of acute expected disappointment of the PAR-mode of beingness. Indeed, the default regression tends to dismantle the natural PAR-process since the latter process relies on the presence and availability of a rapprochement figure. The person experiencing a default regression develops a kind of relational immunity to healing and growth agents—they may turn inward toward self, relating schizoidally, or outwardly, in a borderline-like fashion, or in some combination of the two, depending upon variances in the posture and positioning of the contemporary external object of attachment. The following charts provides an overview of the four phases of motivation.

FIGURE 6: HOW PEOPLE CHANGE: A FOUR-STAGE DEVELOPMENTAL MODEL

	Definition	Pre-Conditions	Mode of Being	Examples
Primitive Motivation	Fear of loss of real parent(s) and family, introjected parents, and those negative aspects of introjected family enated by contemporary significant others. Reparental-other figure is external and predependent. If person acts in ways that are significantly different from parents or parent-like others, the fear of losing the parent (or spouse) arises.	Lack of individuation from family-of-origin, enmeshed with family, even if cut-off. Loyalty to family, psychologically. Dependent on parent or parent-introjects.	Survival by loyalty to parents, parental introjects, or significant others who resemble parents, and significantly not to values. Attachment is to **any** parent or parent-like others.	Children until ages 5 or 6, where maintenance of proximity and more rigid personality structures are normal. Fundamentalist religion or cult members. Child abuse or neglect.
Externalized Motivation	Fear of loss of presumably positive reparental others (therapist, spouse), transference figures, is what motivates the person. If person behaves in ways that are out of sync with view of the reparental other, fear of losing that reparental other arises.	Attachment sufficiently built to reparental others who contain needed missing growth inputs with identification and introjection of re-parental other.	Survival by loyalty to a healthier set of values or principles, as offered by reparental other. Survival by loyalty to family of creation or family of choice. Attachment is made to **the** parent, that is, distinctions are made (e.g., I respect this reparental other because of who s/he is as a person and what s/he represents).	Healthfully dependent children. More rigid sense of right and wrong and of moral development. Conventional religions.

HOW PEOPLE CHANGE: A FOUR-STAGE DEVELOPMENTAL MODEL

	Definition	**Pre-Conditions**	**Mode of Being**	**Examples**
Internalized Motivation	Fear of loss of self is what motivates the person. The real self is defined by a set of values and principles congruent with one's behavior. If person behaves in ways that are incongruent with the wishes of the true self, the person fears being false and losing touch with his or her real self.	Reparental other is introjected and fully internalized that the introject is synonymous with the person. The person has discarded aspects of the reparental other that are not congruent with emerging true self. There is a completion of the integration between reparental other and the person.	Survival by loyalty to the real self: you live your life in accordance to your true standards.	State of true independence. May operate in ways that are outside the norm and unconventional, not to be different (as in Primitive Phase) but "to thine own self be true." May easily operate within the norm as well. Ecumenical, integrated religion; secular humanism.
Spiritual Motivation	The person is motivated almost exclusively by the demand characteristics of each situation they find themselves in. One may act in ways that may be very different than what the real self prescribes, without fear. A transcendental state where you can give your self up without losing it.	The real self is so well formed and trusted that there is no worry about losing it. Complete confidence in oneself.	Beyond loyalty formulations. There is no allegiance. A state of being where context is everything. Achievement of goals that are communal in nature is the priority.	The loving states of bliss where one can give up own needs for the sake of others not co-dependently but interdependently. May be misperceived as primitive state just as a codependent may explain their behavior as spiritually motivated. While behavior may be similar, the spiritually motivated person always retains their true self while the primitive codependent has no true self to lose. S/he enacts the behavior solely out of need of the other.

chapter 5

motivation in psychotherapy

Why is it that some clients arrive in therapy in a highly motivated state of readiness for input and change, while others come to therapy displaying resistance to this same input and change? Resistance may be apparent in the first telephone call to the practitioner, before actual contact is made. It is not unusual for a potential client to call the practitioner and then be unavailable when a return telephone call is made. Others may call the therapist requesting to be seen immediately. That very client may cancel or not show up for the first appointment, never to be heard from again. Still others may maintain a high level of motivation for a period of weeks, only to lose motivation in the succeeding months.

There are many potential explanations for these phenomena. Most explanations of resistance are, however, bound to one's theoretical orientation. This book seeks to explicate motivation-resistance phenomena from a more generic perspective, since explanations linked to single orientations involve inherently circular reasoning.

This model is an evolutionary one based on the foundational notion that as human beings we are survival-driven. In other words, our energies are first directed toward self-protection; only with successive assurances of survival do we engage in increased risk-taking behaviors. This model also seeks to link normal and optimal evolutionary development in that the developmental stages that a child enters and exits are similar to that of a client in psychotherapy.

the default regression and the primitive phase of motivation

Most clients present for treatment in the primitive phase of motivation, where the fear-of-loss of the old self, as defined originally by the family-of-origin and later through dysfunctional self-other transactions, is the force guiding change-oriented decision-making. Clients in this phase of treatment tend to operate in and out of, but mostly in, a default regression, punctuated by periods of extreme anxiety and depression or acting out of a default regression in the form of various addictions and the like, forming a core experience of hopelessness and despair about change. These regressions, sometimes referred to as abandonment depression in the psychodynamic literature, or object-loss in the object-relations literature, arise out of an externally triggered internal process where the client feels defeated in his or her ability to be understood empathically by either the introjected parent or transferentially by the therapist. The default regression is a state of *absence* of motivation which may include or be manifested by resistance, which is an *active* process of avoidance. Demotivation may also, and perhaps more commonly, look like indifference or avoidance. This reflects the fact that the opposite of love is not hate but the *absence* of love, which *may* manifest itself as hate, but more commonly, indifference.

In this state of demotivation one is not advancing either behaviorally, affectively, or cognitively. If a forward-moving state is morphogenesis or evolution, we may consider the state of demotivation a kind of de-evolution. In this schema, one cannot remain static; one is either pushing forward, challenging oneself or one is slowly drifting backward. In this sense, therapy is a part of a progressive and evolutionary spiral of personal growth but in no way represents a completion or a cure. Psychotherapy in the best sense is like good parenting; it offers a template from which future growth processes may emerge.

When this state of demotivation manifests itself in adulthood, we refer to this as the default regression. One cannot move forward while in this state of being, because to move progressively requires the presence of a good-enough inner object (parent) and/or the presence of a penetrating good-enough outer object (reparental agent, therapist, spouse, mentor). Progressive movement is predicated on the availability of this inner (introject) or outer (extroject) object because of the normal fears associated with forward movement and development. In the absence of this penetrating object the person will either not move forward or will proceed toward goals and developmental tasks that are nonprogressively oriented.

Progressive movement is defined as an innately healthy process, whereby the person seeks increasingly greater challenges. The demotivated client, for example, may remain in an unsatisfying marriage without seeking another relationship and without seeking intimacy within the current relationship. This same client may choose to leave his or her partner and find someone to replicate a similar relationship, or its psychological opposite via a role reversal. Advancement toward increased levels of psychological challenge and development is central to this model and requires an adequate level of motivation. Again, the absence of such motivation is the state of default regression. The default regression may occur as a temporary state or become a fixed part of the person, depending upon the specific personality structure of that person.

I have separated these personality structures into two basic types, A and B, and then, further into AA, AB and BB. The B personality tends to experience the default regression as a temporary state in that they are for the most part in touch with and uncomfortable with the feelings of hopelessness and despair. The default regression is experienced as dissonant: something is wrong, or missing.

The A personality, on the other hand, tends to be unaware of even being in a default regression. He or she tends to have more stable coping mechanisms, consistent with a schizoidal-type personality structure. The A-type tends to find a more stable introject substitute like a chronic addiction pattern, either to substances or people. The B-type is a more borderline style of coping and relating. Neither is intrinsically better or healthier.

For example, the B-type may also abuse substances and engage in codependent relationships, but likely in a more risky, binge-like fashion. The B-type experiences object loss and temporary object fulfillment, whereas the A-type relates to others in a way that, while not fulfilling, satiates *enough* so as not to experience complete object-loss. They may realize that something is missing from their experience of life but the default regression is experienced as much less dissonant.

The AA-type is an exaggeration of A found in more classic schizoidal personalities whereas the BB-type is an exaggeration of B found in more classic borderline personalities. Thus, while the default regression manifests itself very differently in A and B typologies, and, more importantly, presents different therapeutic dilemmas, the process of object-loss remains similar.

The role of the default regression in the maintenance of psychopathology and pathogenic relationships cannot be overstated. While there is a plethora of precipitating factors involved in various forms of psychopathology and dysfunctional relationships, including genetic vulnerability, constitution, and the like, with the exception of the role of traumatic life events such as incest or post-traumatic stress, object-relations formulations provide the most complete basis for understanding the motivational process. Even in disorders with clearly biological origins, the willingness to seek out and to comply with needed treatment is paramount. Under-motivated depressed patients who respond well to antidepressant medication often have irregular patterns of use, stop abruptly, or become overly sensitive to otherwise benign side-effects. I have had much more success in having antidepressants prescribed toward the end-phase of treatment, once the motivational difficulties have been mastered. Treatment compliance and tolerance of side-effects are high and self-reports of mood are much more accurate.

When antidepressants are prescribed too early in treatment, often the best result is that the client introjects the medication (instead of the therapist or spouse). The worst result is that the medication may bolster mood beyond what the client's self-esteem allows, which creates a kind of PAR-experience, resulting in some form of self-sabotage via medication non-compliance.

This brings us to an interesting question. What is the relationship between depression or anxiety and the default regression? A default regression may occur and present as a depressive episode or dysthymia. Moreover, a person may be in a default regression and experience depression concomitantly. If one has a predilection toward depression, the default regression state, with its sense of hopelessness and passivity, may exacerbate chronic dysthymia or fuel a depressive episode.

Moreover, one may be depressed and not be in a default regression. Although hopelessness is a hallmark sign of depression according to the DSM-IV, I view the cycle of hopelessness, despair, and faithlessness as a separate process related to motivation that may worsen depression. But, as I stated, the default regression may be easily mistaken for depression. Depression may respond to any number of potent therapies, including cognitive therapy or interpersonal therapy. A PAR-regression once properly identified will respond to any number of supportive therapies or therapeutic monitoring and guidance. The default regression, however, responds only through being provided with a penetrating good object, reparenting, if you will. This may occur via the therapist, spouse, or the original parent(s).

This sense of object-loss becomes embedded into the personality of the child, and later in an older child or adult can be triggered quite easily by similar loss-inducing stimuli. The process of the adult returning to this early state of object-loss, the default regression, must be distinguished from what we refer to as the PAR-regression. But before we move further, let us examine more closely the subphases of the primitive phase.

the primitive subphases: a typology

Traditionally, we have several classification systems for grouping clients who present for psychotherapy. We may categorize clients by their presenting diagnosis. There are several problems with such a system (Schacht, 1985). First, our diagnostic methods, while improving, have questionable reliability and validity when transferred into clinical as opposed to research settings. Second, even when we can reliably diagnose a client, effective treatment may vary greatly for different clients. Most diagnosable populations are more heterogeneous than homogeneous with regard to the multitude of factors relevant to the *treatment* process, most significantly in our model, the motivation to change.

Third, contrary to expectations, the *beginning* of treatment is probably the worst time to diagnose, since many of the client's difficulties may be associated with the motivational cluster of problems related more to self-esteem and self-other relations than to psychopathology. It is only with the clearing away of motivational difficulties that "clean" diagnosable disorders and psychopathology emerge. (I shall elaborate further in Chapter 6.) Fourth, the act of diagnosing may be antithetical to the precepts of good therapeutic relating, that is, the creation of an us-them, "not-me" mind set. This is a point the humanistic tradition in psychotherapy has repeatedly made.

The literature on personality disorders, as illustrated in Axis II of the DSM, provides another method of classification. These personality disorders suffer many of the same limitations as the aforementioned Axis I psychopathology, but perhaps even more so. Labeling a client as having a personality disorder is even more off-putting therapeutically than labeling a client as phobic or depressed. Personality disorders tend to be labels that stick, since there is so little consensus about how to treat these disorders and when there is, treatment tends to be lengthy and arduous. We should not label what we cannot adequately treat. The lone exception is the category of Borderline Personality Disorder, which is a label with a good deal of clinical utility and a developing consensus on treatment (Chathman, 1996; Goldstein, 1995; Heard and Linehan, 1994; Linehan, 1993; Share, 1994; Tobin, 1995).

I must state emphatically, however, that I am distinguishing here between clients who display borderline-like traits and a true Borderline Personality Disorder. The psychotherapy literature is replete with reports of clients who are described as "BPD" yet an objective reading suggests that these clients are more reminiscent of a more prototypical psychotherapy client (e.g., Masterson, 1988, pp. 140–148). Borderline Personality Disorder, in my view, is best thought of as a syndrome that appears to take on a life of its own, analogous to alcoholism say.

Since motivation is our core construct, I contend that motivational difficulties impede the development of the personality and that we should outline our classification of personality types on that basis. Certainly other practice-relevant classifications systems are possible (e.g., Blatt and Felsen, 1993).

Underlying the four major types of clients who present for therapy in the primitive phase of motivation is a narcissism which I simply define as an absorption with the survival concerns of the self. I do not see narcissism as a separate personality disorder per se; all clients in the primitive phase are narcissistic. This narcissism may be acted out interpersonally in one of two ways: as *codependent* narcissism or, more classically, in *entitled* narcissism. The codependent narcissist gives up his or her own needs to feed and fuel the needs of the other, while the entitled narcissist, usually the fed object of the codependent, treats others as objects to feed him or her and sees people as extensions of self.

If we conceive of narcissism as an underlying, essentially *intrap*ersonal phenomenon of the primitive phase, that is, self-obsessiveness in the entitled narcissist or obsessiveness-with-other in the codependent narcissist, then our typology may be distinguished by more *inter*personal phenomena. Distinguishing clients on the basis of interpersonal phenomena is a more useful distinction for therapists, since therapy itself is an interpersonal event.

Our typology is a continuum of interpersonal and therapeutic relating. At one pole we have the AA-types which we may classify as more classically defined schizoids who are the most nonreactive to the feelings of themselves and others in their interpersonal worlds. At the opposite pole we have BB, the classically defined borderline types who are *highly* reactive to their own feelings and to the operations of others and events in their interpersonal worlds. At the extreme ends of these poles we have what I referred to previously as syndromes. For example, the BB pole is the classic Borderline Personality Disorder: difficult to treat, prone to severe forms of acting out and rages, severe reactions to separations, etc. At the AA pole we have the classic Schizoidal Personality,[1] a syndrome defined by extreme distantiation from the feel-

---

1. I am reluctant to label the schizoid as a true disorder since the literature and research are much less conclusive than for Borderline Personality Disorder.

ings of self and others, usually accompanied by a strangeness of affect, cognition, and behavior that arises out of continued and repeated isolation of the self from emotional and life experiences.

The large majority of clients who present for treatment, however, are not at the two poles but are either A's (schizoid-like) or B's (borderline-like). Their personality type is not a syndrome but rather a collection of traits and patterns that form tendencies useful for clinicians to recognize. I have further refined the types into *hard* A's and *hard* B's, fairly stable tendencies that remain steady over the course of treatment, even when great transformation is made. The soft A's and soft B's, otherwise known as the AB admixture, are clients who display enough aspects of both types such that there is little consequence for the course of treatment.

The preponderance of these types over clients presenting for therapy is hypothesized to fit a normal curve such that the AB type represents the modal psychotherapy client with the A- and B-types representing the second highest proportion. The AA-and BB- types are the outlayers in terms of incidence.

Again, our core construct is motivation, so neither grouping is seen as more inherently unhealthy or dysfunctional. A highly motivated AA client, for example, will make greater progress than an unmotivated A client. There is no hypothesized or even suggested correlation between motivation level and client type. Each client type may pass quite differently through our phases as motivation increases, but that may be the only significant relationship in this model. For the most part, it is best to conceive of this typology as various subphases of the primitive phase of motivation. Let us now examine the major A-B distinctions relevant for treatment.

A-type subphase

The A-type clients may fool the therapist in that they tend to present as healthier than they are. This is so because they have a more developed false self. This false self helps them in certain life transactions where playing a particular role(s), such as in their jobs, may bring success. These are clients who may be functioning at very high levels in their careers but are highly underdeveloped in transactions of life that require more realness and role flexibility to be successful, such as love relationships and child-rearing. Even their careers, however, may suffer from difficulties, especially when there is a major upset or crisis, since they may have a difficult time adapting to a change in roles. Moreover, their identities may be tied directly to their careers (or role) so if they lose their job, for whatever reason, they may be unable to rebound. In fact, this is when many A's present for treatment. Their presentation for therapy is usually around a particular issue as opposed to the more diffuse complaints of the B-types. Curiously, though, since there are so many other issues the client is not in touch with, the presenting problem may never quite remit.

For example, a very polished and successful young woman executive came to me for therapy to work on finding a love partner after a lack of success in that area. She appeared bright and eager to work directly on issues of meeting men, dating, choosing an appropriate partner, and so forth. Two years into treatment, we had worked on her highly enmeshed family-of-origin relationship, which she did not mention in the first three months of treatment, and on coping with a career crisis brought about by a merger at her firm. We worked on the issues related to her social life but not in the way the primitive A-type might have expected when first entering treatment.

The A-type, like all primitively phased persons, has default regressions but their tendency is to find coping mechanisms to manage or defuse them. These coping mechanisms tend to be more stable, which keeps the A-type from bottoming out as the B-type might. Things never become so bad for the A-type because of these stable coping mechanisms which often include intellectualization as a primary defense. The A-type will self-talk their way out of a default regression by reading a self-help book, for example.

The A-type may also *progress* their way out of a default regression by focusing on or looking forward to some future goal like a new job, a new house, or a vacation, usually objects or things, whereas the B-type may attempt to "P" their way out of a default regression by focusing on an object in the form of a person.

If the A-type is in a relationship to cope with the default regression, it tends to be a stable one with few highs or lows. If they abuse substances or alcohol, their pattern of abuse is also stable (e.g., the alcoholic who drinks a six-pack of beer every night) versus the unstable binge pattern abuse of the B-type (e.g., the weekend warrior who hits bottom, then rushes to "clean up his or her act," only to binge again). Because the A-type does not hit "bottom," the default regression is difficult to see. We may say, though, that he or she exists in a constant default regression protected by a more developed false self.

When these clients begin to recognize their default regression, they often remark that they do not even know what they feel or even who they really are. Prior to this point, though, the false self is engaging enough to allow others to be "in" with them. However, their modes of relating are essentially false and others are kept at a particular distance, best described by Guntrip (1968) as the schizoidal compromise—not close enough to engender fears of engulfment and not far enough to engender fears of abandonment.

In therapy, the practitioner will have the experience of never quite getting to know the client or constantly remaining at the same level of closeness. Overall, their relationships tend to be marked by distantiation. They may be married to another A-type, becoming a picture of stable distantiation or to their B-type counterpart, functioning as the stable member of the relationship. Many A-types arrive in therapy as the partners of the identified client, the B-type mate or child.

The therapy relationship of the A-type is best described as weak, watered down, and distant but perhaps good enough to keep going. The relationship is not particularly charged until therapeutic penetration is achieved. On the other hand, the therapeutic relationship with the B-type may be highly charged and marked by more extreme closeness and neediness and then more extreme distance, but rarely in-between, especially prior to penetration.

This difference exists because of the contrasting default regression processes of the two types. The tendency for the therapist of the A-type client is to enact *too safe* a posture where little connection is made because the A-type's manifest fear of engulfment may signal and impel him or her to retreat into a schizoidal-compromise position.

The practitioner of the B-type client will tend to make errors in the opposite direction, being in too unstable a posture, or in other words, overreacting to the B-type client's more extreme signaling or soliciting of the therapist to "come here *now*" or to "get away *now*", for example. The A-type client requires the therapist to be more intrusive and playful, then distant again (i.e., to move in and then out) whereas the therapeutic posture appropriate to the B-type client needs to be more stable and present, less reactive to their sharper movements toward and away from the practitioner. Therapists whose countertransferential tendency is to resist penetration may be in danger of creating long-term unproductive dependent relationships with A clients, who may leave and return to therapy again and again over a period of several years.

B-type subphase

As I've stated, the B-type therapeutic relationship will be more highly charged as the less tepid transferential relationship develops, because the default regression for the B-type client is marked by periods of despair and hopelessness punctuated by a temporary lifting of the default regression mediated by an interaction with a substance, love object, new job, or reparental agent (e.g., healer, guru). These coping mechanisms are similar to the ones utilized by the A-type, but they tend to be much less stable. In the default regression, the B-type is often impenetrable whereas the A-type does not move far from penetrability but remains in the schizoidal-compromise position.

The B-type has an inadequate false self that makes role flexibility difficult and all but the most routine functioning may be problematic. The B-type will have a difficult time with maintaining career progression, for example, because if they become deflated or hopeless, they tend to give up completely. The A-type client may undergo the same vicissitudes but they may be so out of touch with the experience that they modify and adjust themselves to suit the demands of the situation. Instead of quitting their job in a default regression the A-type will simply adjust their expectations downward and go on. This unhappiness may remain below the surface, whereas the B-type is more reactive to experience with periods of happiness and sadness. There is, however, an all-or-nothing quality to the happiness or sadness. When the B-type is "happy" everything is fine; when they are sad, *nothing* is fine.

The B-type client appears more *real* in that they enact their experience (e.g., if they're in a default regression, you know it) but perhaps too real, in that they have a difficult time adapting to changes in their environment. In contrast to the A-type, they may be highly engaging interpersonally when *not* in a default regression or highly disengaging interpersonally when in a default regression. The same may be said for their level of denial and defensiveness. They may go from being very open emotionally to extremely shut down and closed. Therefore, the B-types tend to have closer but more volatile relationships with significant others (like family-of-origin and friends), particularly with other B-types in love relationships. In contrast, the A-type will tend to have more stable but distant relationships with friends that are often circumstantial. When circumstances change for A-types, there may be a complete but reasonably calm cut-off.

The following charts offer contrasting portraits of the four distinct primitive subphase types along several key dimensions relevant to treatment. Keep in mind, however, that our hypothesized normal curve of the generic client population suggests the *modal* client is a soft A or a soft B (an AB admixture).

FIGURE 2: CLIENT DYNAMICS AND THERAPIST RELATIONAL POSTURE

	Foundational Fears	Intimacy Dynamics & Posture	Dependency Dynamics & Posture	Power Dynamics & Posture
AA	Engulfment exclusively	You cannot press on abandonment fears. They will let you get as far away as you want. If the therapist moves *closer*, even slightly, the client experiences it negatively.	Client is highly counter-dependent. Therapist must strongly encourage dependency.	Therapist will be seen as weak and unimportant. Therapist must become more overtly omnipotent, directive, and active in the life of the client.
A	Engulfment primary and manifest Abandonment secondary and latent	It's harder to press on abandonment fears. Therapist *begins* in a more distant posture, but moves closer with increasing trust. Therapist attempts to create more proximity and mastery of intimacy.	Client will be passively dependent. They will tend to not discuss and enact their dependency by *not* asking questions, seeking advice, phone calls, etc. Encourage dependency.	Therapist will be viewed as less powerful and important. Therapist will move in the direction of being more central, omnipotent, directive, and active in the life of the client.
B	Engulfment primary and manifest Abandonment secondary and latent	It's harder to press on engulfment fears. Therapist begins in a closer posture, but tends to move away with increasing trust. Therapist attempts to help client achieve mastery through separation.	Client will be actively dependent. They will own and enact their dependency by asking questions, seeking advice, phone calls, etc. Don't *discourage* dependency.	Therapist will be viewed as more powerful. Therapist will be, with time, encouraging of the client's owning their power by becoming self-directed and claiming their authority.
BB	Abandonment exclusively	You cannot press on fears of engulfment. They will let you get as close as you want. If the therapist moves away, even slightly, the client will react negatively.	Client is highly dependent. Therapist will need to discourage dependency and set firmer and clearer relational boundaries.	Therapist is seen as very powerful. Therapist must tend to discourage this by being less omnipotent, directive, and active.

FIGURE 3: THERAPEUTIC BONDING, PENETRATION AND TRANSFERENCE

	Bonding Pentration Posture	How Penetration Occurs in Therapy	How Trans-ference Occurs in Therapy	Type of Transference
AA	Nurturance is most needed but there is no emotional allowance for it. In the meantime a neutral/ confrontational posture to bond is required.	They will *hate* the therapist. After therapeutic penetration, they will *love* the therapist.	Transference reaction is minimally seen. The client may be in a negative or positive transference but it will be difficult for the therapist to know since the client cannot translate their experience.	Therapist will be seen as weak and unimportant. Therapist must become more overtly omnipotent, directive, and active.
A	Generally confrontive to bond and nurturance to penetrate.	They will *like* the therapist. After therapeutic penetration, they will either love or hate their therapist.	Transference will occur outside of session. They will tend *not* to react to therapeutic intervention during the session but mostly *after* the session.	Positive transference more overt ("I like you"). Negative transference is present but covert.
B	Generally nurturant to bond and confrontational to penetrate.	They will tend to love and hate the therapist. If they hate, they will terminate. After therapeutic penetration, they will love and hate the therapist.	Transference will occur in the session and be quite intense. Therapist will be able to read transferential reactions and cues, although they may be difficult to deal with.	Negative transference (suspicion and hostility) more overt. Positive transference present, but more covert.
BB	Confrontation is most needed for growth but there is no emotional allowance for it. In the meantime a neutral/nurturant posture to bond.	They will *love* the therapist. If they *hate*, they will terminate. After therapeutic penetration, they will like or appreciate the therapist.	Transference reactively is very high, quite intense, and obvious to both therapist and client.	Positive transference only. If transference switches to negative, client will terminate.

FIGURE 4: THERAPY PROCESS FACTORS

	Progression/ Regression Dynamics and Posture	Real/False Self Dynamics and Posture	Flow and Rhythm of Therapy	Stamina for Therapy
AA	Regress exclusively. The client is already too progressed.	Break down the false-self facade of the client. Encourage any *real* expression of emotional experience (e.g., dreams, journaling).	Highly predictable, formulated, and controlled. Sessions tend to be "dead" and very boring.	Very poor. The client will always be one step out of the door. If they terminate, they will tend not to seek therapy elsewhere.
A	Emphasize regression. Some progression.	Break down the false-self facade of the client. Let overt default regression emerge. Then penetrate as you would a "B" client.	More predictable sessions and sameness. Lots of anecdotes and story telling (content material) that is repetitive. Too much reporting. Even a rhythm to latenesses and cancellations. Little progress at times.	Good. If they terminate, they will tend to return to the same practitioner even if little clear progress has been made.
B	Emphasize progression. Some regression.	Build up fragile facade to protect client from experiencing consistent rejection in the environment that leads to default regressions.	More unpredictable and a lack of sameness. Highly charged sessions followed by unproductive sessions. Lots of acting out and process material. Irregular attendance patterns.	Good. If they terminate, they will likely return to therapy but to another practitioner.
BB	Progress exclusively. The client is already too regressed.	Build a false self where none exists now. Teach client how to "play the game," adapt flexible roles, and suppress real emotion.	Highly violative, lots of upset and crises brought into therapy sessions. Therapist serves as a container and holder for the client.	Too good. They will remain in therapy indefinitely and never want to leave. If they terminate, they will find another practitioner, with whom to seek a similar relationship.

FIGURE 5: SELF-OTHER FACTORS

	Prototypical Family of Origin Role	Client Descriptions of Family of Origin	Coupling Transaction	Rearing Transaction
AA	Outcast and isolated from parents.	Client is largely unable to describe their family-of-origin experience: "It was okay, I guess." "I don't remember."	Either no relationship or highly unfulfilling relationship. Sometimes "weird," (e.g., different cities, together 15 years and never married.)	Cold and distant parenting. Children may continue to return to parental introjects and real parents to get needed input.
A	Parentified caretaker. Peacemaker. Family therapist.	Generally positive descriptions. Even if negative, it is placed in a positive context ("they did their best.") Client *believes* in their family and the family's way of doing things and overlooks negative.	Tends to stay together in an unfulfilling relationship. Acting out is quiet (e.g., covert, long-term affairs).	As parents they tend to mimic own parents' style. ("It was good enough for them.") Not much real struggle or thought goes into parenting role.
B	Parentified scapegoat. Identified patient, sick, ill, crazy, bad, survivor, "different than."	Generally negative descriptions. Client recognizes the unhealth of the family and acts as the "truthsayer." Client is persistent in discovering and uncovering family secrets. "They're fucked up."	More volatile relationships. Break-ups and acting out which is noisy (i.e., brief overt affairs).	As parents they struggle to do things differently than their own parents yet are inclined to enact the "flip side" of their own experience. (e.g., overly nurturing, lack of discipline for abuse survivors).
BB	Outcast, yet highly enmeshed with one (or both) parents.	Highly ambivalent. Client talks of how negative their family was and is and how much they hate them, but returns to the family home to live or goes on a group vacation. Enmeshed, dependent, and negative.	Extremely volatile. Long-standing never resolved crises. Leavings followed by remarkable calming down periods.	Lots of projection and projective identification with children. Good/bad child. To individuate child rebels by leaving. Claims to do things differently than own parents, but does not.

PAR-regression and the external phase of motivation

PAR-regression is a component of an essentially healthy process of growth and development in which the regressed experiences may seem quite similar to the experience of the default regression. The critical distinction is that the PAR-regression occurs in the presence of growth-inducing stimuli which challenge the previously defined ceiling barriers, prewired capabilities and programming of the older child or adult. The adulthood correlate of a PAR-regression might be the experience of anxiety, fear, or even terror at the prospect of increased intimacy in the form of a marital engagement or the expectation of increased competency in the form of job promotion.

A default regression, on the other hand, occurs in the absence of such progressive stimuli and is triggered by an object-loss that is similar and familiar with an abandonment experienced in early childhood and often reexperienced throughout later childhood and adulthood. This default regression may be momentary or last up to several months or years and may be acted out in the form of an addiction to a substance or person, or acted-in, in the form of depression or anxiety.

The distinction between the default regression and the PAR-regression becomes especially important for psychotherapists to recognize since therapists seek to impinge upon the growth processes of their clients. Like a parent, teacher, mentor, or coach, the therapist is in a position as a built-in figure of rapprochement, to help the client through a PAR-regression. The role of the therapist is very different when a client is experiencing a default regression, as the client is in need of the missing-object fulfillment of the primitive phase. Clients vacillate between progression and regression (default and PAR) throughout any treatment process.

The default regression may be considered a state of demotivation, where hopelessness and despair predominate. Clients who arrive in therapy in this state of demotivation are particularly challenging for their therapists, but less so if the therapists understand their clients' need for object fulfillment and gratification. To accomplish this, the therapist must penetrate the patterned defenses of the client which have over time become a kind of false self for one subgroup of primitive clients (the more "schizoidal" clients or A's) or a kind of self-destructive acting out for another subgroup (the more "borderline-ish" B-clients). Most clients have aspects of both subgroups.

Some clients arrive in therapy already in a PAR-regression. This is not surprising since the seeking out of a rapprochement figure, like a therapist (or minister, parent, or spouse) at a time of life-change-induced stress is both expected and positive. The client in this state of PAR-regression is highly motivated and primed to introject the therapist as a kind of a new mentor figure. This is positive because the client will be open to the techniques, advice, and direction of the therapist and therapy.

The therapist will not need to penetrate the false self of the primitive A client or directly impinge upon the acting out of the primitive B client, since this client comes to treatment in a psychological state of, for lack of a better word, realness and potential readiness to face the progressive and regressive challenges ahead. The role of the therapist is to catalyze this natural health-seeking process.

Clients who arrive in therapy in a PAR-regression are said to be in the external phase of motivation, where the motivation to grow and to change is dependent upon the close involvement of another, generally speaking, a therapeutic other. If the therapist assumes an appropriate relational posture, the client may remain in this PAR-state of regression vis-à-vis the therapist, but more likely will return to their more typical state of motivation (the primitive phase) within a short period of time. This explains why many clients, despite forming positive alliances with their therapists, drop out of treatment after six to eight sessions before meaningful change is accomplished. This phenomena has also been inadequately referred to as "flight into health."

Others may remain in treatment but often to the chagrin of the therapist are now listless and hopeless regarding change they were once hopeful and optimistic about. This is partially a transferential phenomenon as the presence of a new parent figure fuels the positive expectations of healing old wounds. When this does not fully occur after a period of time the negative expectations that, "my needs will go unfulfilled" are once again fueled.

I will discuss such transferential phenomena throughout the book not in the usual psychoanalytic framework but with respect to clinical decision-making. Indeed, the kind of therapy I advocate is best thought of as an active psychoanalysis, first suggested by one of Freud's disciples, Sandor Ferenczi, in the 1920's (Ferenczi, 1921; 1928; 1931; see also Balint, 1968).[2] The therapist here attempts to fill in the gaps

---

2. Ferenczi was considered one of the most brilliant clinicians of his time. However, as Fenster, Rachman and Wiedemann (1990) point out that for a combination of historical, political, and personal reasons, Ferenczi has never been credited with being the originator of many ideas that foreshadowed much of what was to come in psychotherapy.

and deficiencies for the client's family-of-origin experience within the therapeutic frame.[3] This reparenting may be active and directive (advice or behavioral suggestion, for example), as well as passive and nondirective (mirroring or reflection).

In this model, depending upon their family-of-origin experience, their current level of development in the various transactional areas of life like independence (e.g., career), and upon their current level of motivation (primitive, external, internal, or spiritual) a particular relational posture is selected for each client . The client's level of motivation will, of course, change over time. The primary role of the therapist is to assist in increasing motivation so that he or she eventually becomes self-initiating (the internal phase) and, if they choose, become willing to give up their selves for others (the spiritual phase).

Thus, to a great extent, the primitive and external phases are more relevant than the internal and spiritual phases in the therapy process. The primitive phase is the bonding and penetration phase of therapy (which, depending upon various factors, may last three sessions, three months, or three years) and is vaguely reminiscent of the very early childhood experience of the client. It involves the impingement upon the default regression during which the client is in a position to slowly discard and replace various dysfunctional parental and familial imprints (e.g., "I am bad or unworthy when my needs go unfulfilled"). This may appear straightforward or even simplistic. But the client may, sometimes accurately (depending upon the level of familial dysfunction), believe letting go of the dysfunctional maps and programs means they must let go of the self. The self they believe they must let go of, however, is not the true self, but the self that was imprinted with the introjected message of "Your needs go unmet because you are unworthy."

The client who is able to psychologically, and sometimes physically in the form of individuation, distance him or herself, the real self, from the dysfunctional imprints, may now enter the external phase of motivation. If the client comes to therapy without having more or less completely accomplished this, the therapist must become the new mentor or reparental object for this client. Otherwise, the client will not be able to enter the external phase of motivation, as the progressive stimuli inherent in these movements toward growth will lead to PAR-regression.

---

3. Historically the originators and purveyors of what I would refer to as the active depth therapies have tended to be branded as wayward renegades, perhaps even unethical charlatans. In the case of Ferenczi this is an unfair characterization; however, in the case of John Rosen's diret analysis (Rosen, 1975), this assessment is quite accurate (see Masson, 1994).

Like the young toddler taking its first independent steps away from their parents, the adult will look back to the rapprochement figure for positive signals and reassurance. For the adult this figure may be their introjected parent(s) or those in their contemporary life (e.g., a spouse) who may enact the role of the introjected parent(s). This other may assist the person in going forward by providing good-enough reparenting imprints. This may take any number of different forms depending upon the nature of their relationship and the particular needs of the persons involved. Conversely, the other may discourage positive progressive movement perhaps, not coincidentally, in the same way as the original parent, thereby undermining attempts toward growth.

An example may be in order here. Dan, a very creative and talented middle-aged male client felt stifled in his current position working under a very controlling owner-manager. Much of his presenting psychological symptomatology revolved around his boss's treatment of him, which not coincidentally mimicked his relationship with his father. His boss would, as had his father, make grand promises about his future but virtually never followed through by giving him either appropriate remuneration or control over his own destiny. The boss would, for instance, encourage Dan to proceed on a business deal, and then after Dan did all the preliminary work and negotiation, would make last-minute changes that had the effect of undermining Dan's credibility and authority with his client. When Dan would confront his boss about this, his boss would imply that he was too sensitive. Not coincidentally, this was precisely what his father said to him after similar experiences.

An opportunity for Dan to start his own business presented itself when one of his colleagues recognized his abilities and suggested a partnership. There was some risk involved since initially there would be a decreased base salary. There existed, however, an opportunity to profit in succeeding years and, more importantly, give him control over his own future.

While he knew this was a great opportunity, he was frightened at the prospect of leaving the predictability and familiarity of his current situation, as uncomfortable as it was, and began to compulsively focus his decision on the initially decreased salary. He would have protracted and at times obsessive conversations with his wife (Rita) who, while supportive of either decision, never came down firmly on the side of the new business opportunity. Dan kept going to Rita, essentially searching for an elusive "go" signal in the form of "This appears to be what you really want. Go after it. You'll make it work. I'm scared, too, but I'm behind you 100 percent and together *we'll* find a way to make it work. Let's sit down and figure out the finances. But it's what you really want and I want you to go for it." While she was supportive, she never provided the good-enough reparental input "It's okay; you're okay. I trust you and I have confidence in you. I'm here for you and I believe in you." Dan really needed the unswerving "go" signal since he lacked that introject within himself. Instead, what he kept hearing was the introject of his father: "I have confidence in you to a point, but when push comes to shove, I have no faith in you to make things work."

Indeed, this is why he remained in a dysfunctional work relationship where his boss continually enacted this introject. Dan knew something was not quite right when his boss would undermine him but lacked the self-confidence to truly believe in his own instincts and himself. When he would confront his boss after one of these incidents, his boss would (like his father) make some vague, veiled threat like, "Well if you don't like it, you can always leave." Dan would get the message, panic at the notion of loss (i.e., job and livelihood but more importantly, loss of father's approval) and then cave in. This created the default regression and is how he arrived in therapy, a mass of confusion, self-doubt, and self-recrimination which took the form of a kind of generalized despair and loss of hope and meaning that mimicked a clinical depression.

Interestingly, his wife suggested they come to therapy when she became alarmed by his reluctance to address his depression. While his wife was well-intentioned, her panic would be triggered at the very point her husband needed her to provide a "go" signal. She would panic because she grew up in a family in which Dad had all the overt power (although her mother "enacted" the role of the helpless wife for the husband's denied helplessness).

Thus, when she sensed that her husband was "weak" or in a regressed position of "Please take charge now. Let me know it's okay to proceed since in my fear-of-loss state, I need to introject your strength." She, too, became frightened at the prospect of having to relate to his now frightened, and in her view, "weak, regressed" man. Interestingly, and again, not coincidentally, when he enacted this very real fear (what she interpreted as weakness), *she* became scared of enacting her submerged powerful side and of giving him the strong "go" message. Her internal program was that women are weak, and if they behave powerfully and overtly they will be abandoned. This was the dynamic of her parents' marriage.

As I said, Dan came to treatment in this essentially demotivated, or in our model, the primitive state of motivation, a state of stuckness and fear of losing one's family-of-origin, familial introjects, or aspects of those familial introjects enacted by contemporary persons in their life (e.g., boss, wife). My initial task was to bond, form a therapeutic alliance, and ultimately penetrate Dan's psychological space so I could become a potential reparental agent. Thus, at the time the new professional opportunity became available (five months into treatment), he sought me out as a new rapprochement figure, albeit tentatively at first, since his wife was his natural imago-rapprochement figure. But, because of the limitations of her family-of-origin introjects my attempts to catalyze their natural healing processes were unsuccessful. Although I had formed an alliance with her, I had not psychologically penetrated her. In her view, she had not initiated therapy for herself, but was there for her husband.

At a key point in this intrapersonal and interpersonal transaction, I gave him the appropriate "go" signal of belief, trust, and confidence in him along with assurances that I would help him with his fears as he was transitioning into this new progressive arena. This new input was enough to allow him to take a "leap of faith" into himself while quelling his fear of abandonment with my assurances of empathy and direct help.

As one might expect, I had to continue to provide these inputs. The night before he was to give his resignation to his boss, that is, confront and leave his "father," he had a full-blown panic attack. Both he and his wife interpreted this to mean he was making "an awful mistake" and should reconsider. During an 11:00 p.m. telephone call, I had to strongly reassure both of them, explaining why this was all so difficult and that it was okay to proceed forward.

This model of therapy offers a somewhat unconventioanl view of the therapeutic relationship. In more conventional therapeutic relational paradigms, the therapist would not inject him or herself so fully into the intrapsychic and actual life of the client nor take the strong reparental stand, "It's okay to proceed." Many depth-oriented therapists might view the dynamics I have described in similar ways, but not see their role so actively.

A failure to press the conventional boundaries of therapy by giving an active "go" signal may result in the client's avoidance of forward progress and an opportunity for growth may be lost. Moreover, by *not*

providing an active "go" signal, the therapist may be unwittingly enacting the original familial introject even if the therapist is operating in
significantly different ways than the parents did.

The possibility of working through negative transference may be
lost as well. This client, at a certain point in this process, expressed the
fear that I was controlling, he did not say, but could have, like his
father. Instead of his father telling him what was "correct," his therapist was. Indeed as therapist and client we were mimicking the original
father-son transaction. I say "we" because there was a natural tendency
on his part to unconsciously organize this very transaction, in an
attempt, as Freud first posited, to change the ending of the repetition
compulsion (see Freud, 1914).

I did not interpret this transference as much as I impinged upon
it by participating and hence reenacting it while indeed changing the
ending, which Freud saw as fruitless. The ending of the repetitious
transferential transaction changed not by the client's ultimately being
successful and satisfied in his career (which he in fact did), but in his
ability to *trust* that a parent-like figure had his best interests at heart,
believed in him, and sincerely wanted him to succeed. That experience
was at once frightening and healing.

As negative transference was worked through, a new and healthier introject took form. This introject represented the therapist's confidence, trust, and belief, and replaced his father's lack of faith in him.
For some time the client needed this input *externally* from the therapist.
When the client still needs healthy input to be present in the form
of another person in this way, the client's level of motivation is said to
be external.

When the goal of introjecting the healthy input is reached, the
therapist's input is no longer needed or is needed on a less intensive
basis. The client must be ready to let go of and separate from the therapist. When the client is relating to the therapist in this mode, he or
she is said to be in the internal phase of motivation, where growth decisions are self-guided, perhaps in occasional consultation with another.
But essentially clients in the internal phase serve as their own rapprochement figures, giving themselves the needed "go" signal. At the
same time, the client gets his or her regressive needs met in an intimate
love relationship where the lover may also serve in the rapprochement
role, in the sense that the couple on some level, serves as one interlocking organism.

The guts of growth in therapy, though, is in the external phase where PAR-movements take place. Generally, progressive movement and a successful PAR-process in one area of life create the possibility of PAR-experiences elsewhere, since the essential change occurs in the transferential dynamics and the provision of needed reparenting by the therapist. At this point the client will quite naturally seek the therapist out and be open to a host of therapeutic inputs.

In this particular client's case, for example, he started talking about disappointment in his wife for not providing enough strength in the marriage and deferring to him too often. He wanted her to take more control in decision-making areas of family life. While he had said similar things to her in the past, after the successful PAR-experience, he communicated his desire and need with more confidence and assurance. Again, to follow through he needed consistent external input from the therapist since he would panic at the thought of strongly communicating this need to her, for fear she might reject him. In the actuality of their relationship, this indeed did occur, partially because he communicated the need so tepidly and partially because she feared becoming more "powerful."

In therapy sessions, I would role-play with him where first he played himself. He would easily get frustrated with her, lose confidence in himself, become quietly angry, and then sullenly retreat. If he retreated too far away from her, she would seek him out and they would "make up," in a sort of compromise that served to maintain the homeostasis of their marriage, until the process started all over again. He would become increasingly disenchanted with her lack of strength. Then I played him and he played his wife. I enacted the stronger position, saying to "her": "I don't feel like you're listening to me" and "I need you to hear this—it's really vital to me," basically not giving up until "he" was successful at penetrating her defense of denial.

He thus got to experience the fear she was experiencing, as well as introject the therapist as the healthier self-believing object. As he transferred this learned behavior into his marital life, his wife's defenses began to dissipate. She began coming to sessions and speaking from a new psychological space: "Maybe I have some issues of my own here; maybe I'm *scared* of being strong." This provided an opening to impinge upon her PAR-process, where the progressive stimulus was her enactment of strength.

In turn as she introjected the strong parent he was able to regress more with respect to her and became, as she said, much more emotionally available and in touch with his feelings. Ironically, but not coincidentally, this is something she had wanted and complained about not having for many years. Prior to these experiences, he was unable to relate to what she was talking about.

In the external phase of treatment, a vast amount of synergistic change can occur as growth in one area organically spurs growth in many other areas, virtually simultaneously. This is the essence of transformative change as opposed to the modification of patterns that often occurs in therapeutic models that do not allow for the impingement of the PAR-process. Again, however, this can only take place by moving the client out of the primitive phase and represents a more painstakingly incremental kind of therapeutic change as the relationship between therapist and client deepens.

To undo past learning, the client must now rely on a new guide, coach, or parental-substitute so s/he can learn new, presumably healthier roles. The process of learning new ways of thinking, patterns of behavior, states of feelings, and modes of relating is anxiety-producing, the fear of the unknown versus the familiarity of what is known. A close and dependent relationship must develop between the client and therapist in order to assuage the experience of fear.

In the external phase, the therapist becomes central to the life of the client. This is significant, since the therapist's involvement with the client during different phases of growth may vary considerably. The degree of therapeutic involvement in the external phase calls for the implementation of relational postures that many schools of therapy do not allow for: direction, advice-giving, additional goal- as opposed to crisis-oriented extra-hour support, etc. Indeed, what is needed in the external phase may even be deemed *inappropriate* by some schools of therapy since the transcendence of conventional therapeutic boundaries is possible, if not desirable. But it is this very transcendence of therapeutic boundaries that allows the client to introject the *love*, for lack of a better word, as well as the relational values, of the therapist. The client can then pull away from the practitioner without arousing fears of "unlove" or abandonment. Above all, the client becomes self-loving and able to function as a whole person independently. S/he can now truly love others for one can at once retain and lose the self in an intimate relationship. This is the hallmark of the *internal* phase of growth.

corrective transactional experiences and the internal and spiritual phases of motivation

Thus, as the client's reliance on the therapy for support, guidance, and direction diminishes, the introject of the therapist solidifies and merges with the real self of the person. The influence of the therapist as an external being becomes either redundant or superfluous. The client no longer depends upon or needs the therapist, because the gaps and deficiencies in the family-of-origin-experience—nurturance, discipline, and programming—are largely filled in. The client will likely seek out a new love object, either in the current partner, or in a new partner whose tendency is to *not* mimic aspects of the original parental introjects, but rather embodying the new, more positive healing introject.

Even though the partner may have aspects of their personality and interpersonal transactions that resemble the negative parental introjects, the client will be less inclined to enact these because the mechanism involved, the repetition compulsion, is based on the person's fruitless search for a positive introject. Since a positive introject from the therapist has been sufficiently attained, the client is more *conscious* of positive needs and has an awareness of how to attain them, a new consciousness based on experience rather than intellectual insight.

The corrective transactional experience of getting one's regressive needs met in an imperfect but good-enough fashion provides a template to transfer onto other relationships. It replaces the old template of the repetition compulsion, the drive to seek out potential reparental agents in search of the missing healthy aspects of self, and creating an interpersonal reality (e.g., "my husband does not understand me") that is reminiscent of one's childhood experience (e.g., "my mother did not understand me").

As the corrective transaction replaces the repetition compulsion, along with the default regression associated with it, the client is able to experience increasing levels of intimacy which provide more loving inputs. This love, whatever its form, becomes internalized by the client, who then has more love to offer others. The client in turn becomes motivated by the desire to provide love, because the regressive drive to seek love from others lessens. As regressive needs diminish, the love received tends to become more outer-directed, since the client has an internal experience of being filled up sufficiently. When the client reaches these states of fulfillment, self-interest diminishes accordingly.

The client's motivation is then fueled by interests greater than self and significant others. In this *spiritual* phase of motivation, the transcendence of self occurs through a letting go of self-interest that represents a trust and faith in the goodness or rightness of the world. This ability to transcend self-interest provides a kind of spiritual growth that propels the evolutionary drive toward completion.

This trust in letting go represents the opposite of the futile wishfulness of the repetition compulsion and resulting default regression, in that the person fully expects and creates positive outcomes. When less than optimal outcomes occur, the person will tend to see the positive aspects of the outcome and proceed forward with renewed vigor. This tendency may be referred to as morphogenesis.

The spiritual phase is not meant to describe an endpoint to successful therapy; rather, it is offered as a possibility based on my observation of transformative change processes. There appears to be a natural tendency toward altruism in the evolution of the self after the self is actualized, and, to whatever extent possible, gratified and individuated. It is not a necessary step in the evolution of a therapeutic client. However, I tend to favor psychotherapeutic orientations that lead people in this direction whenever possible. Indeed any responsible approach designed to change people must take into account possible endpoints, and be partially evaluated on that basis.

role of the therapist as motivator

The role of the therapist in this model may be considered that of a motivator. In endeavors other than psychotherapy like business, athletics, or education this role is better understood. A good manager in business, for example, oversees the operations of his employees while offering the materials, skills, support, and structure to reach mutually agreed-upon goals. A good athletic coach provides inspiration, goal-setting, nurturance, instruction, confrontation, and vision.

We tend, though, not to want to view the role of the therapist in a similar fashion. In fact, therapists who operate in this way are often viewed suspiciously, thought to be promoting some agenda different from the client's intentions. This is unfortunately the case in some treatments. However, therapies that tend to be overtly nonmotivating, less active or activating, often fail for that very reason. Yet their failure is merely less obvious; they are more likely to be seen as a failure on the part of the *client*, since responsibility for change is assumed a priori to lie with the client.

My view is that the responsibility for change lies fully with both the therapist and client. The responsibility for providing *motivation* to change, though, lies clearly with the therapist, since inadequate motivation is at the very heart of the client's reason for being in therapy.

The function of the therapist-as-motivator is to charge or recharge the motivational spark of the client. When the motivation is rekindled, we may return to what I would call the technical aspects of the therapy, the work, just as a swimming coach, say, might confront or discipline an Olympic swimmer for being late for a scheduled practice. Once an understanding is reached, the athlete and coach return to the technical aspects of the training. This is not to suggest that either motivation or work is more important than the other, simply that without motivation, the work cannot take place. The work aspect of therapy must be completed for successful treatment to occur, and motivation is the fuel necessary for engagement and maintenance of that work.

Why is providing motivation to grow and change the role of the therapist? Should this not be the role of loved ones in the client's life? Couldn't the therapist help the client find and maintain satisfying relationships outside the treatment situation? The answer here is yes and yes.

Most clients present for therapy because of the failure of loved ones to provide these needed inputs. We are wired to receive these inputs from family, according to our basic nature, so I usually assume that the client's engaging of me as a therapist occurs after more natural, pre-wired, avenues for seeking love have not worked. Going to a therapist for help, support, and guidance remains a somewhat difficult, sometimes embarrassing event, a step not taken easily, and often only after other avenues have been blocked. The very purpose of the therapist's providing these needed inputs is so that the client may have the *experience* of receiving love, of being psychologically penetrated so that they may become capable of seeking it from others. As a therapist, I assist wherever possible in spurring this natural process. The experience of receiving love, a particular kind of love, creates a sense of familiarity within the client. This familiarity, along with a newly acquired sense of wholeness, opens up the possibility of growth and change.

I often pose the reverse of the question: Why should this not be the role of the therapist? Our notions of the appropriate role of the therapist are surprisingly poorly delineated in the field. Therapeutic

role behavior is mistakenly assumed to be directly associated with theoretical orientation; in other words, that the theoretical orientation of
the practitioner prescribes a particular therapeutic role. Role of the
therapist is more related to his or her views on issues of the limits of
therapeutic responsibility and the like, and these may or may not be
correlated with theoretical orientation (Rappaport, 1988; 1991b). The
relational postures presented by the major schools of therapy, it has
long been noted (Fiedler, 1950; Strupp, 1969; Sundland, 1977;
Sundland and Barker, 1962) are stereotypes of actual practice, which
tends to be more fluid and eclectic.

In this model, the role of the therapist is, or has the potential for
being, central to the life of the client. If the therapist maintains only a
peripheral role in the life of the client, then his or her sphere of influence will be limited accordingly. We are interested in positively influencing the client and see therapy as a process of social influence. Since
this is such a potentially powerful position, we attempt to ensure that
influence is representative of the wishes and desires of the true self of
the client. In this sense, the therapist acts as a container and a voice
for the real self of the client until that self can discover its own voice.

This suggests that we are promoting agendas that the client is
actively resisting or avoiding. We presume, however, that this resistance is rooted in the client's fears of change. Therefore I maintain a
kind of "disrespect" for the expressed wishes of what we consider to be
the false self. So while I may be actively promoting an agenda the
client is resisting, I experience it as an embodiment of the battle
between the real self and the false self of the client. A Gestalt therapist
may encourage the client to play each part of the self to gain emotional insight, with the therapist facilitating in this process.[4]

In contrast, in this model, we take on the role of the reparental
agent voicing the motives of the healthy, real self to gain influence, a
role which the Gestalt therapist would not care to assume for many reasons, not the least of which is that it takes responsibility out of the
hands of the client and puts it onto the therapist. While this is un-
doubtedly true, the therapist's taking this level of responsibility for the
wishes of the true self becomes introjected by the client. Eventually,
the client becomes the guardian of the real self when the introjection
of the reparental guardian is realized.

---

4. I may utilize a two-chair techniqe as well. I do not, however, expect resolution of the
ambivalence on that basis, if the client is in the primitive or external phase of motivation.

Despite some views to the contrary, we do not see clients as highly susceptible and prone to easy influence. In our experience, due to the fear-of-loss of the familiar as well as fear of the unknown, clients tend to be suspicious and find change to be quite difficult. Except in a small minority of more disturbed clients, influence may occur only after a bond is made and trust is appropriately constructed. There are a number of adequate safeguards against the therapist's exercising an inordinate or negative influence, not the least of which is the client's ability and willingness to end the therapy at any time.

All this raises the question of how a therapist determines what the true wishes of the client are, particularly if the client is not voicing them. First of all, many clients are indeed aware of the intentions of their true selves and request help in attaining them. For example, a client may present in therapy desiring a more fulfilling, intimate, and productive relationship with a spouse, a parent, or a child. They may be quite honest about their difficulties and fears in attaining this but are steadfast in their desire for growth. Of course, clients alternately lose and regain this motivation to grow, and the therapist must, even in the best of cases, strongly embody and safeguard the positive goal for the client.

In other therapeutic situations, the therapist must initially set the goals. If, for example, a client may come to treatment with a series of complaints about his spouse, claiming "everything would be just fine with me, if it weren't for her nagging." I might respond, "You really don't have a clue how to be intimate, or for that matter how to get your needs met, with your wife. Perhaps we could work on *that*."

Again, if the client experiences the therapist as off-base or out of tune with what s/he wants, then s/he may question, challenge, argue, cancel, miss sessions, or terminate treatment. The client may engage in any number of active or passive resistance strategies. The therapist must detect these and process the client's resistance, concerns, and fears.

The notion of the therapist as the guardian of the real self is not a new construct, as many of the depth therapies offer parallel concepts. The idea of therapist as a *motivator* of the real self does suggest a more active, directive, and at times confrontational relational stance on the part of the therapist that has not received much attention in the psychotherapeutic literature.

In the absence of stated true-self objectives or if the client is presumed to be voicing goals or desires that are founded more in fear (as manifest by the false self), one may then ask how the therapist draws conclusions about the intentions of the true self?

There is one set of assumptions we make about the intentions of the real self which provides a template for growth and goal-setting in treatment. This template is a model for optimal, as opposed to normal, functioning. We are uninterested in normative constructs of health, which typically infer the absence of pathology. We are interested, rather, in constructs associated with personal and interpersonal growth. These constructs include, but are not limited to, goals of increasing levels of intimacy in a primary love relationship (the coupling transaction); provision of nurturance, discipline, and programming to children (the rearing transaction); and a satisfying and successful work experience (independent transaction). For this to occur we emphasize, on the one hand, *individuation* processes—first from the pathogenic aspects of the family-of-origin, second from the pathogenic aspects of the primary love partner that tend to resemble the family-of-origin; third, from the growth agent (the therapist) and finally, from the pedestrian interests of the self (transcendence, spiritual).

This oscillation between increasing levels of intimacy and increasing levels of individuation, and the ability to engage fully in either process depending upon circumstances and need becomes the layer of health that is superimposed over each case. This layer of health is compared with the client's current functioning and development to determine appropriate progressive (P) expectations or treatment goals as well as concomitant expectations for regression (R) and normal abreactions (A). This process of goal-setting and therapist-client rapprochement is termed PAR, which I will discuss throughout this book.

The real self revelations of the client are measured and judged against the PAR-model of optimal functioning, based on the assumption that the broad goal of increasing levels of intimacy, for example, is a common desire of the real self of human beings, generally. Some may argue against such omnipotent or even arrogant assumptions, but I do not offer this as a truth with a capital T. Consistent with co-constructivist epistemology and philosophy (see Speed, 1984), I merely suggest that this is the most useful assumption to make. In any case it is impossible *not* to make some assumption, and it is my observation and that of others who study human behavior that there seems to be more of a basis in reality to this one than to other potential assumptions.

chapter 6

separating motivational and psychopathological phenomena:
the role of theory in psychotherapy

There was once a time when the notion of unitary explanations for psychopathology, personality development, and psychological change was thought to be a useful enterprise (London, 1986; Omer and London, 1988). The first wave of explanation of human behavior derived from psychoanalysis and its varied offshoots, the depth therapies. Behaviorism, the second wave, posed a direct challenge and antithesis. The third wave, humanism, stood in opposition to the previous two waves, albeit in different ways. Other viewpoints have emerged, including family systems theory, and cognitive therapy, along with biological psychiatry, providing other counterpoints to the prevailing mainstream of theory and practice.

At the time of each of these paradigm shifts, it seemed as though what would emerge would be an improvement on previous knowledge and treatments. To a great extent this has indeed occurred. A client who is depressed today can choose among a vast array of treatment possibilities. S/he may try any number of antidepressant medications or pharmacotherapeutics, cognitive therapy, or interpersonal therapy, all of which have proven track records of efficacy. If the person believes or is convinced by a practitioner that the depression is related to some other factor (see Addis, Truax and Jacobson, 1995) like an unsatisfying marriage, they may benefit from couples-oriented treatment. In fact, people who are depressed have benefited from various kinds of psychotherapy. Of course, some treatments perform better in outcome studies of specific disorders for large samples of clients.

The fact that some treatments tend to outperform others has led to the sensible viewpoint that matching clients to particular treatments based on a range of factors may be a superior overarching approach. This research-driven notion is largely atheoretical in nature (Lazarus, 1995). If we amass enough data, including theoretical and case study as well as research, that supports a particular intervention for a particular therapeutic problem, then we should abandon other theoretical approaches that prove less effective.

While there are problems with such a viewpoint, including the reliability and validity of measurements of a positive outcome, difficulties inherent in such research, particularly the applicability of a research paradigm to a practice paradigm (e.g., manualized treatment), it is difficult to argue with its basic premise. If, for example, behavioral exposure theory is proven effective for clients presenting with phobias, then no matter what our preferred orientation is, we should offer the client the apparently superior treatment.

This is not always so simple, as our theories may determine whether we even construct a particular pathology; a given analytically oriented therapist may not "see," let alone attempt to treat with systematic desensitization, a phobia. As we work toward a common language for psychotherapy (Goldfried, 1995) though (and DSM-IV, which as atheoretically as possible defines psychopathologies is one step in this direction), we can establish a reasonable basis for the corresponding application of certain treatments.

The proponents of technical eclecticism, as well as many others, find the concept of a unitary theory of psychotherapy an unnecessary, impossible, or an irrelevant endeavor. The complexity of human behavior and the philosophical incompatibility of competing models are cited by many as the primary reasons for abandoning the unitary-theory idea (Neimeyer, 1993).

There has been a consistent minority voice among what have been called common-factors integrationists. Bolstered by the spate of outcome studies that led to the dodo-bird verdict, that is, that all theoretical approaches have won and all must have prizes (Luborsky, Singer & Luborsky, 1975), meta-analytic studies (Lipsey and Wilson, 1993; see Schmidt, 1992 for a discussion of merits of meta-analysis and cumulative knowledge in psychology), and the theoretical persuasiveness of authors like Frank (1982), Garfield (1992b), Schofield (1964), and Strupp (1978), common-factors integrationists continue to view psychotherapy as a generic enterprise emphasizing commonalities and the blurring of differences among approaches (see also Patterson and Hidore, 1996). Of these commonalities, much attention has been given to common theoretical factors like exposure, abreaction, and catharsis. For example, despite the fact that the construct of exposure has its roots in behavior therapy, virtually all theories of therapy involve, overtly or covertly, some form of the gradual exposure of a client to some feared and/or avoided situation.

Another set of common factors has been identified post-hoc. Listening, attentiveness, and the therapist's belief in his or her approach are common to all schools of psychotherapy and while once viewed as an inert ingredient and seemingly nonspecific to the treatment, common-factorists argue these are the elements that account for most of the positive outcome variance (Hanna and Puhakka, 1991).

The common-factors viewpoint can be both compelling and satisfying in its attempt to explain the narrowness and limitations of particular approaches to psychotherapy. The problem with the common-factors viewpoint lies in the implication that, if the theoretical and technical endeavors of the therapist are somehow less important, we should then worry less about developing new theories and advancing new innovations or techniques. Further, the integration of theories and techniques is less than meaningful (see Colapinto, 1984) if theory and technique matter so little. At its extreme, such thinking tends to digress into the kind of extreme antireductionism exemplified by Hynan (1981), who claims therapy is nothing more than a kind of friendship. Conclusions like these can lead to therapeutic laziness, a mindset that whatever one does in therapy is okay, as long as one is attentive and empathic, for example. Even if we discount the outcome research that shows that certain approaches do seem to be more effective for certain kinds of clients, our experience and intuition have taught us that human behavior *is* complex and that this complexity must hold meaning. For example, our increasing knowledge of the effects of childhood trauma and dissociation has led to better treatments for that population. Experienced practitioners will support the idea that therapeutic attentiveness or empathy is not enough to secure a positive outcome for post-traumatic stress disorder, for example. We may say the same for a host of presenting difficulties, ranging from substance-abuse problems to marital dysfunction and eating disorders.

And yet, specialists in those disorders continue to discuss the similarities of these clients to more heterogeneous client populations. An appropriate therapeutic credo may be to recognize the differences but to always keep in mind that you are always treating a human being who has much in common with others, such as difficulties in maintaining intimacy, finding satisfying and meaningful work, dealing with families-of-origin, etc. There is certainly a point at which all client populations blur and therapies of the alcoholic, anorectic, and the affected come to have great similarities.

If we overemphasize the differences then we may continue to reinvent the wheel, a common criticism of theory-driven approaches (e.g., cognitive theory's "discovery" of emotions). If we blur the differences and emphasize the similarities among groupings and approaches, then we lose our scientific edge and the necessary thrust toward innovation, halting development in the field.

One may look at this dilemma historically. Has innovation, the development of new approaches and techniques, helped us? The answer is an unequivocal yes. If you are depressed, in a difficult marital situation, a survivor of childhood abuse, or struggling with sexual orientation, you are much better off now than you were in 1930, 1940, or 1950. Greater knowledge and the understanding of differences among client populations has led to vastly superior models and approaches. As a field, we have developed and honed a body of techniques to aid in the treatment of our clients. Role playing, psychodrama, dialoguing, eye-movement desensitization, paradox, thought-stopping, journaling, sculpting, and mirroring, have all enriched psychotherapeutic practice and the lives of our clients.

Yet, we also know that often clients improve in psychotherapy whether we use specific techniques or not, and some clients do *not* improve even when we do use appropriate specific techniques. There must then be some marriage of the specific (theory, technique, approach) and the nonspecific (common factors that are seemingly unintended)(Karasu, 1986). One recent trend that has addressed this issue is what Omer (1990; 1992) has called making the nonspecific specific. These common factors should not be treated as static inert entities, but activated as constructs and techniques.

For example, if we accept Frank's (1971) notion that any healing enterprise "works" in part through the practitioner's own belief in that enterprise, which presumably inspires that hope, faith, and belief in the client, we must examine ways to insure that this process occurs. The development of therapeutic models and approaches that address these critical common factors then becomes an important next step. In this sense, we gain the advantage of technical eclecticism without falling prey to its indifference to theory.

I am uninterested in any theory of therapy that offers unitary explanations (psychoanalysis, behavior therapy, Gestalt therapy, object-relations, family systems, or any of their representatives), or in the integration of these theories like psychoanalysis and behavior therapy (e.g., Wachtel, 1977). I am interested in interventions that are embedded within a clear and consistent, but not stifling, set of values of health. Values about the nature of health, not theoretical orientation, guide the clinician to decide what to do when.

In fact, I am partial to all theoretical orientations; I like them all. But as approximations or attempts to explain and simplify complex behavior, theories are only abstractions. To base what we actually do on these approximations and simplifications is nothing short of bizarre. Because our knowledge and data base in clinical psychotherapy is so limited every single case must inform theory-building, not the reverse. Now if we integrate the active commonalities that appear to cut across orientations to one degree or another, like empathy, exposure, and transference, and place them alongside the supposedly inert, but activated commonalities, like instilling in the client faith in the treatment and certain aspects of the therapist-client relationship, a unitary theory of psychotherapy that is at once expansive and adaptable may emerge.

What *is* the appropriate place for theory in psychotherapeutic practice if theory is such a poor guide for selecting interventions? Theory is a belief system, a set of ideas about particular affective, cognitive, and behavioral processes. I've rarely met a theory I didn't like. I find most to be valid to some degree.

Cognitive therapy seems to explain cognitive processes and their effect on psychopathology, particularly depression and anxiety states, very well. Then again, theories about serotonin-receptor processes explain certain categories of depression. Trauma theory explains the effect of childhood abuse on adult psychopathology quite well. Systems theory explains how symptomatology is maintained by one or more members of a family. And so on.

These theories are not necessarily competing, but rather compatible, particularly if we consider the not atypical psychotherapy client: the adult survivor of childhood abuse, with a possible genetic predilection toward depression, in a dysfunctional love relationship and struggling with an enmeshed contemporary family-of-origin. Our theories of psychotherapy only get us into trouble to the extent that they tend to claim unitary superiority, as when the family therapist says, for instance, that the hypothesized dysfunctional family system is *the* cause or significant correlate of the problem and therefore must be the focus of treatment.

The ultimate solution in finding unitary explanations may be via the integration of theories, an endeavor I support despite its enormity and complexity. We may be at least fifty years away from reaching consensus on integration, especially in light of the recent gloomy forecasts about the viability or even necessity of such endeavors. The seeds for this integration may rather be found in specific treatment plans for specific populations and special problems. For example, Liddle and his colleagues (Liddle, et al., 1995) propose a model of multidimensional family therapy for treating adolescent substance-abuse among minority, low-income youth. Such integrated treatment modalities may be considered "case studies" for further research and theory development (Rappaport, 1995a).

Even if we developed the perfect explanatory theory, that theory should remain in the background because what motivates behavior are not mechanisms proposed by theory. Even if we could say, for purposes of simplicity, that biochemical processes influenced all behavior and all behavior can be reduced to such processes, and if we could develop a psychopharmacological treatment package for all disorders, each patient would still have to decide whether to accept that treatment. Some would take the pill(s), some wouldn't, and others might take them intermittently. If that is so (and there are those health professionals and patients who see mental processes through this biochemical lens), how do we explain why some will take the pill and others not?

We might say that some clients resist to seeing their problems as biochemical in nature, for whatever reason do not wish to improve, or are receiving "secondary gain" from their symptoms. We might even develop as part of a treatment protocol some psychoeducational component where the patient is taught the rudiments of biochemical processes to help understand why taking the medication is important.

There are parallels to this in physical pathologies due to behavioral processes. For example, cancer and emphysema are no doubt biological phenomena. Cigarette smoking is a behavioral choice influenced by psychological and physiological addictive processes. Continued cigarette smoking can lead to lung cancer. Some smokers continue to smoke cigarettes even after such a diagnosis is made, while others quit well before such a diagnosis is made. Some of those quit smoking and then restart any number of times. We can say that lung cancer may be caused by continued cigarette smoking. Indeed, there is a well-established base of research to support this theory. This established *fact* (and we have few established facts in psychology and psychotherapy) can lead to preventive and educational programs that teach people cigarette smoking is harmful and life-threatening. Since the mid-1960s, this message has been given with varying degrees of success. Some listen and heed the message, and others do not. Some are affected in more complicated ways.

My point here is that theory is helpful only to a point. No matter what theoretical forces or combinations of forces (biochemical, cognitive, social, systemic) operate upon a person, as long as we live in a relatively free society, the locus of control lies within the individual.

No matter how good or complete our theory is at explaining *why* that person is engaging in a dysfunctional endeavor, we still, quite accurately and necessarily, view ourselves as free to choose. We may say that person X is an alcoholic because he has an "alcoholic gene," he grew up in an "alcoholic family system," that he is "self-medicating" his depression, or is coping with a dysfunctional relationship. We may say the true answer is that he is an alcoholic because of some combination of the four explanations. And we may be right. We may even someday be able to identify the alcoholic gene through genetic testing. Similarly, we may unambiguously show through twin studies and other kinds of research that growing up in an alcoholic family increases the chances of alcoholism by a high percentage.

I am optimistic that with time we may reach conclusive evidence citing if not causation, then certainly correlates of psychopathology. This needs to occur for us to develop better treatments (see Arkowitz, 1993). And in fact, this has already occurred. We do not, for instance, view alcoholism as amoral or will-less behavior as we once did. We have a much greater understanding of alcoholism than ever before. The same is true for a host of psychological disorders. And so, we no longer recommend or select psychoanalysis as the treatment of choice for alcoholism.

Increased understanding helps us create better and more complete treatments but it does not help us in getting clients to enter, engage, and commit to those treatments. Better treatments will tend to lead to better results. Treatments that are based on better knowledge will make more intuitive and intellectual sense to the client leading to increased compliance with treatment protocols. But ultimately, decisions about entering, engaging, investing, and committing to treatment are made by the client for a host of reasons.

This "host of reasons" involves the rubric of motivational processes, which is best viewed as unrelated to the quality of the treatment. Again, this is not to suggest that the quality of treatments is
unimportant or that any reasonably motivated person will succeed in
virtually any good-enough treatment. Treatment quality is essential.
Motivation to enter, engage, and commit to treatment is essential.
Each is necessary but insufficient alone. My point is simply that as a
field we have not focused sufficiently on the motivation question.
While treatment quality is still a vital issue in need of investigational
pursuit, our understanding of the motivational process of psychotherapy, which is rudimentary at best, needs to catch up.

Motivation involves issues of self-esteem, self-valuing, self-
appreciation, and self-love. (Because of the varied uses of 'self-esteem'
in the existing literature, and because of its colloquial associations, I
prefer the term self-love. Because it is so widely used, however, I will
continue to use the term self-esteem.) Although, the evidence is
ambiguous (cf. Basic Behavioral Science Task Force of the National
Advisory Mental Health Council, 1996; Jones, 1996; Main, 1996), I
claim that psychopathology and self-esteem are essentially unrelated.
But just because the absence of self-esteem is not necessarily highly correlated with psychopathology, it does not mean that increasing self-
esteem is not an important goal of psychotherapy since, in my view,
increased self-esteem will lead to increased motivation to enter,
engage, and commit to any sort of change process or procedure. If we
as therapists can positively affect the self-esteem of our clients, they
will tend to become more motivated to address their particular
pathologies. Of course, even when the client is motivated, we must
provide quality treatment or they will become quickly disillusioned.
This is at the crux of the relationship between increased self-esteem,
i.e., motivation, and our psychotherapeutic interventions. Both must
be present for successful treatment.

If I had to choose between emphasizing the treatment of self-
esteem/motivational processes and the treatment of a particular psychopathology, I would choose the motivational since the client may seek
out other forms of intervention or help from any number of sources to
deal with their psychopathology. I've had cases where I believe I helped
the client feel better about themselves and increase their sense of self-
esteem, who then left therapy to become the motivated client of another therapist or therapeutic agent, who could better treat their particular
pathology. Similarly, I've had motivated clients come from other thera-

pists, who successfully helped these people feel better about themselves, and who were better helped by my theoretical and technical help.

When the client has had continued experience of failure in seeking help, s/he becomes hopeless and disillusioned about change. I have referred to this as the default regression, which can often take on a life of its own, not unlike alcoholism, where the stress and problems that may have led to drinking behavior originally become indistinguishable from the problems that excessive drinking has created. In other words, a syndrome develops. A cycle of disappointments (or default regressions) creates a pathological response which may include an acting-in of the default regression, in the form of dysthymia and anxiety, or acting out in the form of "addictive behaviors," along with certain relational patterns (avoidance, clinginess, blame, projection). All of this dysfunctionality affects one's sense of self and notably, self-esteem.

Thus, I am not suggesting that psychopathology cannot or does not bear upon self-esteem. I am merely suggesting that we separate the two for the purposes of this model. Importantly, we can distinguish intervention strategies designed to increase self-esteem and hence, motivation, from those designed to impinge upon certain aspects of psychopathology. A depressed client with low motivation does not need a treatment of antidepressants or cognitive-behavioral therapy. A depressed client with low motivation needs increased self-love. My first clinical goal with that person is to address the question why this person is so hopeless, self-hating, and generally despairing about life? In this model, I provide the client with a certain kind of relational experience designed to address that despair and to provide hope.

Some might suggest prescribing the depression treatment of choice (e.g., Prozac), as that, too, may influence the depressive syndrome. If less depressed, presumably the person's zest for living and sense of hope may increase. I am not opposed to this strategy, except on the grounds that a negative result may occur if the treatment "works," for the client may introject Prozac as his or her source of hope into the self-esteem/love structure.

I prefer not to impinge upon motivational or self-esteem processes with a psychological, technotherapeutic or psychopharmacological intervention. I wish to impinge upon motivational processes directly with "love from other" (or therapeutic reparenting); which, I posit, becomes the client's image for self-love and ultimately a willingness and will to love significant others.

If I successfully impinge upon this process, I may find that this "depressed" person is no longer depressed and that their depressive symptomatology was for the most part a motivational and self-esteem issue. Sometimes, I find the person does not need a specific kind of treatment whether Prozac or cognitive/behavioral interventions. At this point, the client is more motivated to enter into, engage, and commit to treatment, which increases compliance and ultimately success.

Indeed, this is why I, too, believe that "all treatments have won and all must have prizes," (Luborsky, Singer and Luborsky, 1975; Stiles, Shapiro and Elliot, 1986), or why, as Strupp and Hadley (1979) have found, that untrained college professors do as well as professional psychologists in attaining successful psychotherapy outcomes. The factor impinged upon so often in psychotherapy is the default regression cluster: hopelessness, despair, low self-esteem, which I posit arises out of a therapeutic *relational* experience of love. The client will then either spontaneously remit symptomatology (at a swifter rate, I must point out, than with placebo or no treatment), or will be open to quality-treatment in the case of more severe accompanying psychopathology.

But I disagree with many interpreters of these same outcome studies who claim that since theory, technique and professional experience matter so little, we must question the value of psychotherapy. Such interpretations tend to unfairly disregard psychotherapy's potency. While I accept the conclusions of these studies, although one could argue against them from a methodological standpoint, what this literature says to me is that we must focus our attention on the potency of the therapeutic relationship and develop models of therapy where that relationship is central and responsible for change. Too often these results are offered as reasons to doubt the efficacy of psychotherapy or to present psychotherapy as some vague or even mystical enterprise. Many of the common-factors integrationists have made this error by assuming that psychotherapy works because it is a socially sanctioned context for psychological healing (e.g., Frank, 1973). These theorists suggest that any kind of validated treatment will work since psychotherapy theory and treatment are rituals of change, akin to shamanistic healing in other cultures. "If the client believes it will work, then it *will work*" is often offered as a reasoning for the success of so many different kinds of psychotherapy and psychotherapists.

This notion of therapeutic intervention as a ritual and the therapeutic relationship and context as curative is interesting from a cross-cultural perspective and should be incorporated into our understanding of psychotherapy. However, this generic explanation does not account for as much of the successful-outcome variance as its adherents suggest. This is particularly true if we consider positive outcome to be less related to remission of presenting symptomatology or problems.

In our model, alleviation of the presenting problem is a target, but not necessarily *the* target, of treatment. Increasing the motivational level of the client to grow in life is the major goal of therapy. If the client's motivation increases, the presenting issue will either remit spontaneously or diminish in importance. As well, motivation to address the presenting problem will increase to such a degree that the problem becomes more manageable. It is important to note though that in times of intrapsychic or external stress, the symptom may reappear, and with it a corresponding sense of hopelessness. Interestingly, in this model, as in many depth therapies, *more* problems or symptoms will tend to arise during treatment as the client becomes increasingly *motivated* to raise them and allow them to surface in the presence of a safe, strong, and helpful therapeutic agent.

For example, a client may come to therapy with diffuse complaints of anxiety easily diagnosed with DSM categories, but end up focusing on their distressing marriage. This leads to talking about disappointments in their childhood and then back to the original anxiety that brought the client to treatment. My goal as therapist is to impinge upon the motivational processes such that the client is invested in dealing with every significant aspect of life. The areas I consider to be most important are primary love relationships, relationship(s) with children, doing meaningful work, and relationships with family-of-origin.

Whether the client chooses to work on those areas in therapy or in therapy with me is less relevant than the fact that they have an expanded opportunity to do so. My job is to help them become more motivated to grow in life, to increase their capacity to give and receive love and to engage in meaningful work. This may sound humanistically vague and inadequate but the purpose of this book is to operationalize the process.

This question of enlarged or expanded treatment goals versus targeting presenting complaints also confuses the issue here. Expanding treatment foci in the way I propose does not preclude a client from entering or engaging in treatment so that they improve and exit treatment before "owning" the treatment. It is simply their choice to end therapy at some point along the continuum of what they consider to be adequate motivation. I do not believe there are harmful effects or feelings of failure on the part of the client for not continuing the change endeavor, if the factor of motivation to grow is offered as a lifetime, not as a now-or-never undertaking. Of course, such rationalizing begs a question I sometimes confront my clients with: if not now, when?

Psychotherapy is a biphasic process with regard to treatment focus. It is useful to separate those two parts of the processes so we may integrate them coherently. On the one hand, we are concerned with psychopathology, the specific problems and symptoms the client brings into therapy. Included here are eating disorders, addictions, phobias, depression, post-traumatic stress, etc. I am not interested in the specificity of the DSM categories but rather in broad-spectrum problems. Most clients do not easily fit Axis I or Axis II categories. Many overlap or may mask unspecified symptomatologies or problems (Benjamin, 1993). In time, I believe we will reach consensus for treatments of choice for each of these phenomena. For the most part theories that have previously been thought of as competing are compatible and explain different aspects of the phenomenon or syndrome in question. While some theories may account for a larger proportion of the variance of explanatory or prescriptive power, each theory possesses some degree of validity.

As stated, one's degree of psychopathology is not highly correlated with one's motivation to grow. Indeed, there are many nonclients of psychotherapy who do not have much psychopathology, if any, but are extremely resistant to growth. Similarly, there are many nonclients of psychotherapy who may easily fit several DSM categories who are reluctant to change, often evidenced by their refusal to try therapy.

Psychopathology is rooted, I contend, in a set of biological and biochemical predispositions. Basic temperament and tendencies toward anxiety and depression, while not biologically fixed in any way are predetermined by sets of vulnerabilities. Parenting and caretaking can minimize or exacerbate these vulnerabilities in various ways that may influence the course of psychopathology. Better or worse parenting may serve to create the overt manifestation of these vulnerabilities. As a result, a psychopathological syndrome may develop.

While parenting and caretaking (and significant for our model, therapeutic others) have some effect on the development and pathogenesis in the child and the emerging adult, parenting has an even greater effect on the child's self-esteem, self-love, as well as on the emergence of the true self and identity. We could say that self-love covers a multitude of pathologies, meaning that the truly self-loving person is better equipped to deal with a host of problems and crises.

How does one become self-loving? When a child is born, s/he is at the mercy of their caretakers' capacity and ability to provide love. This love takes many forms: first, bonding, nurturance, and responsiveness (the first year or so) and soon after, regularity, predictability, and protection from harm (the toddler years) and then teaching, guidance, direction, and expanded opportunities (later childhood).

Each child is unique and tends to need given input in a particular sequence in time. To the extent that the child internalizes these loving inputs, s/he becomes self-loving. The *introjection* of loving inputs is determined by the readiness, steadiness, and appropriateness of care and the ability of the child to hold onto the parent's love during periods of separation, ending with the late adolescent's launching into a career and love relationship(s). This constitutes the child's individuated life.

The child's search for and experience of love from others becomes their template for self-love and their love of others. To the extent that the child is self-loving there is increased motivation to grow. If the child is not loved in some good-enough fashion, then the child remains fearful of losing the love that s/he has, and their focus tends to become survival-oriented, as opposed to thriving-oriented. This happens because the parental introject remains incomplete and the child continues to engage in a mostly fruitless search for the missing inputs (Balint, 1968; Dicks, 1967; Fairburn, 1952; Freud, 1914). Motivation to grow is thwarted by the child's engagement in this process. To be more precise we may say that this person is motivated to grow, but that their motivation is primitive. Their *motive* is to search for the missing reparental inputs.

This is not unpromising. If one is continually searching, one may ultimately find these inputs. The process of finding them is not so easy, however, since the primitively motivated person must adequately attach and become dependent upon a therapeutic other who is different enough (that is, possesses the new inputs) from the original introjected parent(s). This requires trust and overcoming the fear of losing the known (the original introjects) for the unknown (the reparental introjects). Replacing the old introjects means discarding familiar ways of relating and values. No matter how poorly these values may be working, there exists a fear-of-loss.

In times of crisis, where it is obvious that the old and familiar values are inadequate, faulty, or inhibiting, life steps in and poses "new" opportunities that were previously present but easily denied. The new opportunity for change may be signaled if the person is willing to discard old programming in favor of new. The willingness to do so may increase because the fear of letting go of the familiar is supplanted by a new and larger fear, the fear of losing the needed input which is now too present to deny. This is the role of life crisis in change. Life crises set up clear choices and decisions to be made. These choices were always present, but now the denial becomes more difficult, although not impossible.

It is here that the relationship between psychopathology and motivation assumes its greatest significance for psychotherapy. We know that life crises, like marital separations, propel people into treatment. Often the person's response to the crisis is the development, exacerbation, or rekindling of a psychopathological symptom, like intense anxiety, depression, addiction, or an eating disorder. Sometimes the person comes to therapy in anticipation of the crisis, in the midst of a crisis, or well after the crisis, in a period of despair. If they come to therapy in anticipation of, or during the crisis, the therapist is in an advantageous position. After a crisis has been adequately resolved, the therapist is in a less advantageous position. I will discuss all these possibilities and their attendant strategies in Chapters 8 and 9.

For the purposes of our discussion here, I will simply point out that the psychopathological response is a sign of stress from the crisis, and that the remediation of that symptomatology need not be the central goal of therapy. Rather, the psychopathological response creates an opportunity to increase the person's motivation to grow, a far more valuable commodity than the remediation of the immediate, even if chronic, psychopathology. The crisis state brings a new-found openness to experience regression, dependency, and trust. It is in this atmosphere that therapeutic reparenting may take place. There is an openness to new loving inputs as the person realizes the old familiar inputs are inadequate to *grow through* the crisis. I am not suggesting that all clients consciously want or decide to grow at this point. Some merely want to feel better and be done with the crisis and the therapy. Again, I will discuss therapeutic strategies for dealing with such situations in Chapters 8 and 9.

Suffice it to say that the role of the therapist is to provide new reparental inputs or set the stage so that the client's motivation to receive the inputs is increased. So we have seen that psychopathology can be viewed as a helpful signal in the motivational process (also see Benjamin, 1993). It is also a great inhibition to growth, in that if not significantly affected, can lead to feelings of despair and hopelessness regarding change and life's possibilities.

Thus, the therapist must be proficient at understanding the nature of the client's syndrome and the need to disrupt the psychopathological symptomatology. In this model, symptoms are viewed as functional or in the service of a larger purpose, a viewpoint which is consistent with several humanistic and early family-systems formulations. I do, however, tend to view symptoms less romantically. A dialectical balance must be achieved between the therapeutic attention to symptomatology and motivation, both of which are significant to the work of therapy.

The initial focus of treatment then is to impinge upon the default regression process of the client with the intended objective of replacing its hopelessness and despair with hope and possibility. The therapist is central in this regard, as this process is largely interpersonal in nature. Despite the good intentions and metaphoric appeal of the inner-child and self-parenting paradigms, it is simply a misnomer to suggest that one can parent oneself (e.g., Bradshaw, 1989). Parenting is an *interpersonal* phenomenon. Love is predicated on the notion of a giver and a receiver. In therapy, the practitioner is the giver of love and the client, the receiver.

Let me clarify the use of the word love here (also see Coen, 1996, for a review of love in the analytic setting). As a term in the field of psychotherapy, love is unfortunately affected by its associations with sex. Some therapists consciously or unconsciously associate the word "love" with Eros and sex, and therefore avoid its use in describing psychotherapeutic activity. Sexual acting out by psychotherapists is no doubt a problem that the field must address and in part may be related to the very phenomenon I am discussing. Because love is a part of the therapy process, as well as for other reasons, erotic feelings on the part of the therapist toward his or her client may arise and become inappropriately acted upon. I am however referring to *nonerotic, nonsexual* love.

In Chapter 9 we will explore how love is expressed in psychotherapy as a corrective transactional experience. Let us first examine the principles that underlie this work and which offer an operationalized definition of love that forms the core of therapeutic relating.

chapter 7

the therapeutic basis for selecting interventions:
the place of values in psychotherapy

a basic philosophy of treatment

The astute reader may have noticed what seems to be a flaw or contradiction in my argument. On the one hand, I am promoting an eclectic viewpoint that eschews theory; at the same time I am advocating a particular "theory" of psychotherapy. I wish to make a distinction between conventional psychotherapeutic theory (e.g., psychoanalysis or behavioral therapy) and the ideas presented in this book. I am not invested in any particular theory or in sets of theories as in theoretical integration.

What I am offering is a system of values designed to guide therapeutic practice and decision making. This system of values includes notions about the nature of healthy functioning both within and outside of relationships, intimacy, responsibility, power, and dependency. This value system is the overlay of health that we superimpose over each case to determine what's missing or needed, and in what direction to proceed, in other words, the goals of treatment. After this basic operational philosophy is applied to the case, we are free to utilize any valid theory to explain and make sense of the case. Before we proceed further, I wish to state the basic philosophy of treatment:

1) The unitary basis of life problems, including some elements of psychopathology, is one of inadequate and poorly directed motivation toward personal growth and development. For there to be adequate motivation toward personal growth the person must be willing to exit unproductive but familiar operational sets and enter potentially productive but unfamiliar operational sets.

2) The reason for deficiency in motivation toward personal growth arises from fears associated with detaching from what is *familiar*, aspects of which are inadequate for growth-seeking behavior—the introjected family, the actual family-of-origin, or pathogenic aspects of the latter as manifested in the family-of-creation. Progressing in the direction of growth requires an abandoning of these pathogenic intro-

jects and extrojects and embracing healthier introjects and extrojects, in the form of a therapeutic other (therapist, spouse, mentor, etc.).

3) Healthier introjects and extrojects are identified by a particular system of values which include:

(a) Movements toward increasing levels of intimacy without unhealthy enmeshment in primary love relationships. Intimacy is defined as acceptance of the true self of the other while being accepted for one's own true self. The false self and the false self of the other are not accepted.

(b) Movements toward increasing levels of providing love toward one's children, accompanied by greater demands upon the self in the caretaking role.

(c) Movements toward greater levels of responsibility-taking for the separate growth of children and the primary love relationship.

(d) The willingness to experience increasing levels of dependency and the concomitant issues of trust and power to achieve increasing levels of intimacy and responsibility-taking.

4) Woundedness, and a corresponding decrease in motivation toward personal growth, occurs in the context of an interpersonal relationship. Healing, and a corresponding increase in motivation, occurs in the context of an interpersonal relationship.

5) The natural context for both healing and woundedness is primarily the family-of-origin, secondarily, the primary love relationship and various therapeutic others, and more vicariously, the rearing of children. The invented or culturally created context for healing (as well as woundedness) is the psychotherapeutic relationship.

6) The role of the therapist is to fill in the gaps and deficiencies of the client's family-of-origin experience through a kind of reparental experience within the protected therapeutic frame. It is recognized that for healing to occur, that is, for the client to experience the therapist's provision of love as real, the traditional boundaries of therapy may be stretched, crossed, but never violated. Love is defined as the provision of nurturance, confrontation, and guidance.

7) Healing and personal growth are lifelong processes. While therapy may serve to remediate psychopathology, therapy is viewed as an essentially transformative process designed to increase each client's level of motivation to address impediments to personal growth. Remediation is seen as a valued and at times life-saving endeavor, but preference tends to be given toward transforming the client's motivational processes. Transformation of the self is viewed as difficult and

risky, and it is understood that few will engage in such risk-taking actions in the absence of a penetrating good-enough object. The therapist in this model is encouraged to become this good-enough object, despite the difficulty, risks, and courage required.

8) The therapist is 100% responsible for bringing about change. The client is 100% responsible for bringing about change. This principle is parallel to a useful construct in couples therapy. That is, each partner does not, as is commonly suggested, contribute 50% to the problem or solution. Rather, each partner contributes 100%, or stated differently, is fully responsible for 100% of their contribution to the problem and solution.

9) The client's seeking and contracting for psychotherapy is viewed as an evolutionary event, a natural request for a change in approach to life and relationships. Significant therapeutic change, such as individuation from family-of-origin, or challenging the homeostasis of one's primary love relationship, as well as separation from the therapist, are essentially revolutionary. In revolution, power differentials are equalized and the status quo is upended. Others in the client's life may, of course, perceive the client's development toward personal growth as an infringement upon their own sense of well-being. Because of this, it is a moral imperative that the client be made fully aware of the potential costs of personal development in the form of upset, anger, or estrangement from others. Furthermore, the therapist must also consider the impact of the client's treatment upon the significant others in the client's system.

10) Therefore, the individual treatment of a married partner (or partner in a committed love relationship) must not exclude that spouse. Individual and marital therapy with the same practitioner must always be an option available to the spouse. It is in the interest of both partners (and their children) to grow together synergistically. Those significant others in the client's system in one-down hierarchial power relationships with the client are also considered to be "clients" of the therapist. It is imperative that the therapist think through the potentially deleterious effect of each intervention on the out-of-power person. This is a shared responsibility of the therapist and client.

11) Preference should be given to therapeutic interventions that are as *direct* as possible, but it should be understood that this is a therapeutic ideal not possible in every case, or for many, in the beginning phases of treatment.

12) The person of the therapist strives to be as *real* as possible and not merely assume a therapeutic role. This, too, is a therapeutic ideal not possible in every case, or for many, in the beginning phases of treatment.

13) The therapist's obligation is to these principles and values and to the client before them. The self-interest of the therapist is irrelevant. Loyalty to particular theories, pet ideas, and techniques is inappropriate.

14) It is expected that some clients will challenge and stretch the limits of the therapist. It is incumbent upon the therapist to explore his or her own countertransference, defined here as the tendency for the therapist to act in non-therapeutic ways such as inadequately appreciating, respecting, or loving the client. It is also necessary for the therapist to attempt to live his or her own life in accordance with the principles and values implicit and explicit in this system. The therapist must never request an intervention they themselves have activity or passively avoided, as this would not be genuine.

15) Therapy should be viewed as a completely voluntary process. The client may exit the therapeutic relationship at any time. Therefore, this model is not appropriate in court-mandated therapeutic situations, at one extreme, and may or may not be appropriate in situations where one is expected to attend therapy by someone else (parent, spouse, employer).

the relationship between values and theory

These principles and philosophy of treatment are therapeutic values, not psychotherapeutic theory. These principles supersede theory. From these overarching principles many valid or useful theories may emerge, depending upon factors like the nature of the presenting problem, the uniqueness of the individual client in terms of family and cultural background, and the level of motivation to change.

We may borrow certain techniques from virtually any school of therapy to assist the client in specific areas, as long as this occurs in the context of a healing reparental relationship, and the principles that define that relationship are consistent with the model. This therapy is defined by the specific relationship established and developed between therapist and client. Specific change strategies are highly flexible and may be based on the extant psychotherapy literature (theory, technique, and research) and practice (experience, one's own and that of others), but the reparental therapeutic relationship remains the consistent core.

As healing therapeutic agents, we may utilize any number of treatment strategies. But therapy is not the mere utilization of a "bag of tricks." In fact, the provision of therapeutic care and love referred to previously constitutes most of the "ert" or active substance of change. These include *nurturance* (unconditional positive regard, congruency, mirroring, prizing), *discipline* (confrontation, limit-setting, toughness), and *programming* (guidance, advice, direction), all of which must, of course, be provided with an empathic understanding of the true self of the client. These may be viewed as "techniques" but if delivered empathically tend not to be experienced as such by the client.

While the client may recognize the therapeutic situation or context for these inputs, they tend to be experienced as real and emanating from the true feelings of the therapist. If, for example, I am attempting to provide the client an experience of increased intimacy and provide a deeper connection with the real self of the client (as manifest perhaps in the regressed, child-like self) fearful of engulfment, I may move my chair closer, maintain more eye contact, and decrease "adult"-like verbalizations. Even if the client views my movements as "technique," they tend to be correlated with my true intentions. My movements are *ultimately* seen by the client as emanating truly from me as a person in this therapeutic context. If this does not occur for the client, the "technique" is of virtually no value to them.

Moreover, if the therapist does not act empathically and in a sensitively timed manner the client may lose perspective and experience the event as demeaning or hurtful. This is called a true therapeutic error and must be corrected. Even when done properly and timed well, the client may experience the event negatively, perhaps even traumatically (if, for example, the therapist is operating from inadequate information). This experience may constitute negative transference and will need to be worked through with the client. The therapist here takes on the role of the facilitating parent figure, separate from the perceived offending parent. This oscillation between therapeutic role behavior and real behavior occurs throughout the therapy with the goal of decreasing role-bound behaviors and increasing real behaviors.

when theory is not working

Psychotherapeutic theories can be wonderfully elegant and useful. Their major drawback is that they are only good when they work. While it is necessary for therapists to be well-schooled and versed in the major approaches to therapy, this is in and of itself insufficient for helping clients to change. Therapists must also be schooled in what to do when the major school(s) of therapy are ineffective.

Unfortunately, an inordinate amount of attention is given to theoretical formulations and an inadequate amount of attention is given to what to do when the studied implementation of these theoretical formulations is insufficient to produce change. One answer, of course, is to be flexible, eclectic, and willing to abandon a theoretical formulation that is not working. We may even have an integrative system for choosing among alternate paradigms and treatments. This is a step in the right direction. But we also need a system of understanding all the processes involved in treatment success or failure.

This model cites motivational processes at the core of treatment success, both the client's and the therapist's. But models invoking processes other than motivation as core are certainly possible.

What *is* the place of theory in this model? I tend to choose theoretical models on the basis of two criteria. First, the theory must be able to fit into the values and goals of the treatment. This is generally not an issue if one is willing to abandon certain elements of the theory I consider irrelevant. Orthodox adherents of these theories would be troubled by this, but my allegiance is to my clients, not theories. This allegiance is part of my therapeutic values or principles and treatment philosophy. For example, like many practitioners, I find transference to be a solid, important, and useful construct to explain certain positive and negative distortions in the therapeutic relationship. Yet I do not operate relationally as a blank screen, the supposed prerequisite for a "clean" kind of transference to emerge.

One of the underlying principles of this model is for the therapist to value simplicity and eschew theoretical formulations that are unnecessarily complicated. Therapists are bombarded with a multitude of stimuli and potential data from which to select in formulating a plan of treatment, and have a vast array of possible theories to explain and make sense of this data.

Some of these therapeutic theories are competing but most are compatible, even epistemologically, since many theories deal with different pools or levels of data. A cognitive therapist, for example, need not argue with a psychoanalyst about the nature of psychopathology and change, since the epistemological system they are operating from applies only to the data each is uniquely concerned with (Wright and Medlock, 1995). The cognitive therapist deals with the effect of dysfunctional thoughts on affect and behavior, not with the inner psyche of the client, as an analyst does. This is not to suggest that the cognitive therapist agrees with the operations of his or her analytic colleague, but that they are dealing with two different realms of human functioning. The challenge of psychotherapeutic integration is not with agreement or disagreement about theory and techniques, but rather with the question of compatibility. Where we do need agreement is in the area of therapeutic operational values and philosophy. The debates that have dominated psychotherapy continue to center around theoretical correctness instead of the differences in values which usually underlie the debates. Again, much of actual therapy practice is value-driven although it is not usually identified as such.

deal with what's in your face

But if theory does not guide our clinical decision-making and values, how do we decide what sets of data we apply these values to. One generic approach to decision-making in therapy is what I refer to colloquially as "deal with what's in your face" (or DWF). When determining a therapeutic direction or strategy the practitioner will typically do one of two things. Either s/he will apply a preferred model of treatment no matter what, and make the data fit the theory, or, if s/he is more eclectic, will select and adapt a model that best fits the data presented. In either situation, though, the selection and application of an approach is at least a step away from the level at which the problem is occurring organically. A notable exception to this is Lazarus' technical eclecticism which eschews theory in favor of responding to the presented treatment foci. But even Lazarus may be a half-step away. Although he claims to use social-learning theory as a broad-based operational model, he also seems to choose interventions based on an as yet unidentified set of values.

It has long been noted that one's preferred theory will illuminate particular sets of data (e.g., dysfunctional thought patterns for the cognitive therapist) and obscure other data sets (e.g., the client's dreams and fantasies). Those in the integration movement (as well as everyday practitioners) have identified this as problematic and have attempted to develop models that combine essential elements of various schools of therapy. While this effort may expand the data pool to account for more client variability, the integrative therapist remains theoretically bound.

Constructivist-minded psychotherapists have pointed out that theories are constructions of reality as opposed to more or less accurate discoveries of reality. They, too, tend to eschew theory and focus on how the constructed "stories" of the client may inhibit their growth and constructing more useful narratives could spur natural change processes.

While appealing as an emerging philosophical viewpoint, constructivism as applied to psychotherapy practice is problematic (see also Held, 1995). Clients (people) are not motivated by their ideas, theories, or thoughts. They are directed by their values, what they believe is right or wrong for them. Consciously or not, they come to therapy with value dilemmas, not narrative theoretical problems, constructed or otherwise. Moreover, these values, such as notions about relating and intimacy, are not insignificant or easily altered. The potent presenting problems that clients bring to therapy, what *they* talk about and what concerns *them*, are questions of values, loss of meaning, and spiritual dilemmas having to do with how to best lead their lives.

Too often therapists search for the meaning of symptoms and question *why* people do what they do. At worst, the behavior or problem is explained by a diagnosis, which serves to label the person, however accurately according to valid operational standards, but offers little direction with regard to treatment. To say a person has a narcissistic personality disorder may be descriptively useful but unhelpful in determining a course of treatment. While DSM-IV is offered as an atheoretical classification system, it is clear that people who meet the definition of dysthymic disorder, say, are more different than alike with regard to any number of significant characteristics, particularly characteristics, such as level of motivation, that are relevant to the treatment process.

When a supervisee presents a case to me and attaches one of these elaborate theories to their presentation, my response tends to be uniformly the same and on the order of, "Yeah, sounds good. Could be true. Sure. Maybe, I don't know; do you know?" The reason I offer these ambiguous responses is to help my supervisee shed the concern, and at times obsession, with *why* this problem may or may not be occurring. I similarly will dismiss my client's formulations since intellectual insight or understanding no matter how brilliantly and correctly formulated, will not lead to a change in feelings and behavior, or lessen dysfunction.

At best, insight will help the client develop a better understanding of the problem so that their level of motivation to directly address it may increase. At midrange, insight and exploration offer the therapist and client an interesting and subculturally sanctified diversion to engage in while the therapeutic relationship is unfolding. At worst, insight may lead the stuck client into believing they are making significant therapeutic progress when they are not. Insight, in my experience, is best understood, applied, and utilized *after* the necessary changes in operation are made.

When the therapist applies a theoretical formulation to a client's dysfunction, then the problem is framed or reframed. That frame imprisons both therapist and client unless the specific change prescriptions gleaned from that theoretical frame offer a relational and value correlate. Sometimes they do, but most often they do not.

Let us consider an example that I will present as simply as possible to support this position. A theoretical formulation applied to anorexic adolescents is an adaptation of family therapy, where the therapist views the dysfunctional eating pattern within the context of the teenager's family. One of the primary technical elements of this model has the parent(s) feeding the child in the presence and with the guidance of the therapist. This approach, most often called Structural Family Therapy (SFT) is well conceived, with a strong history of research and practice to support the application of SFT in such therapeutic situations. According to an encouraging body of research, SFT for anorexic teenagers is quite effective, with high success rates.

My interpretation of these positive results, while not diminishing the underpinnings and application of the SFT approach, is that we need not accept its assumptions to accept its success. Confronted with the same therapeutic presentation, I would involve the parents in the treatment not because I speculated there may be a structural problem in the family (although I'm not necessarily opposed to the notion that there may be one) but because I am making a specific value judgment. Simply put, that value judgment is that if one's 15-year-old daughter is having serious life difficulties, it is the *responsibility* of the parents to do whatever it takes to help her with the problem.

The reader may wonder about the difference between the two interpretations, particularly in practice. These differences are significant. I do not need to accept the primary SFT assumption, that there is a structural problem in the family. A technical eclectic would also be unimpressed with this assumption since s/he may say, I, too, can apply SFT techniques without accepting the SFT theoretical baggage.

While this is true, and Arnold Lazarus makes this point as eloquently as anyone, the problem arises when the client(s), in this case the family, *resist* the treatment(and as one may suspect they often do). A popular axiom of clinical practice supports this: those who resist treatment tend to need it the most. If the parents, say, refuse to get involved, or only participate minimally, or cancel sessions on a routine basis (all possible, even likely), then we must abandon the SFT approach or technique for another one. Again, we may or may not accept the theoretical assumptions and explanations of the new model. But if the technical eclectic chooses models based on relevant data and SFT is the therapy of choice, what new context will s/he use in selecting the second or third approach?

In my value-based viewpoint, I have the flexibility and further options of technical eclecticism without abandoning a coherent overarching structure. I do not hold the parents responsible for the problem; I simply hold them responsible for becoming part of the solution. Indeed, I expect them to be part of the solution. If they are not motivated to do so, to whatever extent, then *this* becomes the problem in my face. I may, depending upon the unique circumstances of the case, confront, cajole, encourage, induce guilt, or scare the parents into full participation in treatment, because I view it as their responsibility. Their resistance (lack of motivation) is a part of what I must work with. I am attempting to increase their level of motivation specifically and directly to help their daughter, but broadly and less directly to help their marriage, themselves, and other children in the family.

Again, I do not do this because I accept the assumption of the tie between members of a system or subsystems (For me this may or may not be true; the most I can say is that it is as good, if not better, than any other theory). My own approach is values-driven. For family members to take responsibility, especially parents for children, is viewed as a productive and positive approach to living.

In one such case, after confronting a resistant mother on why she was avoiding completing an important task of therapy in helping her anorexic daughter, she began to weep and talk about how hopeless she felt, not necessarily about her daughter, but of having the kind of loving relationship she dreamed of having with her husband. Her husband, when confronted, spoke of feeling estranged from the family. In time, the daughter's symptoms dissipated. Whether the anorexia was related to this set of developments that ultimately took place in therapy is an interesting theoretical question, but immaterial to me as a practitioner. The daughter's anorexia was no doubt a problem that needed to be addressed, but I did not have to frame the treatment with this problem. That people in this family were not responsibly and adequately loving and being loved was the only overarching frame I found useful. Their motivation to address this lack of loving and responsibility taking was thwarted by a host of factors.

DWF is based on a system of relational values and therefore, may take on tones of "should" and "should not." Standard therapeutic practice eschews the therapeutic discourse of moral imperatives, at least as overtly expressed. (But how one can avoid values imposition and engage in a relationship with the client is a question I still cannot answer.)

Values are what guide my clinical decision-making. I have definite ideas about what a healthy marriage looks like (generic not specific notions). If, for example, a client is having a covert marital affair, I will challenge the client directly.[1] While I am certainly interested in exploring the reasons for the affair, whether it be the avoidance of intimacy, triangulation, or any combination, I deal with what's in my face, mainly a spouse who is lying. What do I have against lying if that's what the client chooses to do, and if, as I hypothesize, the spouse, who may or may not be my client, chooses to covertly collude or condone? Actually, I have nothing inherently against lying in and of itself. It is not a moral issue to me in the sense of breaking some established commandment. Rather, I assume that the client, if truly motivated toward personal growth, would be hard-pressed to lie and would see lying as dystonic with a healthy approach to life.

This is not a moral issue per se. I have no inherent problem with overt or mutually agreed upon affairs. The component of an affair that is incompatible with the motivation toward personal growth is the lie and the deception involved. The overt affair may be possible for a cou-

---

1. Again, I am not suggesting that I do anything so unusual. Therapists confront clients on such issues all the time. Moreover, I am just as sure the basis from which these therapists operate from is rooted in their *values*. I challenge the reader to find an established therapy model in the literature that proscribes this. Many theorists who do describe the value-based motives of therapy and discuss particular values (e.g., Peck, 1978) tend not to offer prescriptive help to clinicians.

ple who is each positively motivated toward personal growth. This is highly unlikely, but in the context, for example, of gay male couples, open nonmonogamy is at the very least a theoretical possibility. Because monogamy is not necessarily a basic assumption in gay communities, generally speaking, if a gay male client comes to me and tells me untroublingly about a sexual affair, I do not consider that to be "in my face" (Rappaport, 1993b).

Consistent with this values approach, I want the client to introject my values about integrity in intimate relationships, since I present them in as personal a manner as possible. Traditional therapeutic theory views personalized confrontations like saying or implying that a client is engaging in behaviors that are "wrong," or "hurtful to others" as inappropriate. Instead, we tend to codify such ascriptions as "dysfunctional" or "unhealthy," but health is largely determined by particular sets of therapist-determined *values*, rather than by some objective scientific standard.

For some therapists, confrontation merely means clarifying what the client is doing, pointing out antecedents, or relevant correlates to the behavior. I certainly am not opposed to these milder, even benign, forms of confrontation, if they are appropriate for that particular situation. I am simply stating that all confrontation derives from the same source: the values of the therapist, no matter what the conscious intent or system of those values is, i.e., theory, research, or practice.

I tend to prefer direct and personalized confrontation for several reasons. First, it is more honest in that I am offering my viewpoint without subliminal messages. Thus, if the client disagrees, my viewpoint is laid bare rather than being embedded within a codified language difficult to contest. These disagreements may even lead to my altering my own views, a process that I see as the co-creation of therapeutic values and goals. Second, if my intention is to have the client introject a set of values, it is best to present those values as unambiguously as possible. The more I offer them in a personal frame, the more likely the client will be to introject them clearly.

It is not unusual for me to label what a client is doing as "fucked up." I prefer the phrase "fucked up" because it is common parlance and more genuine, reflecting more accurately what I am really thinking. (I give myself the freedom to think more like a "person" than a "clinician.") It's also nonpathologizing language and gives the client a level playing field to challenge me on, if s/he chooses. I could refer to the client as "narcissistic," "self-destructive," "thinking dysfunctionally," "enmeshed," but such terminology only distances me from the client.

Some therapists may say it is inappropriate for me to term a client's behavior as "fucked up." Some clients must make meaning for themselves, it is often argued. While I agree with the notion that clients always make meaning for themselves (even more perhaps than the proponents of this viewpoint), therapy is unabashedly a process of influence, whether that influence is conscious or unconscious, overt or covert, direct or indirect. I simply favor influencing processes that are direct, overt, and consciously planned.

I often tell my students to stop thinking like a therapist: think and feel like a person, but act as a clinician. The caveat, of course, is that one cannot think and feel like just any person, but only as an emotionally stable, strong, and loving relational other. Quite often, a student presents a complicated, perplexing, and seemingly hopeless case, starting and finishing with, "I don't know where to go, or what to do next." I usually respond, "What if this client were your child? You're their (healthy) parent; what would you want for them? What would you like to see happen, and what might you do to help them?" This tends to clear the muck that not only the pathology but our theories of psychotherapy can create.

I do not mean to oversimplify psychotherapy here. The pressures, demands, and patience required to be "like a parent" or in a reparental posture are enormous. However, if we hold the therapeutic relationship to be the central mechanism for change and consider our theories and techniques a distant second and third, the therapy process becomes much clearer.

The therapy relationship that I propose is best thought of as therapeutic relating. Therapists invented therapy, but therapeutic relating is a quite natural process that predates Freud and the advent of psychoanalysis. Natural therapeutic agents have more to teach therapists than the other way around. Therapists are hampered by the fact that they learned quite odd modes of relating from teachers and other therapists (supervisors) who in my estimation are not particularly good at relating in a perhaps necessary but quite peculiar frame: the professional once-a-week 50-minute psychotherapy session.

chapter 8

motivating clients in the beginning of therapy

If we keep in mind our biphasic approach to the client's presenting problem, namely, separating the cluster of self-esteem, self-love, and motivational issues from psychopathology, we get a clearer picture of the critical beginning phases of treatment. Since we know that motivational difficulties negatively affect a client's willingness to deal with his or her problems, our central interest is impinging upon the motivational process.

If a client comes to therapy deflated, hopeless, and despairing about life and change, we say they are entering treatment in a default regression. The client who enters treatment in the primitive phase of motivation, or the client who returns to the primitive phase after a period of time in the external phase, is difficult to treat. By definition, they will tend not to engage well in the process of therapy whether that involves producing content or material necessary in the psychodynamic, humanistic, or experiential schools of therapy or accomplishing assignments or tasks necessary for the cognitive and behavioral schools. They may even be reluctant to take a psychotropic medication, overly sensitive to its side-effects, and unimpressed with its intended effects.

Some in the psychodynamic, experiential, or humanistic schools of therapy would contend that the fact that many clients come to therapy in undermotivated states is not surprising. It is simply part of the treatment process and the therapist must accept the client, reflecting empathically or interpreting back to the client.

While I accept the premise that lack of motivation is not an unusual or unexpected state of affairs, we must remember that most clients will not continue in therapy if they remain hopeless. The process of empathic reflection and interpretation tends to be slow and arduous. Few clients will experience less directive and more neutral relational paradigms as emotionally penetrating and inspiring enough. Those clients who do tend to remain in therapy because they feel more hopeful; the vast majority tends to drop out prematurely.

attitudes about premature termination and therapy failures

Different therapy models, in particular models that de-emphasize motivational phenomena and eschew formulations of resistance like the constructivist and narrative schools, may tend not to consider premature terminations as relevant. I consider a termination "premature" according to a standard of therapeutic outcome that holds the ultimate goal of therapy to be not only resolving the presenting difficulties (whether based in self-esteem or in psychopathology) but also attaining the internal phase of motivation, where one becomes more self-directed. The extent to which the presenting problem and motivational difficulties are interwoven may vary. The presenting problem may resolve itself quickly with the therapy becoming more self-esteem-based, or the presenting problem(s) may not resolve until very late in the treatment, only after a great deal of motivational work has been accomplished. All things considered though, while this standard is high, it is not a lofty or unrealistic one.

Moreover, I am unimpressed with therapies that do not recognize or tend to rationalize failures (see also Bugental, 1988; Stricker, 1995). While more is not always better, people who *stay* in therapy tend to improve more than people who do not stay in therapy (Seligman, 1996) although, of course, some deleterious effects of psychotherapy may occur in approximately 10 percent of clients (Strupp, Hadley and Gomes-Schwartz, 1977).

A rough but excellent measure of therapeutic success correlates with attendance and continuance in treatment. We must discard the neo-romantic and pleasant sounding platitudes about the "difficulty of life's journey" and the "many roads one must take along this journey (which do not include therapy)" that I often hear as apologetic, post-hoc explanations of premature termination. These kinds of explanations attempt to reframe the failures and excuse the therapist of responsibility for it. There are many therapists who at worst simply do not believe therapy works (and sometimes use their clients to prove their thesis) or are highly skeptical of the therapy process. While I am sympathetic to a skeptical viewpoint of therapy, a person who holds such a view should not be actively functioning as a professional therapist. Unfortunately, the field of psychotherapy is replete with large numbers of would-be philosophers and ministers. Although it may serve many functions, therapy is primarily an *activity* and *procedure*. If I had heart disease, I would consider a range of alternative treatments, but if I decided to undergo a bypass operation I would choose only a surgeon who strongly believed in the efficacy of the bypass procedure. I would consider the opinions of specialists who counseled against the bypass, but I certainly wouldn't go to them for the procedure.

Of course, the briefer therapies by definition have different goals, and client termination after four, six, or eight sessions may not be deemed failure at all. These therapies may successfully address psychopathology but will not impinge upon motivational processes. In briefer cognitive and behavioral therapies more active participation is necessary and motivation is a more overt factor. If the client is insufficiently motivated, the therapist is forced to employ other approaches to engage the client (Omer and Alon, 1989; Lineham, 1988).

emotional penetration and the infusion of hope

Many of these other approaches revolve around the concept of hope-building. The infusion of hope is necessary, but not sufficient, in every treatment. This is my first consideration when working with any client, especially a primitively motivated one. How do I get this person to believe in what we're going to do? How do I help him or her to see the possibilities in life and in change? This is the therapist's first job.

We cannot expect the client to help us much in this endeavor. The client may even resist our every effort because they do not believe that life can really be different for them. However, as therapists *we* must believe. If you are a therapist and do not believe in the possibilities of life, you should not be a practicing therapist, an agent of change. One cannot infuse hope in another without having hope oneself. One cannot love another without loving oneself. One cannot motivate another without being motivated oneself. My first duty is to provide the hope that change is possible, so that the client may gain faith. That faith at first is *in me*, as the person who I am and the person they *need* me to be.

Their construction of me is based partially on transference, an organization of me into a familiar parent-like figure providing new and needed inputs for growth. As the transference resolves and I gradually become less of a transference figure and more of a real person providing real inputs (i.e., love) then this faith transfers away from me and *onto* the client. Faith needs to be placed in the therapist before it can emanate from the client. This is because the state of demotivation and self-hate represents an object-deficiency, and this object-loss is reexperienced as the default regression. One cannot be one's own inner self-loving object without first experiencing an other-loving object, whether a significant other or therapeutic agent. Self-love emanates from a successful experience of love by an other.

The task of therapy is conceptually simple (although in practice not at all straightforward), when a client first presents. One has to determine how to emotionally or psychologically penetrate the psychological being of the client. How do I penetrate the psychological being of this person is the question the therapist must ask h/herself. The reason to penetrate is to infuse a sense of hope I've been discussing to give the client a recognition that they have found someone who can really help them in their life, and not necessarily just with specific problem X.

the importance of bonding and role flexibility in therapy

Before this can happen, though, we must create a bond with the client. If the person comes for therapy in the primitive phase, the practitioner may not immediately penetrate since the process of penetration feels overwhelming to the client. The therapist must first prove to be worthy, trustable, loveable, knowledgeable, and strong, a good-enough re-parental agent, if you will.

There is an ongoing oscillation between bonding and penetration: at first bonding must be emphasized; then later deemphasized in favor of penetration. With time and progression into the external phase, the therapist can pull away from active involvement which assists the client in claiming the healing introject.

In bonding, the therapist assumes a relational posture that mimics what the client experienced (negative and positive) in their family-of-origin. This gives the client a safe sense of the familiar. In addition, the client will virtually always attempt to organize the therapist to mimic their family-of-origin experiences through the process of projective identification (enactment) and transference. The therapist actually has difficulty *not* being in this role.

A common example of such a bonding posture occurs with clients who have had abusive backgrounds, whether physical, emotional, or sexual. Depending upon other factors, a necessary element of bonding necessarily includes a toughness that may *mimic* abuse. A typical error that many therapists make with clients who have had abuse in their backgrounds is that they tend to be overprotective or "too nice." Such a posture weakens the connection between therapist and client.

People who have been abused commonly tend to cathect in one of two ways. They either find other transference figures to be sadistic or abusive and victimize them. This includes supervisors, lovers, or friends. Alternatively, through a process of identification with the aggressor, they may play out the role of victimizer to another (e.g., a lover) who represents themselves as a child.

In therapy, the practitioner must be careful not to be experienced either as the "abuser," by being too tough in his or her posture, or, on the other hand, too soft. Both will lead to premature termination. The "too-tough" posture will engender fears of annihilation; the "too-soft" posture will engender fears of abandonment. The practitioner perceived as too nice will hear pretermination complaints of "nothing's happening here." Each of these responses is rooted in fear and therefore will easily lead to cancellations, no-shows, and premature termination. But, as I stated, the client will signal us as to what they need from us. We must, however, attend to the key signals.

If one's therapeutic orientation prescribes a relational paradigm that does not allow for active toughness, confrontation, and challenge we will be unable to mimic certain negative aspects of their childhood experience. Contrary to the popular conception of overly powerful therapists manipulating defenseless clients, most clients lose motivation and terminate therapy because of their perception that "nothing (or not enough) is happening." In general, clients are quite well defended, far from the defenseless patients often depicted in the popular media. Most therapists err on the side of doing too little rather than too much and in the direction of overpassivity, underactivity, and nondirectiveness. Some clients (in this model, the BB personality type) thrive within such nondirective postures, but the great majority do not.

There exists a myth in psychotherapy, perhaps even in the entire human-services field, that we should provide clients with the opposite of their negative experiences as they were growing up. This view holds that a client who was treated disrespectfully by significant others in childhood needs to be treated with an abundance of respect by the therapist; this is necessary, and may even be sufficient, for healing. While I agree with the basic premise that *ultimately* therapists must provide these kinds of positive inputs to supplant and replace the negative introjects of childhood, it is the client's *experience* of the input that is critical. Providing positive inputs of unconditional love, positive regard, nurturance, and mirroring, for example, to a client who is filled with self-hate and in the primitive phase of motivation will *not* be experienced by the client as empathic. In fact, the client may experience such well-intended interventions as noxious or at minimum, unhelpful.

Alternatively, this same client may experience confrontation or toughness as quite empathic. Too often we give clients what we *choose* to give them rather than what they need. The lay addiction field led by recovering addicts, has known this for quite some time. To motivate most addicts one must penetrate what is often referred to as their denial. I believe these practitioners are not impinging upon the addict's denial as much as penetrating the emotional experience of the addict.[1] This provides the client with an internal experience that "s/he knows and understands me; I feel connected to him or her." This stops the default regression process, although perhaps only temporarily.

The recovering-addict/counselor is able to do so not by mirroring or providing respect; rather, s/he is challenging and tough. If we viewed a videotape of such a confrontation, we might recoil at the seeming lack of respect. I have attended workshop presentations where such material was presented to negative audience reaction. But it is the *client's* experience of the interaction that is crucial. At other workshops where the client in question was present and offered a positive view of the confrontational encounter, many in the audience overrode the client's own perspective and experience.

There appears to be a bias in the field against more active, directive, and confrontational relational paradigms. This bias has never existed in the field of drug and alcohol abuse, however, and for all their difficulties and failures, they have outperformed more traditional professional approaches in treating substance-abuse. It is often necessary to penetrate the self-hating and self-destroying introjects of the addict, and once the self-hate of the client is pierced, nondirective interventions may be very effective and experienced empathically.

The course of treatment may follow this oscillation in posture. Interestingly, as the addiction field becomes professionalized with programs run by psychologists and psychiatrists, there has been a shifting

---

1. I have treated addicts who are not in denial, who know precisely what they are doing to themselves and yet do not care and remain hopeless. They are unwilling to change it because they remain in a primitive-phase default regression.

away from confrontational interventions. The more the addiction field views substance abuse as comparable to a medical illness and frames multiple problems in living in terms of "dual diagnosis" and the like, the naturally therapeutic confrontation traditionally used by ex-addicts diminish. While recovering-addict/counselors can easily err by overidentifying with the addict, professional therapists tend to *underidentify* with the client's self-destructiveness and self-hate. Natural therapeutic agents utilize a wide variety of postures when relating. Unfortunately, therapists tend to limit themselves to a single cluster of more nondirective and less active postures. Therapists have more to learn about relational healing from natural therapeutic agents than vice-versa.

Although therapists may see themselves as experts in relating, they tend to be poor motivators. The postures prescribed by the major schools of therapy and learned through acculturalization in graduate school and during training experiences are quite limiting. If we consider the natural therapeutic agents and motivators that exist in the larger culture, several images come to mind: the wise grandmother who, with a relevant story provides a strong message and a dose of unconditional positive regard to her grandchild, without any mirroring, dialoging, or technique of empathic listening; the gruff basketball coach who "rides" a certain player all season by being tough and "getting in their face" when that player fails to utilize his potential; the teacher who brings out the best in a student by praising their abilities and seeing his or her raw talent before anyone else.[2] This teacher may become a kind of booster or cheerleader similar to the mentor who takes a special interest in someone on a lower rung of the ladder. This mentor uses his or her knowledge of the field and helps the mentoree profit from his guidance and his own mistakes. The mentor is a kind of guardian angel who advises, consults, and leads the mentoree in the direction that s/he thinks will lead to success and satisfaction.

The enactment of these roles by natural therapeutic agents is ubiquitous. Because of the fractionalization and disintegration of communities, we need more such natural therapeutic agents. It has been suggested that the increased demands placed on psychotherapy have occurred because therapists are expected to fulfill many roles that were

---

2. By no means am I suggesting that natural therapeutic agents relate in superior ways or are always correct in their mode of relating. I can certainly think of many situations where that same coach, for example, was not tough and confrontational but cruel and humiliating or the teacher who was ignored by the pupil s/he was trying to help.

once handled by community leaders, extended family, and religious figures. But how much do therapists actually enact these roles? I suspect, quite a bit. For the most part, though, apart from the odd metatheoretical paper here or there (e.g., Riebel, 1990), these roles are not integrated into our models of psychotherapy.

Because of the demands of hour-by-hour psychotherapy and the confidential nature of the enterprise, therapists do a lot of things that go unreported in the literature. I am not speaking of the unethical or the irregular, although that, too, occurs, but rather of the therapist's going outside the bounds of his or her orientation to engage in operations that are intuitively driven (Rappaport, 1991b; 1993a). There are many problems with this, including the inherent lack of accountability and the rigorous scientific dictum that *ideally* every intervention of the therapist should be data and/or model-driven. The therapist should be able to defend each intervention as purposeful and transferable to other cases.[3] Moreover, if the therapist only operates intuitively, the therapy will tend to be idiosyncratic if not sloppy.

The kind of therapeutic posture I am proposing utilizes what practitioners tend to engage in quite naturally. I am merely attempting to provide a rationale for selecting a posture for a particular client in a particular situation with particular goals in mind. Lazarus (1993) has referred to this process as being an "authentic chameleon." I've acted as the helpful mentor, the tough coach, the wise grandmother, and many other roles. Obviously different clients require different stances. The genuineness of the intervention is not determined by the intent of the practitioner but by the experience of the client. This is particularly so in the beginning phases of treatment, when mistakes are costly and timing is everything. For most clients, as treatment progresses, the therapist often switches relational paradigms depending upon the demands of the situation.

At the very beginning of treatment (i.e., for the first several sessions and often longer) the therapist must find the particular relational paradigm that is at once familiar and healing to the client. Roles are a good way to define the early relational paradigms. As therapy pro-

---

3. In this sense, each therapy case becomes a source of data for the scientist-practitioner that can be applied or not applied to other cases on the basis of success or failure. Ideally, this data collection should be disseminated to other practitioners. Unfortunately, this tends not to occur because such interventions are non-theory driven. A bias exists against their dissemination which inhibits the flow of innovation in the field as a whole (Rappaport, 1993a).

gresses, these roles will tend to give way to more real relating because it provides more direct healing. Therapeutic role-relating is best thought of as stabilizing and indirectly healing, or a necessary precursor for the penetration of the true self. Once the client's armor is penetrated the true intentions of the therapist and the real self of the client may merge to create moments of relational transcendence that humanistic theorists like Carl Rogers (1957) spoke of so eloquently. These real therapeutic interactions, whether as brief translucent moments, a set of those moments, or incrementally provided throughout treatment, are potentially transformative.

In the primitive phase, though, there are few, if any such moments. In the primitive phase the therapist is less real and in one of many possible roles. The framework for choosing that role is based on the notion of reparenting, the filling in of the gaps and deficiencies from the family-of-origin experience.

In some cases, the role we choose may be obvious. A client recently came to me worried about losing his job because of the interpersonal difficulties he was having with coworkers. He needed coaching, help in understanding what was happening, developing a strategy, along with advice on how to handle certain situations. It is significant that he did not *ask* me to coach him; he simply, but despairingly, told me the problem he was having. This may sound simple, but rarely is anything in therapy simple. He obviously needed this kind of help, if only to save his job which he said was very important to him, but was resistant to accepting it.

Why? Because his experiences of being helped in an active way brought up fears of powerlessness. He could not trust that I could have his best interests at heart. Indeed, his lack of trust was one of the reasons he was in danger of being fired and was at the heart of his interpersonal difficulties. He tended to misinterpret things I said, believing (although not necessarily saying so directly, as is typical of the primitive phase) that "(I) was on their side" if I tried to explain his boss's viewpoint to him. Thus, I had to be a "coach" without appearing to be too much in that role. I inserted the coaching into a bonding-oriented relational framework that was familiar to him, one that mimicked his experience with his mother who, in such situations, would provide a kind of supportive sympathy to excess. With elements of the bonding posture in place, he increasingly accepted more coaching, which helped him greatly alter his work situation. Significantly, he began to accept me as a potentially helpful person, and in time began to come to therapy more open, asking questions, and actively seeking direction.

When a client reaches this point, we say they are moving from the primitive to the external phase. What this client let go of was his skeptical view that *anyone* in a position of power would abuse him in some way, and he no longer needed to defend against that transferential expectation especially of men. Giving up the destructive viewpoint(s) from the family-of-origin for a new view of the world, that people may be trustworthy until proven otherwise, was the exit for him out of the primitive phase. He was able to accomplish this by incrementally trusting me more and this became a corrective transactional experience for him until he could trust himself.

The coach or mentor role is often appropriate for men who have had distant, uninvolved fathers. These men tend to feel lost. They'll talk about not knowing the rules of life, not knowing what it means to be a man, feeling like other men seem to know things that they don't. These men had little guidance. Some may have had closer relationships with their mothers, although they may have been embarrassed and conflicted by that. In their embarrassment, they may have attempted to avoid close contact with their mother. In any case, there is only so much a mother can do in teaching a son about manhood.

These men come to therapy emotionally hungry. This hunger may be manifest or latent. If it is manifest the work of the therapist is, of course, much easier. These clients need to be *claimed* by a reparental agent. Claiming is a process that occurs in normal gender development when the critical parenting shifts to the parent of the same gender as the child. The child is claimed by the parent as theirs—their project, their primary responsibility. With these clients, I claim them not by saying but by doing, becoming "like a father" to them, teaching them about life, the world of work, women, etc. This creates an experience of specialness which all clients need to experience before moving from the primitive phase. Ultimately, each client must hold a special meaning to the therapist.

I spoke of two kinds of cases that involve the primary therapeutic role of coaching, but coaching is a part of virtually every therapy to some degree or another.[4] In our model, flexibility for the therapist to

---

4. The cheerleader/booster function is another important motivating role for the therapist. Providing encouragement, moral support, and positive reinforcement can be very helpful if a client lacked that kind of input growing up. The message, "you can do this," ultimately becomes internalized as "I can do this" in the internal phase.

switch roles based upon client need without excessive worry that the treatment process will be disrupted, is essential. In psychoanalytic therapies, for example, if we were to actively coach a client we would be interfering with the flow of transference. In our model determining the correct role at the correct time and understanding its impact on the transference are important cofactors.

the value of encouraging dependency

But how does the therapist's assuming these roles serve to increase the client's motivation to grow? The short answer to this question is, it doesn't. What the role accomplishes is the creation of a healing bond to the practitioner, the kind of reparental relating that I've spoken of previously. The client's *inner* motivation to grow is, for the most part, unaffected. Moreover, the client's focus and attention shifts to the practitioner and to the treatment as a source of new constructions, new modes of thinking and experiencing, and new ways of living. There develops an openness to the practitioner that aids in the healing process. We view this as a essential step in the process of increasing motivation to grow. In this particular step, the therapist becomes a more central figure in the life of the client and thereby an important motivator.

It is important to note that the therapist is not replacing the client as primary motivator, nor is s/he usurping the client's inner positive drive or motivation. Positive aspects from the family-of-origin and elsewhere that the client has introjected and healthfully enacted contemporary manifestations are supported and encouraged to flourish. The therapist must be careful to distinguish which attitudes and behaviors of the client are growthful and which are more survival-driven. The survival-driven operations of the client are targeted for change since these are based on negative introjects and unrealistic expectations (e.g., "the world is a uniformly dangerous place where I get hurt and victimized").

Of course, when the therapist adopts the role of motivator, it is with an expectation that some dependency upon the therapist will develop (or alternatively, a counter-dependency), one which must be addressed. In general, dependency is viewed negatively by psychotherapists. In solution-focused, narrative, problem-solving, cognitive/behavioral, and humanist/experiential therapies, dependency is seen as antithetical to growth; these therapies seek to bolster the client's existing, if subterranean, self-competency rather than exalting the therapist as expert or healer. While many of these therapies are active and involve activating processes, the therapist assumes a background role, serving as more of a change consultant. In the depth-oriented therapies, like psychoanalysis, and its offshoots, such as object relations therapy, client dependency is viewed as an expected component of the treatment. Despite this expectation, dependency is not viewed positively, nor is it encouraged. Rather, it is something to be processed, analyzed, and understood by the client. In working through transference, the client is expected to see that dependent feelings that s/he holds for the practitioner are related to regressed aspects of the personality. While dependency is not directly discouraged, the client is given the message, covertly if not explicitly, that dependency is not a positive aspect of treatment.

In our model, we view dependency differently. The client is switching allegiance from the negative introjected aspects of the family-of-origin and its contemporary manifestations to the therapist and the therapy. If dependency does not occur, the therapy remains unpenetrating. While the client may certainly make changes that seem to remediate the presenting complaint(s), transformational change is not possible, nor are dramatic shifts in motivation.

The first shift in motivation in our model is from the primitive phase to the external phase. While some clients do this more easily than others, all clients require some amount of time in the dependent, external phase of growth to receive new inputs and develop new ideas and skills. A small number of clients may achieve transformative growth with the therapist remaining in a less active relational role, like consultant. To the extent that this can occur, that is fine. But most clients require the therapist to assume more active, directive, and intensive roles, which will in and of itself create both therapeutic dependency and a reaction to it, counterdependency. The client's emerging motivation may now be to ally with the therapist, to get closer to and please him or her. We need not question these motives, which are to be expected, nor view them negatively. This may be congruent with some psychoanalytic theorists who posit that when the therapeutic relationship is going well, it is unnecessary or unwise to focus on it (Reik, 1948; Fromm-Reichman, 1950).

The client is, to a large degree, creating us. In other words, s/he shapes the interactions by organizing and projecting onto us disowned or undeveloped positive aspects of themselves. Through the process of projective identification we enact these positive aspects for him or her.

The therapist becomes the holder for what the client wishes. The problem is that much of the time the client on the whole is ambivalent about these goals, and the therapeutic process becomes a battleground for change, with the therapist representing positive growth and change and the client representing stagnation and homeostasis. Such struggles are normative (see Omer and Alon, 1989, for a parallel discussion related to therapeutic strategy).

This occurs because the client cannot hold the positive (loving) aspects of the self while the negative (hating) aspects of the self have not been sufficiently affected. At the beginning of therapy with primitively motivated clients, the therapist holds virtually all the positive goals and wishes.[5] With time, the client may reclaim the projected wishes as their own and as motivation increases, the practitioner becomes less of a container for the client's positive goals and wishes. The ultimate goal of therapy is reached when the therapist no longer holds any such wishes for the client.

impinging upon the default regression process

The therapist *stops* holding these positive aspects only when the client exits the therapy, which we read as the truest statement of the client's intentions and wishes. Otherwise, our role as therapists requires the steadfast belief in the client, especially when the client no longer believes in him or herself. For example, if a client who comes to therapy while in the external phase of motivation (however brief) may say to me, "Help me learn to be more loving, positive, and intimate with my spouse." They are organizing me to hold this goal for them. I expect that two weeks or two months later that same client, after some disappointment with his wife, may say, "Fuck her—I'm tired of trying, I give up. I'm not coming here anymore." It is my job to hold the client to the loving introject he once directly handed to me and is now attempting to withdraw. I may say to him (in a way that he can accept, of course), "No. Fuck *you*. I know this is hard, but you're giving up so easily. It's only been two months and you're so willing to give up . . . This is exactly how you got into this trouble in the first place—you get frustrated and then you give up."

---

5. At the beginning of treatment with a primitively motivated client who comes to therapy because "my wife thinks I need it" and nothing else, the therapist is a 100% container. The same client who two months into treatment says, "I guess I could be nicer to her," may project 85%, onto the practitioner, and so on.

Such an interaction is designed to pierce the default-regression process and penetrate the client emotionally. This client needs to be confronted and to be held accountable by the therapist. We cannot expect the client to provide this function by themselves, since self-discipline (that is, resiliency in the face of achieving a positive goal) is not likely to be in their repertory. Being frustrated and giving up may be the familiar (primitive) response. It is only when the client reaches the *internal* phase that they can provide this function for themselves. Thus, the therapeutic contract, both the initial one and the contract that develops over the course of treatment, is very important, for it establishes the therapist as the holder of the goal along with the client. The therapist then must determine what role will best serve this particular client as s/he attempts to reach his or her particular goals.

In the default regression, the client experiences object-loss, and s/he has an internal feeling of aloneness in the world. We typically hear statements like "Why bother trying; nothing ever works for me anyway." "I have to do this myself." "This is all too hard." These are statements indicating the client is experiencing a default regression. In clients who are biochemically prone toward depression, such a state may overlap with or become a major depression.

Since there is a loss of object, the therapeutic task here is a simple one, to penetrate the real self of the client. If the therapist has already penetrated the client, then s/he must repenetrate. It is not unusual for a therapy to be punctuated by a series of default regressions over a long period of time. The therapist must not become frustrated and give up on the client. "Giving up" may include knee-jerk referrals to other practitioners, premature recommendations for medication or psychological testing.[6] The client will quite correctly experience such recommendations as abandoning. The default regression is marked by a hopelessness and despair which can engender the same feelings within the practitioner. The client is essentially recreating their childhood experience of abandonment. If the therapist participates by allowing him or herself to play the role of the abandoning parent, it will be a suc-

---

6. In the twists and turns of real-life psychotherapy, however, the client may come to us with the latest popular magazine article in hand proclaiming, for example, "I'm A.D.D.—it says it right here . . ." With certain clients, giving them "permission" to seek out assessments that are not indicated or inappropriate treatments may also be experienced as abandonment if the client's *motive* arises out of the default regression. Of course, in certain situations it may be strategically necessary for the therapist to approve the suggestion in order to maintain the therapeutic relationship.

cessful recreation and the client will likely remain in default regression. One can view the essential dynamic of the default regression as the client's simultaneous fear of and wish for abandonment.

Why would someone wish for abandonment? The pain associated with the unknown is more acute than the chronic but familiar pain of what is known. The client, we must remember, is virtually certain that s/he will be let down, disappointed, or abandoned. To them it is only a matter of how and when. Organizing and creating the abandonment themselves at least gives them some sense of control over the process, if not the outcome. To them the outcome is all but assured anyway. Some clients attempt to convince the therapist that they are unworthy of help while others are convinced that change is not possible anyway, at least for them.

No matter what the manifestation, and there are many, these are all indicative of a default regression. The client may unwittingly and unconsciously engage in this maneuver over and over again. The therapist's response must be steadfast, unmovable, and patient. Metaphorically, the therapist is in the basic relational stance of the solid parent of the two-year-old who throws tantrums or the five-year-old who claims, "You don't love me" when the parent disciplines the child. In other words, the therapist is responsive but nonreactive. The helpful response both for parent or therapist, is to provide hope in the face of hopelessness and faith in the face of faithlessness. This hope and faith must be inspired by a particular belief system. The therapist must believe in the healing possibilities of the therapeutic process, the healing possibilities of him or herself as a therapeutic agent, and most importantly in the healing possibilities for each client. If the practitioner does not believe in these three elements, then s/he cannot genuinely infuse hope and faith, and successfully intervene in the default regression.

In a default regression, the therapist will interject him or herself into the client's psychological space to offset the object-loss inherent in the default regression process. Therapy models that discourage increasing levels of therapeutic involvement as well as client dependency rely on the therapist communicating this message in other, less overt, ways. This will be adequate enough with some B-type clients, and with BB-clients, may be the relational posture of choice. Most B, and virtually all A and AA clients will not introject the therapist's hope, faith, or belief in them or change the process. These clients tend to require a more active and direct impingement when they are in a default regression.

It may even be necessary for the therapist to maintain outside-of-therapy-hour contact with the client. It is not unusual for me to suggest to a client that they call-in daily for any number of reasons (e.g., to chart progress towards a particular goal, or to report on a daily depression or anxiety log). For obvious reasons, as much as possible I prefer to have the client simply leave a check-in message, with occasional call-backs arranged for special needs. The underlying reason for the call-ins in the late primitive phase is to provide the client with object-constancy in the face of object-loss. Their experience may be that as soon as the session is over, I stop thinking about them and no longer care about them. Of course, what the client is really saying is that they cannot psychologically hold me in their own psyche. The call-ins provide craved for object-constancy and continuity of care. Common therapeutic worry centers on insatiable clients who would overuse and abuse such a stretching of therapeutic boundaries. While this may be true for BB- (borderline) clients, for the great majority there is an overt reluctance to request, along with an underlying but manageable hunger *for*, such outside-the-hour contact.

The true reparental metaphor would be for me to call them and check in to see how they are doing. Besides the obvious awkwardness of doing this, the client would experience this as intrusive and a crossing, rather than a stretching, of the therapeutic boundaries. Still, from time to time a few clients have requested that I do this, and in cases where I deemed it appropriate and potentially healing, I have called a client unprompted. The basic rule of therapy involves assessing the client's fear of engulfment and need for counterdependence ("I can do this myself"). These acts of meaningful loving must be experienced by the clients as real and genuine. We know the therapist has been successful when the client says something like, "I thought I was just another client to you but now I see that I am not."

In other words, the client feels *special* or unique and loved for their specialness to the therapist. I have referred to this process as therapeutic claiming. An important function of parenting is for the parent to claim each of their children as separate, distinct, and uniquely wonderful. The therapist must provide each client with such an experience when they are in a default regression since the default regression indicates an absence of feeling claimed. Indeed, the client may feel remarkably unspecial, unimportant to him or herself, or to anyone else. For a client to grow, s/he must first matter enough to someone else, especially the therapist.

Of course, we are talking here of degrees, not absolutes. Virtually no one grows up without feeling special to someone at some time. I have worked with clients who have had childhood experiences of abuse or abandonment who do not experience the depth of isolation that another client from what appears to be a more fortunate background does. I am not attempting here to explain this phenomenon, except to say that it is a complicated one, mediated by many factors, not the least of which are the client's particular *experience* of their childhood, the presence of psychopathology (e.g., a serotonin-depleted biochemical system) and level of motivation. Morever there is an inherent difficulty in accurately assessing childhood experiences.

identifying the default-regression trigger in therapy

As complicated as the relationship between childhood events and adult states of demotivation is, we can operate on a simple premise in psychotherapy: if we identify that a client is in a default regression, then we assume that there has been object loss. There is a method for determining the trigger that led to the change from hopefulness to despair which may be a helpful assessment technique when we are attempting to understand the client's often sudden submergence into despair and which can provide at least circumstantial evidence for the presence of the default regression.

If a client left my office the previous week, in a state of "non-default-regression," not necessarily full of hope or excitement but not despairing, and they return for the next session in a hopeless state, I typically do the following: I ask the client, "What happened? When did you start feeling this way?" Most of the time, the client will look at me as if I were crazy since this is such a frequent experience for them. The default regression, like its psychological opposite, transcendence, has a kind of timeless quality to it and when the client is in a default regression, they feel as if they never felt differently. Emotionally, although not necessarily intellectually, there is no memory of better times.

I will then remind them of how they were when they left my office, and slowly, we'll begin tracing back through their week, looking for the *trigger* to the default regression. This trigger is never a life-event, although that may be a precipitating factor. The trigger is always an object-loss. If the client has already been penetrated by me the loss of object is the loss of *me*. Even if, as is often the case, there is a separate loss of some other, their difficulty at the time in connecting to *me* (either psychologically or, more likely, by calling me and asking for my direct input) is viewed as the trigger. If the client has not yet been penetrated by me, the search for the trigger to the default regression is much less important as an assessment factor. We just assume that the default regression is present and initiate the process of therapeutic penetration.

a case example*

The following is a partial transcript of the fourth session of treatment with Jon, 36. In the session, there are annotated highlights of the concepts we have discussed, including the infusion of hope, emotional penetration, therapeutic claiming, the active directive cluster of relational postures, role flexibility, and tracing the default regression.

CLIENT: When I left on Thursday, I just . . . You know, I don't know what happened to me. But I started to get like, you know, a little . . . I mean I saw myself . . . I drove to go to see my old boss and . . . I mean, I wasn't sure about what to say, and what he is going to say to me. I just wasn't ready to do it.[7] What I ended up doing, I ended up talking with him a couple days later, but I saw him on Saturday. I saw myself just pull away, and . . .

THERAPIST: Yeah, describe that to me, like . . .

CLIENT: I did that for days.

THERAPIST: Yeah, describe that process.

CLIENT: It was kind of like withdrawal . . . pull away from any kind of confrontation, or any kind of stressful situation. But I felt sort of . . . just do it. It didn't feel like it was the right thing to do, but it was actually what I was used to doing. I mean I saw myself getting down. I mean, I wasn't running. I wasn't able to run because I thought my foot was going to be the problem, so I didn't run, which I have kind of clung to since the fifth grade, physically working out. And I saw myself . . . you know, eating and not working out, so I felt like I was getting fat . . . To me . . . All that hard work down the drain.

---

* I have discussed elsewhere (Rappaport, 1993a), our skewed impression of everyday psychotherapy practice due to the editing of case material by theoreticians such as myself. The reader is cautioned that the transcripted material presented in this book is not necessarily an accurate representation of my therapy work. I have selected material on the basis of illustrating certain concepts.

[In the default regression, clients will have these kind of vague complaints about overeating, body dysphoria, and the like. It is important that the therapist not necessarily view such data as evidence of particular psychopathology. I see his complaints as a lack of self-esteem and inadequate motivation, and base my interventions accordingly by increasing relational potency.[7]]

THERAPIST: When did this start exactly? You said when you left here?

CLIENT: When I left here. I was feeling good when I left.

[This statement indicates that successful penetration occurred during the session, which had been my experience as well. It is critical to note that once the default regression process is impinged upon directly, the client has been penetrated. Further default regressions are not unusual but significantly, the therapist now has a template for re-penetration.]

THERAPIST: You were feeling . . . How were you feeling when you were here?

CLIENT: I felt good that . . . I mean, after talking to you, that I had accomplished so much, that I was being aggressive . . .

THERAPIST: Right . . .

CLIENT: . . . and I saw myself going right into the passive mode, as soon as I left here.

[This is the beginning of the default regression process]

THERAPIST: Well, trace it . . . I would like you to trace it back. I know you were feeling good when you left here . . .

CLIENT: I got in the car and I was going to go to see my ex-boss and get that out of the way.[8]

THERAPIST: Right.

CLIENT: But I . . . He kind of is like, you know, he was going to be there Tuesday and Wednesday, and that I should call, and I did try to call him. I called him and he said he didn't feel good today, and so I didn't like feel like he was being very receptive to . . .

[We could refer to this real event as the apparent trigger to his default regression].

THERAPIST: So he was kind of unreceptive . . .

---

7. At some point following the adequate impingement upon the default regression process, if such symptoms linger, treatment for depression may be indicated.

8. Jon was to meet with his ex-boss for an exit interview. He was intimidated by this man, a well respected figure in his field.

CLIENT: They told me . . . kind of like . . . you know I don't know . . . He's not here right now. I was going to go and wait for him. But he's not back yet from his appointment. I was going to wait and he may not even show up, and I kind of just . . . went home . . . instead of waiting for him. I said I'll call him tomorrow . . . I will do it tomorrow . . . I'll do it later. And I went . . . it was safer to just go home. It was easier to go home. Because I didn't know how he was going to respond. I didn't know what I was going to say . . . so I just went . . .

[He experienced his ex-boss's apparent avoidance of him as a personal rejection.]

THERAPIST: What were you afraid of happening?

CLIENT: H-m-m . . . I guess him viewing me as being unprofessional. . . not being worthy of his respect, you know, and it turned out he's. . . he was in his own world when I spoke with him, you know, he was more concerned about his illness and his pain. He just like yessed me when I told him what I was feeling, what I felt about everything. I was thanking him. . . he was like cordial, but he wasn't engaging. He wasn't like, "Oh, yeah, I know. I think the same way." He was just like very laid-back. So I mean, I felt better that I just said what I said, whether it got to him or not or whether he understood any of it. He may never.

THERAPIST: But it was fine.

CLIENT: It was fine with me. I mean I left things in a way that no bridges were burned. . . and it was fine. I felt confident because I kind of knew that I was going to be working at somewhere else. So I went in there knowing I had a job. And I. . . uh. . . that's the beginning. That is when it kind of started. . . I kind of scooched around. . .

THERAPIST: Which was. . .

CLIENT: Approaching him. Approaching him.

THERAPIST: But if we trace it back, it seems as though we find a starting point, it's when you called and found out that. . . it wasn't. . .

CLIENT:. . . For him to be there. . .

THERAPIST:. . . A high priority. . .

CLIENT: Right. Yeah.

THERAPIST: So I think what happens to you is, you're extremely sensitive and extremely tuned in to other people's, you know, how they see you or view you, or. . . And the slightest indication of what you're seen in any kind of negative light or disrespected in any way, you go w-h-s-s-s-h and you drop right down. Like immediately. And then you're one step back.

CLIENT: Right.

[Sensitivity to rejection may be symptomatic of an atypical depression (see Kramer, 1993), but at the beginning of treatment, we are most concerned with plugging the default regression. The treatment of psychopathology is second to the impingement of motivational processes.[9]]

[Silence]

THERAPIST: What are you thinking?

CLIENT: I'm feeling bad for myself. I'm feeling sorry for myself. . . that I let that happen. I am very sensitive, and I do worry about what people think. I mean. . . Sometimes, I guess, first, before what I think of myself. Why are some people more sensitive than others?

THERAPIST: Well, I think, you know, I think you first need to accept that you're sensitive. That's just who you are. That's not going to change. And that's fine. It's a good quality to have. It's not a bad quality.

CLIENT: I think I know that . . .

THERAPIST: Good. You know, the idea is that although it is a challenge for you psychologically, it's a challenge because you feel things so deeply and you're so tuned in to what other people think of you. It really means that you have got to, you know, be strong in the face of what you're feeling because you're tuned in to a lot of negative things, that at least you perceive are going on. It means you have to really be self-aware. You have to know what's happening to you, which takes a lot of strength. But the sensitivity, I mean, that's not going to change. You're always going to be sensitive.

CLIENT: What things do *you* do when you doubt yourself, or if you question what someone thinks of you or. . . ? What do you say to yourself?

[Many therapists avoid answering direct questions (cf. Clickauf-Hughes and Chance, 1995) particularly when the client seeks personal advice. At such an early point in treatment, *not* answering the question, no matter how artfully or respectively, would almost surely trigger a default regression, albeit subtle and perhaps undetected. The client is simply requesting more usable input from me.]

THERAPIST: It takes a long time. It took me a long time to be tuned in and be really aware and know what's happening. And things

9. It is significant to note that at the time of this writing one year into treatment, this client is not in a default regression and is firmly in the external phase of motivation. Not surprisingly, there are no signs of depression, or even low mood, indicating that the cluster of symptoms he presented with were motivational in nature.

that used to take me days or weeks to figure out, you know, or get back up to speed, I can do, like, in a matter of minutes. Sometimes even seconds. But it takes a long time to be able to do that.

CLIENT: What is the first step?

THERAPIST: The first step is, like, you got to check in with me. You need to be able to talk about what's happening, to be able to express what you're feeling.

[I am not expecting the client to handle the default regression on his own at this point so I strongly encourage the client to rely on me.]

CLIENT: I've got to learn that?

THERAPIST: Yeah, yeah. Only now there is another layer of awareness that is going to be there. You know, going forward. Like if this were to happen again, you know, what I want you to do is give me a call and we will talk about what's happening, if you start to feel this again, and then in doing that enough times you will be able to determine why's that, and do it yourself. You know, figure out what's happening yourself.

CLIENT: I'm telling you, after I met with you I just saw myself . . . from here just w-h-s-s-s-h. . .

THERAPIST: It's unbelievable how quick a drop, just how fast it happens.

CLIENT: I couldn't wait to come and see you. I probably should have called.

THERAPIST: You should have called me right away.

CLIENT: I don't know, if I had done that. . . I should have called.

THERAPIST: Yeah, I mean, that's what I'm here for. . . That's what we are doing. . . We're trying to prevent that from happening. I mean I don't want to see you waste a week, or even a couple of days. It's not good. It takes the wind out of your sails and ruins the whole momentum that you build. Because you're building the right momentum, you know.

[I am attempting to jump start his PAR-process. (See Chapter 9 for a discussion on synergism.)]

CLIENT: I still feel like I had it going. I mean it definitely let the wind right out of my sails. Emotionally, I just have taken a back seat.

THERAPIST: Is that how you always remember being? Really sensitive to rejection and to. . . the way people think about you or look at you, and . . . even as a kid?

CLIENT: I was always very sensitive. I always had to have some kind of comfort level. . . .I usually always was up. . . to go down is unusual for me, to feel so down.

THERAPIST: You used the word depression. Why did you use that word?

CLIENT: I was depressed. I want to just stay in bed. Just avoid. . . To me that's depressed. I mean, I guess, I saw myself doing that in my relationship with Sharon for the last few years. You know, I was with her, and kind of wanted to escape and to want to just work and go to work and pay bills. I came out of it and said I got to do something. I worked hard at it, doing a lot. I remember being kind of, like, lethargic, escaping. I didn't like it. I didn't like it, being like that. It's just not this year or this month. I have done it before, allowed myself to slip. And stayed in a relationship, which I probably should have said, it's not happening. I mean, I stayed there. My sister seems to think that I go into relationships and I dive in head first. Like with Julie and like with this girl, Bonnie and Sharon, who I was with for about five-and-a-half or six years. We just started seeing each other and right away, I moved in with her. I stayed there five-and-a-half years.

[The default regression, as opposed to depression, can be modulated and partially abated by codependent relationships.]

THERAPIST: How did you feel when you first met Sharon?

CLIENT:. . . Very sexual. . . it was you know, a lot of fun. I just. . . loved it. I was in love, she loved me, and she made changes. She was going to move out down South and she stayed here and I moved in with her. . . and her children. Look what I did with Bonnie and Julie in the beginning. It's kind of like. . . just moving . . . kind of like clinging. . .

THERAPIST: How quickly?

CLIENT: Right away. Spending four or five days in a row together.

THERAPIST: Then what happened in the relationship with Sharon?

CLIENT: With Sharon?

THERAPIST: Uh-huh.

CLIENT: Uh, I kind of resisted marrying her. She wanted to get married. She wanted to settle down. She wanted to finalize everything, and I couldn't do it. I kind of met Julie while I was with Sharon and kind of, like, would call her, go to visit her and bring her flowers every now and then, kind of like of courting her without . . .

THERAPIST: You were maintaining two relationships at once.

[Very mild confrontation]

CLIENT: Yeah, that's at the end. Kind of the end of the past year. Last summer, actually was when it ended. I kind of met Julie.

THERAPIST: You know, I think you get involved in these relationships so quickly because . . . It's interesting that your sensitivity is to rejection. These relationships provide a really secure base for you. A place to feel okay about yourself. Not to say that there aren't other aspects of the relationship, or truly loving feelings or whatever, passionate feelings, but what makes it hard to separate from them is that security that you get. That has been one of your strategies for dealing with this sensitivity of feeling bad about yourself. See what happens when there is a rejection, when you perceive a rejection, you feel like shit about yourself. I mean you feel totally like shit about yourself. Totally. . . You know, it's not like a mild thing. It's a really strong thing. And it's very negative. And you feel very alone. See, I don't even know if depression is the right word to put to it. I think it is more about just feeling so badly about yourself, alone, separate from the world, and these relationships become something to cling to. Somebody who feels good about you.

CLIENT: So that's not a very good place to get self-assured.

THERAPIST: No, no. And it creates problems within the relationship itself, because then you don't know what your true feelings are. It creates a lot of ambivalence.

CLIENT: So the picture . . . should I be seeing. . . instead of that one, being my place for reassurance, should be from me.

THERAPIST: Ultimately from yourself. Right now, here. You know, right now with us. But ultimately from yourself.

[To allow Jon to believe that he could do this for himself now would be a setup for failure. In a sense, I am educating him about the importance of the external phase. Often, therapists, as well as clients, try to move directly from the primitive to the internal phase of motivation.]

CLIENT: From myself?

THERAPIST: Yeah. And it takes a while to get there, you know.

CLIENT:. . . . I don't want to take too long . . .

THERAPIST: Well. . . you've diverted yourself. When you divert. . . Your relationships are essentially diversions, you know, from dealing with yourself. From really looking at this. You know, they almost have an addictive quality to them, you know, where they become the source of your good feelings, your source of feeling good about yourself.

CLIENT: So what do I have to start being aware of?

THERAPIST: For good feelings?

CLIENT: Yeah.

THERAPIST: By reaching your goals . . . You know, going after what you really want. You do feel good when you go after what you want. You feel good when you're aggressive. You feel good when you're out there and you don't let that passivity, you know, wash over you.

CLIENT: You know, I didn't go to that party I told you I was going to go to Saturday night.

THERAPIST: You didn't?

CLIENT: I probably should have gone.

THERAPIST: Yeah, I mean that's a great example, where you kind of allow your passivity to run you; you know, allowing those bad feelings to run you. I really want to see you break away from that, and be more aware of when it is happening. "What am I doing here? Well, I'm staying home because of these bad feelings and I don't want to give in to these bad feelings." . . .That was a long time with Sharon. Five years. . .

CLIENT: Over five years. . .

THERAPIST: That's a long time.

CLIENT: How do you learn from that? What should I learn from that relationship?

THERAPIST: Several things. One is, "I need to feel good about myself. I need to feel that can't come from another person." If it is coming from another person, then it's going to be problematic. Second, you've got to go slow. You've got to go much much slower.

CLIENT: Meaning what is slower?

THERAPIST: [Laughs] Like, you don't move in right away. You don't see her four or five nights a week, you know, or spend four or five days together. It means you're not ready for a committed relationship right now. You need to accept that; you need to put some limits on yourself that way.

CLIENT: What do you mean, limits?

THERAPIST: Like follow this rule: You are not allowed to get involved in a relationship with a woman right now. You can date and you can casually go out with women and so on, but you can't get involved. You're not in a position to get involved with a woman.

[I am attempting to prevent Jon from recreating the same dynamic with another woman. I am also seeding for a progressive goal, the program of three (see Chapter 9).]

CLIENT: Why?

THERAPIST: Because it is going to be . . .You're going to rely on the woman to feel good about yourself. It's going to be too much the source of positive feelings and it is going to prevent you from developing this within yourself. From *you* being the source of the positive feelings. It's too easy. It's too easy to get it from a woman. And you know that.

CLIENT: What else should I learn? Sometimes I feel very very ignorant about it, even though I'm smart and intelligent enough to know I might *want* to get back in a relationship.

THERAPIST: Right. Well, you can't. You're not allowed.

CLIENT: (smiling) Not allowed . . .

THERAPIST: (smiling) You're not allowed.

CLIENT: And that's okay.

THERAPIST: That's good. [laughs] I will kill you if you get involved in a relationship. You know. . . don't do it! It will be a big mistake. A big mistake.[10]

CLIENT: Just date.

THERAPIST: Just date. Just date.

CLIENT:. . . even with Julie.

THERAPIST: Date Julie. Date Julie, yeah. The problem is, if you do get involved, even if it's great, you won't be sure of what your feelings are. You will be ambivalent again. I mean, the problem with Sharon was your ambivalence, because you couldn't commit. You know, you had a very difficult time committing to her. And I think in some ways rightfully so. You weren't sure of how you truly felt about her. Because when the other person is kind of the source of your good feeling, it's like you're not sure. Is this person really a person I truly love and want to spend the rest of my life with, or is this person just making me feel good? And you can't quite distinguish what the difference is. They all kind of run together; all those feelings run together. Dating will give you the opportunity to, from a distance, be able to say what do I really like, what do I really want in a woman. You know, how do I really feel? If you get involved too quickly, you won't know. Even if it is good. And I'm sure it would be good for a while. You seem very capa-

---

10. By the time of this writing the client had ignored my "rule" and recreated the same relational dynamic with another woman. The relationship ended in a similar manner. After approximately nine months of treatment, he began dating women more casually and was avoiding intimate sexual contact. While he finds this very difficult, he acknowledges numerous benefits.

ble of having those kinds of relationships. They're good for a while.

CLIENT: Of what? Romantic, intimate relationships?

THERAPIST: Yeah, yeah, to a point. They work to a point.

CLIENT: I will go into them not being prepared to be in them.

THERAPIST: Yeah, yeah. And then you got to kind of disentangle from them and that could take five years. You know, and the next thing you know, you're. . .

CLIENT: A waste of time . . . Wasted time in a relationship . . .

THERAPIST: I mean, if you *learn* from it, it's not a waste.

CLIENT: I learned things from her.

THERAPIST: Sure.

CLIENT: We shared a lot. But personally I didn't . . .

THERAPIST: Right now, you know, your focus needs to be on yourself and your career anyway. . . . You need to get yourself together that way, before you'd be ready for a relationship.

[Later]

THERAPIST: So, the next time you get this feeling, this feeling that you are being viewed negatively, or rejected, what are going to do?

CLIENT: Call you. Is that what you want me to do?

THERAPIST: Yeah. Yeah. Yeah. I mean, if you are unable to deal with it, cope with it, recognize it, figure out what you need to do, . . . you know . . . because it comes in many forms. That's why it is going to be hard to get a hold of, because it is going to take some time, because it has got many disguises. It will come in all shapes and sizes. You know, a big one is going to be, is this the right thing? Or what should I do in this situation? Or, I don't want to enter into this situation. I mean, it comes in various ways and you have to be really, really tuned in to it. If you get to a point where all you got to know is that if you're slipping within yourself, if you are avoiding something, if you are being passive, if you're procrastinating, not following through on something then you will know you're in it. You know, you're in. It's already past the point, you know. Definitely, at that point, that's when you make a call . . . to me. Because you're already past that point.

CLIENT: Yeah, I was definitely way past the point.

THERAPIST: Yeah, when you called me you were, you know, several days past the point.

CLIENT: I sometimes think that I let myself start to feel bad . . . I hear this little voice saying, "Oh, you're 36 years old; you're going to be 37 years old, and you should have had all this done in your life. You should have accomplished these goals that you're setting for yourself now, years ago." I mean, I feel, kind of like, I failed or I didn't do what I could have done or should have done, like my friends may have done. I mean, they're married and they're having children, and . . . I mean, I know a lot of them are unhappy even though they have done all that stuff. But, I kind of wish sometimes some of those things for myself, too. To have had them, or to have them, or to accomplish them, to find that, too.

THERAPIST: Well, the fact is, you have not had anybody really to help you, you know, in a way that you need.

[Therapeutic claiming]

CLIENT: All right.

THERAPIST: I mean, how *old* were you when your father died?

CLIENT: Six.

THERAPIST: You can't imagine how lost you've been. Can't imagine. I think it is amazing you've gotten to where you *are*. You know. Six is so little. Six is so little.

CLIENT: He was forty years old. My mom, she feels guilty all the time. She feels like she didn't do enough . . . she didn't teach me the right things . . . She still is right there with wanting to see me feel good. I know she doesn't feel that great about herself to begin with. Let alone watching me not feel good.

THERAPIST: It's probably all that guilt she feels and that guilt has not helped. It has gotten in the way of her helping you. Her own bad feelings about herself. Feelings of inadequacy. . . Kind of figured, you know, since you were six years old, that . . . you know, that is like . . . there is a loss there. A loss. You don't have somebody to . . . a man to check things out with, help you, give you confidence and say, "Okay . . . let's try it this way. You know, I'll help you, I'll show you."

CLIENT: I at least got this far.

THERAPIST: Yeah, I said it's amazing that you have gotten as far as you have, really.

CLIENT: Why do you say that?

THERAPIST: I think you're in pretty good shape considering.

CLIENT: . . .There's other people that lost their parents or have lost a father and mother at an early age, that . . .

THERAPIST: That have what?

CLIENT:. . . gotten. . . to the top of the cliff. . .

THERAPIST: Right, you want to show them to me? I would like to study them.

CLIENT: I don't know for sure, but I assume that there's people like that have it really hard growing up . . .

THERAPIST: Sometimes people have others in their life, you know, somebody who steps in to the role and becomes a surrogate father and so on, and you know . . . But six years old; it is little. Not only is it little, little, little, it is a critical age, you know, for a boy, in terms of his relationship with his father. Very critical.

CLIENT: Why?

THERAPIST: It's kind of the age for us to learn, it's like the starting of true identification with a male figure. The little boy starts to really get . . . "Oh, I'm a boy. I'm separate from mom. I'm not the same as mom." He kind of naturally is wired at six years old, is kind of naturally wired to go to dad from that point. Kind of . . . it's like seeking out . . . "Oh, I'm a boy; I'm more like dad than like mom."

CLIENT: My grandfather was there, sort of, not always. He would try to love me, take me under his wing. My uncle, a little bit also.

THERAPIST: I'm sure that all helped.

[Later]

CLIENT: I don't feel like I have set any goals yet. I know I want to have things. Sometimes I feel like I don't have money like some people do, a house, big fancy cars, and I want to have all those things, too. I'm not sure how to keep it all into perspective . . . what I am trying to do. . .

THERAPIST: It's funny, you mentioned that your father died when he was forty. I just thought, you know forty. I'd like to see you at forty. You should be pretty good at forty.

CLIENT: What do you mean?

THERAPIST: You know, in terms of what you will have, you know, is that being a good . . .

CLIENT: . . . Target?

THERAPIST: Yeah, . . . Target . . . vision . . . Not so much like what it is going to be like tomorrow or next month, or the next year, but like at forty, what you're like at forty.

[Teaching the discipline of delaying gratification.]

CLIENT: I will make up for all the things my father didn't have.

THERAPIST: Yeah. It makes sense, you know, you're thirty-six.

CLIENT: That's three years. I am going to be thirty-seven in February.

THERAPIST: That's a good target. What do you think your life will be like at forty?

CLIENT: I'll be married. I would like to have a child, have a nice house, nice car, nice business, . . .I would like to travel, provide for my child and my wife . . . give to my mom, make her life easier. Do all the things that I have to do. Be healthy. Be happy. Have a dog . . . a Labrador running around. Not have to worry so much. People surrounding me, not to have to worry about it.

THERAPIST: These are great goals, so what I want you to focus on right now is getting control of that process that we started talking about, which is you know, how you let that drop. I want you to look for that drop and work at not allowing that to go. If you can do that just right now, it will make all the difference in the world. Right now it's your main form of sabotage, self-sabotage. You get in control of that, and you know, because I see you as really being able to move very fast. The goals you're talking about, to reach those by forty, you got to move really fast. You got to be very aggressive. I see that you are able to do that. The key is getting in control of that process. Do you feel like you could do it?

[The therapist is providing encouragement, coaching, and inspiration in the hopes that the client will eventually internalize this input for himself].

CLIENT: Yeah! I know I can. I know I can.

[The client is highly responsive but will continue to need this input *externally*, from the therapist].

THERAPIST: Good.

CLIENT: I want to.

THERAPIST: Well, I'll do my part, and you do your part, and then . . . if you're committed 100 percent to get it in control, then I'll be committed to doing what I can do 100 percent to help you, you know.

CLIENT: I can't see it not working.

clients who present in the external phase

For a client to be considered to be in the external phase of motivation, there must be a good-enough bond with the practitioner to proceed forward in growth-enhancing work. This work involves engaging in life's varied transactions: career, coupling, and child-rearing. This is essentially not in-therapy work, although an intensive relationship with the therapist usually emerges. Rather, this is outside-of-therapy work that requires a certain kind of relationship with the practitioner that is challenging, transferentially charged, and potentially transformative. The client is expected to progress into unknown or unfamiliar territory pressing up against *a priori* ceiling barriers based on maps and programs from the past. To accomplish this transformation, the client must give up familiar ways of being, doing, and knowing.

When faced with a new growth task, the person becomes imbued with internalized spirit of "I've done something like this before, therefore, I can accomplish this again." In our model we refer to this as the internalized phase of motivation. Positive growth experiences serve to abate the fear of losing the familiar since giving up the familiar, presumably did not result in disastrous consequences (abandonment, annihilation, engulfment). On the contrary, positive outcomes may have occurred, such as increased personal strength or increased sense of self-esteem, even if the actual real-life consequences were unwanted outcomes (e.g., break-up of a relationship, rupture in familial relationship, loss of job, etc.).

However, clients who come to therapy typically do not have strings of positive growth experiences to bolster their confidence in doing the difficult work before them. How do we treat persons with negative or inadequate growth experiences who come to therapy? These persons are fearful of making changes and the perceived consequences. Sometimes, life crises help signal to the person that the old familiar ways of doing, being, and knowing are no longer effective but may be keeping the person from achieving something s/he (i.e., the true self) desires. For example, I've worked with a great number of commitment-phobic men who've come to therapy highly motivated to change during or after the breakup of a love relationship. It is only at this point that these men realize that their pattern of resisting intimacy by avoiding commitment (perhaps because of their fear of engulfment) keeps them from holding onto any kind of meaningful love relationship. Their fear of engulfment, once manifest, is supplanted by a larger fear, the fear of abandonment, once latent and now manifest.

Incremental personal development or maturation can serve or intensify the same purpose. That is, the fear of losing the old and familiar (the regressive trend) is supplanted by the *healthier* fear, the fear of losing what is wished for or desired (the progressive trend). When a client comes to therapy with the progressive tendency realized or potentialized (more likely the latter), then we are in an advantageous position to augment continued growth, assuming the therapist presents as a good-enough rapprochement figure.

This client will present *in need* of the therapist. S/he will arrive with a supply of questions, and a host of interrelated insights. The therapist here does not need to be role-bound in his or her approach; when roles are flexible healing can be provided directly. An early motivation-killer to such clients are therapists who eschew virtually any kind of direction, omnipotence, or advice-giving. These therapists will make the client feel that their requests for direction and even enthusiasm for change are at best, inappropriate to the therapy situation or, at worst, an indication of some kind of manic state. The client may succumb to such a viewpoint, since the psychic territory they are exploring is unfamiliar terrain to them and they are in need of a guide.

What is actually occurring is that the client transferentially is in a naturally regressed position vis-à-vis the change agent. From this position, the client will transferentially tend to view the therapist positively and want and expect the therapist to fill the gaps and deficiencies from their family-of-origin experience. The therapist must not become overwhelmed by the dependent presentation of the client. The primary job of the therapist is actually quite simple, at least in theory here: fulfill the regressed needs of the client since the client requires these inputs to grow forward. The client is able to regress easily in the externalized phase because there is more trust in the therapeutic other. The transference is largely positive, and there are few, if any, negative expectations. While the client may be intensely afraid of the progressive tasks before them, they tend not to be *relationally* fearful of the practitioner.

In fact, we may assume there is only positive transference at this point, a distortion-free belief in the healing power of the other. Negative transference is minimal until, of course, the practitioner lets the person down as the original parent(s) did. This will always occur, unless unhealthily avoided by client or therapist, at some point or other in the treatment, since the therapist is not the all-knowing, all-healing object, just as the client's parents were not. We take advantage of this positive transference by simply allowing it to be. In these cases, we need not encourage it; we simply need not discourage its natural occurrence in the external-phase client. Just as negative transference will organically emerge as the client begins to see the therapist as more human, the quality of the positive transference also varies greatly. Some clients may view the therapist as god-like, others as a savior, true parent, brilliant professional, good consultant, or important friend. The variations are of no great significance. The therapist should acknowledge the particularities of the transference and in doing so, work through its resolution.

progressive movement in the beginning of therapy

In the beginning of the external phase of motivation, the positive transference may be quite intense. This is a good thing as the therapist more easily becomes the rapprochement figure in the growth-regression process. As the early external phase is highly charged, any mistake, whether a genuine error or the occasional result of a misperception, can have equally intense and negative consequences, leading to a premature termination.

Thus, three elements must be present. First, a progressive goal that the client desires sufficiently enough to be willing to discard aspects of the family-of-origin that are no longer operating toward that end. Second, there must be a good-enough attachment to an external therapeutic other to provide guidance, direction, and support while the person is engaged in the progressive movements forward. A third critical factor is the need for the goal or progressive movement to be appropriate for the person. Goals are co-created with the client. In therapy, though, the therapist must maintain veto power, so to speak, since the practitioner is in the reparental and authoritative role. Since the client is free to end the relationship at any time in the truest sense, of course, s/he holds the ultimate veto power. It is important that the therapist exercise this influence when the client is unsure or misguided about what they need to do. Suggestions that the client determine appropriate treatment goals, while politically correct and conceptually or aesthetically pleasing, are not indicated because of the overwhelming fears involved in choosing a goal that will lead the client into unfamiliar terrain.

The therapy is structured by the progressive goals presented in the early external phase and modified throughout the remainder of treatment. If they are determined improperly, the entire treatment will be skewed. I cannot emphasize this point strongly enough. The therapist must not be afraid to set the progressive goals that the client needs to engage in, the subgoals, and various steps in the process of reaching these goals must likewise be delineated.

If the therapist does not clearly establish what needs to occur, the therapy becomes a hodgepodge of disparate energies. Moreover, the therapeutic dependency will not serve the growth of the client, who will eventually and correctly feel that while something may be happening, s/he is not sure what that is or where things are going. A familiar client reaction is to question the length of treatment or to ask about how to determine the end of treatment.

I am not suggesting that the process of establishing progressive movement forward or goals, is a simple one. But it is important that the client accept, on some level, that these goals are appropriate for him or her. Even more importantly, the therapist must have a good sense of what health should look like. I call this process of goal determination the overlaying of health. In other words, we take the case for how it presents and then ask a series of questions like the following: If this person were psychologically healthy and had good self-esteem and self-love, what would they do in this situation, in other situations that they have not presented, and with their lives in general utilizing the principles outlined in Chapter 7.

Some may question whether one can do this since there may be any number of "healthy" solutions to life's dilemmas. Indeed, this is a value position that underlies much of contemporary psychotherapeutic practice. It is, however, a wrong-headed one.

Actually, the *process* of good mental health is fairly monolithic; it is psychopathology that is full of variety, if not in content then certainly in process. Value-based though it may be, it involves the giving and receiving of love as well as the engagement of good and meaningful work. Certainly, there are a host of possibilities to doing good and meaningful work, these can represent principles for living. "It is better to love than not to love" is a principle that guides my practice. If a woman client comes to me and tells me, "All men are assholes" or "Why bother getting into a relationship? They only bring hurt and pain," ultimately I challenge that client. First I need to understand her experience of men and relationships as well as the sources of her frustration, hurt, and anger. But I will not accept her decision as a "healthy solution" since it is not. Indeed, it is one pathological alternative among many. The healthy decision is simple, at least theoretically: to proceed forward *with help* (my own or another therapeutic other's), toward achieving love and intimacy, knowing that she will have to work through the pain that she (re)experiences in even *considering* being with a man.

While this may be obvious to many therapists it is not easy to achieve in practice. Some clients will tend to resist what they need the most since it involves the (re)experience of earlier unwanted pain.

Unfortunately many therapists tend to be non-directive and non-confrontational particularly if the client states their position passionately. These therapists will tend to "give in" to the client's unhealthy solutions. Often when this occurs the client may deflate and experience a default regression because they "won" a battle they did not want to win. They wanted to be convinced (that is, penetrated) by the therapist that this solution was unhealthy. Some therapists may interpret this as "gamey" but if it is it is certainly not a conscious one. The client may come back later and ask the therapist, "Why did you let me get away with that?" With the exception of classically borderline (BB) clients, this is not a no-win situation for the therapist although it may sometimes feel like one.

The process of firmly but respectfully holding to a progressive goal continuously in the face of all this resistance, which tends to intensify the closer the client gets to it, requires a great deal of therapeutic belief in the correctness of the intervention and the strength of the therapist. Unfortunately, many practitioners are inadequate in this regard. The forces of the resistance can be overwhelming. This is frightening to most therapists, who are trained to believe that we are, or can be, neutral and objective. When we feel we are losing our objectivity, we are trained to think that we are operating countertransferentially and therefore need to pull back from all but the most obvious interventions (e.g., suicide- and abuse-prevention). While I do not minimize the negative effects of countertransference, in *our* model, the therapist is *supposed* to have strong convictions. Our personal feelings need not be the reason to pull back from interventions; we may pull back for other reasons. But I am suggesting a different mindset for psychotherapy where deciding what is best for clients is acceptable, if not desirable.

client slippage from the external to the primitive phase

Even in the best of circumstances, no matter how technically correct the posture of the therapist, very few clients who enter therapy in the external phase of motivation will remain in the external phase without returning to their "true" (absent for life-crisis) state of motivation, which is primitive. This represents a key point in therapy and determines whether the client will continue on a growth path.

What creates this slippage from the external phase of motivation to the primitive phase? First, the crisis that brought the person to treatment usually resolves itself, sometimes without intervention. This may be why many wait-listed or placebo-treated research subjects do as well as they do (Lambert, 1986; 1992). Crises, or in our model, PAR's, tend to be short-lived. The client who is wait-listed does not improve in any meaningful way, but in the absence of progressive movement (P) the intensely regressive experience (R) dissipates. There is no need to seek out a therapeutic other to abreact the regressive experience (A) so they can proceed forward. The wait-listed client-subject may experience that "things are better" and not request treatment or if they do come in, it may be with less motivation.

Now this phenomenon may occur very quickly even after the first contact with the practitioner. It is not uncommon for a therapist to return the prospective client's call, only to find that the client, who may have sounded extremely motivated, is no longer, or only mildly, interested in treatment. If we think of therapy as beginning with the first contact, probably the greatest number of therapy drop-outs occur in the period between a person's first considering treatment and the first consultation in the therapist's office.

This is so because it is difficult for a person to remain in a PAR-state of readiness without an adequate rapprochement figure. Successful referrals are greatly assisted by sources who serve as rapprochement figures until a good-enough bond is formed with the practitioner. These therapeutic others will help the client remain in a state of PAR-readiness. Clients who do not have these therapeutic others will have a difficult time remaining in PAR, since this morphogenic state is by definition unbalancing. The forces of homeostasis are strong in all of us, but particularly so for the more dysfunctional. These clients will tend to make compromises and relent to the regressive forces: the old maps, programs, and tapes not in the service of growth.

For example, I was referred a couple whose wife had just discovered her husband had been having a two-year affair. After confronting him she summoned her courage and told him to leave the house despite her various concerns: child-rearing ("If we get divorced, what will happen to the kids?"), family-of-origin ("My mother will think me a failure as a woman"), and financial ("How will we live?"). Underlying all the concerns was a fear-of-loss, loss of the familiar and the known. It is important to note that we often consider this fear to be irrational. But why should she fear to lose the familiar if that familiar is extraordinarily painful, the knowledge that your most trusted other has betrayed you and lied about it.[11] These are often the very clients who argue: "Yeah, but what about the good stuff . . . mightn't it outweigh the bad? . . . He's not all bad . . ."

I agree that such decision-making is complex, and indeed hold the view that in such cases both partners contribute in their own ways to the affair. In determining health and the correct progressive movement forward (P), we take a narrow lens view of how a healthy person reacts when they find out their spouse is cheating, which tends to be more value-based, as well as a broader lens view (i.e., both partners are responsible) which tends to be more theoretical. The narrow viewpoint suggests that the wife's anger and insistence upon the husband's leaving the house was—and here comes the value-laden word—*appropriate*. It is the correct progressive movement.[12] Why? Because a wife with a healthy sense of self-esteem would be outraged at such a blatant betrayal and would display at minimum a *willingness* to exit the marriage, no matter what the circumstances. My client exercised this willingness by telling her husband to leave the house. Some may object that there are a multitude of ways of manifesting this willingness or otherwise responding to the situation, but here I argue that health is fairly monolithic.[13]

To be sure, health is not defined by a single movement, but is determined by a series of movements summed up in an operationalized approach toward life and living. In this case, having her husband leave the house might be considered progressive movement #1. Progressive movement #2 might be expecting thoughtful and heartfelt explanations from her husband. Progressive movement #3 might include examining

11. Denial of the pain of awareness, of course, is fodder for therapy, and many theoretical and technical approaches may address this. The model I propose is relevant for goal determination, value-setting, and therapist-posture prescription.

12. A classic, often feminist, argument against this viewpoint is that since many men hold the bulk of financial and economic resources, there is a power imbalance that may not allow a woman the freedom to exit. This argument sounds reasonable and is sociologically accurate. However, in my experience, economic freedom does not necessarily correlate with psychological freedom. I've had as many women clients who were in a sound enough financial position leave a dysfunctional relationship but chose not to as the reverse. Many female clients will make this argument as well. As a therapist, I tend to be highly skeptical since I've seen so many situations where a female client says, "I'll leave when X happens." X might mean the death of her father, and a sizeable inheritance. When X occurs she still does not leave. Fear-of-loss is a psychological phenomenon, not an economic one.

13. Nor am I suggesting that every person in that situation *should* or *will* display this willingness. I am simply saying that displaying willingness is the appropriate goal for such a client. It may take some clients a great deal of therapy to gain the strength to enact such willingness.

her own behavior to understand what responsibility she might have borne in the marriage crisis. Progressive movement #4 might be offering her husband (and herself) an opportunity to work these issues out in a sensible context like marital therapy. The time frame (two weeks or two years) or the particular manner (their unique dance), in which the couple engages in these progressive movements forward is of little consequence to me as a therapist. However, the movements themselves are intractably healthy and irreplaceable. There are no other healthy alternatives, although there may be a wide variety of unhealthy responses. This is the overlay of health I spoke of previously.

As value-based as this may sound, such a clear conceptualization of progressive movements, unlike the conceptualizations of theory which may be vividly descriptive but not *prescriptive*, provides the therapist with a template to co-determine with each client case—appropriate treatment goals. In addition, these progressive movements are organic and serve a holistic function. That is the wife's *willingness* to end the marriage as evidenced if only for the moment by telling her husband to leave is beneficial for him; a person who lies and cheats is in need of discipline and confrontation as the power (of knowledge) shifts to his spouse. This movement will help motivate him to understand that his actions have consequences, i.e., that the betrayal of the affair has hurt his wife and damaged the relationship. One could imagine the negative effects if his wife did not respond with a strong appropriate emotional response (hurt or anger), and concomitant behavior ("You need to leave"). Such a non-response might refuel the very forces that initiated the betrayal.

While the husband's leaving may be traumatic for the children, we could argue that a (hopefully) temporary upset like this is less traumatic than an ongoing dysfunctional relationship. Having a mother who is empowered and a father temporarily out of the house is better than a disempowered mother and inappropriately empowered father in the house. Again, I am not suggesting that her telling him to leave is the *only* healthy alternative; rather, her displaying the *willingness* to end the marriage is the only healthy alternative. It is difficult though to think of ways for her to manifest that willingness otherwise.

With regard to other synergistic effects on her contemporary family and family-of-origin, the wife may have to face the disappointment of her mother, who she thinks will view her as a failure if her marriage ends in divorce. She fears engaging in the appropriate behavior because she does not want to have an active hand in that occurring.

Yet we can see that if she enacts the correct progressive movement, she faces that fear and challenges her mother; she individuates into an adult who makes her own decisions. Presumably, Sally operated *as if* ending her marriage, even if for appropriate reasons, would mean she was a disappointment in her mother's eyes. Whatever the reality of this, Sally was not acting as a choice-making adult.

Interestingly, in this case, her contemporary mother was supportive when she enacted the movement; Sally's fear appeared to be based on a negative-transference expectation more relevant to her historical (childhood) mother, who because of her own marital difficulties was generally disapproving of Sally. To illustrate the steadfastness and stamina required of the everyday practitioner, Sally reported to me that while she would tell her mother that Roger had left, she would conceal even the most basic of facts. While in some cases, reporting less to a parent would work in the direction of increased individuation, with Sally, I determined such nondisclosure to be an avoidance of individuation (where Sally's stand might be, "Here's the truth, and let the chips fall where they may. If my mom is upset with me, so be it"). Besides exploring her quite rational reasons for not disclosing, I took the position that she must tell her mother the truth. Sally did so, and got maximum benefit from the progressive movement.

So we can see that one correct progressive movement (P) has a multitude of positive holistic effects. One might say that the benefits arise out of the current evolutionary climate that favors growthful movements in the direction of empowerment through individuation and a separation from the pathogenesis of others. One could easily think of times in our history when such a progressive movement would have been foolish.

Thus, Sally told Roger to leave the house (P). She then panicked (R) initially fearful of all the consequences discussed above. Sally knew she needed help, but was not very savvy psychologically, and did not know much about therapy or couples counseling.[14] She happened to have an appointment with her physician that day, so she told him what had happened after she had unexpectedly started crying in his office. Her physician gave Sally a prescription for Xanax and my name (significantly, in that order). The physician knew me only by reputa-

---

14. Psychological awareness (or being therapy-wise) is not really as important as emotional strength, which Sally displayed. Many people are psychologically aware but lack the strength to make changes. Of the two, I emphasize emotional strength, but insight and strength are a potent combination.

tion and thus the referral was not a particularly strong one. Sally took the Xanax but waited before calling me.

By the time the couple (I had asked to see both of them) arrived in my office, Roger had returned to the marital home. Roger felt horribly guilty, empty at the apparent end to the affair, and confused by his own and Sally's behavior. While they both felt anxious after Sally had Roger leave the house (the external phase of motivation) they both appeared deflated and vaguely hopeless (the primitive phase of motivation) about their marriage and themselves at this point. The external phase of motivation, the PAR-state of readiness, may be very short-lived. Perhaps if Sally had a therapeutic other as a temporary rapprochement figure or contacted me sooner, I could have reassured her, as I often do with clients in PAR, that she was doing the right thing (the active "go" signal). Sally believed, of course, based on her disempowered primitive sense of self, that she would lose the familiar (family the familiar love) if she did what *she felt* was best for herself (self-love).

In a PAR-state, the client is emotionally open and ready to accept virtually any rapprochement figure who seems to know what s/he's talking about. The physician in this case, rather than emphasizing therapy as a source of change, offered medication, and indeed, Sally "introjected" the Xanax! In the first session, she told me that "if it weren't for the medicine (she) didn't know how she could've made it through the first week."

In PAR-states, people can introject virtually anything or anyone since in that state they are giving up what is most familiar. When one accepts that the familiar is not working; one is beginning the process of individuation. Yet, the person may have relatively poor judgment since they have so little experience in being trusting and open of new and unfamiliar others. This explains how people discard their familiar values and are susceptible to cults, cult-figures, therapists, twelve-step programs, and the like. Now, this can be good or bad, depending upon the values of the external agent. If the values are progressive, growth-inducing, and include individuation from the external agent, then it is likely to be a good thing. Cults and even twelve-step programs are notorious for creating dependency for its own sake, but we forgive the twelve-step programs, since the replacement of dependency on a destructive substance (the familiar and primitive) by dependency on the twelve-steps (the new and external) is obviously superior.

Sally entered the external phase, however, briefly. It was the crisis of knowing of the affair that forced the issue and the new choice.

She was unable to sustain the progressive movement and the couple returned to a new, albeit, higher level of homeostasis.[15] This higher level, while still primitive, was sufficient to get the couple to therapy. I successfully bonded with each of them, which enabled them to continue in therapy. We dealt with many issues, but because they were primitively motivated, the therapy lacked energy. They were both very fearful of losing each other. Thus, whenever their hurt or anger reached a certain point that even vaguely threatened their homeostasis, and aroused the fear of abandonment, there was some diffuse and weak compromise, then deflation.

An example of this was Roger's complaints about the lack of passion and sexual excitement in their marriage which he felt (and Sally agreed) was a major factor in the affair. When Sally failed to follow through on an initially agreed upon homework assignment two weeks in a row to surprise Roger, he was upset but said he was probably "expecting too much." His familiar map included the notion that couples cannot maintain sexual excitement and passion for each other after the kids are born. I insisted he was not expecting too much and that a healthy marriage is defined by a continuation of passion and romance (a new healthy map). He would retort, "Yeah, but not for us" and this was sometimes followed by a cancellation of the subsequent week's session because, he said, he had to stay late at work. With regard to the affair, Roger insisted it was over and Sally avoided all efforts on my part to talk about her hurt and anger, or push for more details from Roger.

Here is an excellent example of the therapist attempting to provide the progressive movements ("You can have passion—here's how" message) which in their most motivated moments they verbally agreed with. Behaviorally, they were, not unexpectedly, resistant. The beginning months of therapy followed this kind of course.

One day, while Roger was away on business, Sally called me, crying, saying she had found the other woman's telephone number twelve times on Roger's car phone bill. Roger *had* claimed he ended the relationship completely. We processed her feelings and talked about how she wanted to confront the situation. She found herself in virtually the same position as previously, and she chose to handle the situation in much the same way. The difference was she now had a rapprochement figure firmly in place to help quell her irrational fears and encourage

---

15. I say higher state of homeostasis because one cannot remove the knowledge of the affair, which is potentially useful information to the couple.

her to proceed forward through the PAR. She confronted Roger and again told him to leave the house.[16]

Roger called me and we discussed what had happened. Roger struck me as different than the emotionally flat and calm person he presented as before. He was scared and therefore more emotionally open to input. Gone was the deflated victim-self and in its place was the clear manifestation of Roger's true self, the self I had attempted to reach previously in the primitive phase. Roger realized that he had "fucked up royally," and understood now how he could no longer deny his feelings or his needs. He said he had called the other woman before he called me and ended the relationship (this time I believed him; previously I had been skeptical, despite his claims to the contrary). He said he wanted to make things work with Sally and remarked (only half-jokingly) he would come to therapy every day (he ended up coming twice a week for two months). Previously, I might add, the couple claimed that money for therapy was a problem. In the external phase of motivation, priorities are re-ordered.

Addressing the couple's difficulties, personal hurts, and woundedness appropriately became a top priority. Interestingly, at this point, Roger supplanted Sally as the driving force at work in therapy. The overt power balance in the system shifted toward Sally. While motivated to work on her own issues, she was appropriately skeptical of Roger's intentions, once claiming, "He's just trying to win me back." At other times Sally would look to me for "go" signals, questioning whether she was being "too much of a bitch" by not trusting Roger. I very clearly told Sally that her skepticism was warranted and that she was being tough, not bitchy. In Sally's *familiar* map, being a powerful woman meant being "a bitch."

Sally's newfound "true" detachment replaced the old enmeshed, unhealthily detached Sally. As she pulled away, Sally became much more attractive to Roger because she was less needy and clingy. Curiously, but not unexpectedly, these changes seemed to fuel a new passion in the relationship. With my assistance, Roger began to pursue and court Sally. Roger would typically become hurt and angry at Sally

---

16. Real-life psychotherapy is replete with unexpected twists and turns. This case is fairly straightforward and useful for illustrative purposes. I have worked with couples in this situation where the husband, for example, refuses to leave the house and the wife calls me to ask, "What do I do now?" Therefore, the reader is cautioned not to view the cases I present as directly transferable. Rather, I am offering a way of *thinking* about, not necessarily *doing* psychotherapy.

if his courting did not yield immediate rewards, like Sally's trust. Several times, I confronted Roger on his immaturity and unrealistic expectations, teaching him, in a sense, to delay gratification for the pursuit of his larger goal.

Prior to the second discovery, Sally would never pull away emotionally enough for this regeneration to occur or for Roger to follow my suggestions that he participate more fully in the therapy. My attempts to "push the P," as I call it, in the other direction, by having Sally "surprise" Roger also fell flat since there was no motivating drive on either side to change. Similarly, while attempts at having the couple dialogue about their needs at times served to stimulate the therapy, it had little carry-over effect beyond distracting the couple from the fact that not much was actually changing in their marriage.

In the external phase, change is fluid and organic. The therapist makes sure that the progressive movements are correctly formulated, keeps the client on track, and serves as a rapprochement figure when regressive fears arise. In the next chapter, we will see how the change process develops through the guts of the treatment, in the midphase of therapy.

chapter 9

motivating clients in the midphase of treatment

One of the major advantages of determining the particular motivational level is that we will have some a priori expectation of what interventions tend to work and what interventions yield little or no success. Particular interventions or approaches will require more or less motivation than others. Many therapy failures occur because the therapist or the treatment model fails to take into account the motivation level of the client.

Most treatments are based on an assessment or a diagnostic model. The basic assumption is that if we can accurately define the client's problems, we can select an appropriate intervention. Besides the multitude of problems with diagnostic systems, overlapping diagnoses and the accuracy of diagnostic methods, my contention is that diagnosis is best not established at the *beginning* of treatment. We cannot determine which of the client's difficulties are associated with inadequate motivation and low self-esteem until later in the treatment. It is only with the resolution of motivational problems that we can ferret out true, diagnosable difficulties.

A client, for example, may come to treatment with many of the symptoms of depression. The problem is many of those symptoms can be explained by the default regression cluster of symptoms: aloneness, hopelessness, and despair. Even if we could offer a reliable biochemical depression screening and found problematic serotonin production, this would not prove the existence of a depression per se only that the client had inadequate levels of serotonin that may be associated with or manifest themselves as depression. This is an important distinction.

I am not attempting here to venture into a debate about the causes of depression. Suffice it to say, there is a biochemical correlate and motivational or self-esteem correlate. The correlate I am most interested in at the beginning of therapy is the motivational one, since I am less interested in psychopathology at that point. Depression, anxiety disorders, eating disorders, drug and alcohol problems, all of which may be debilitating or life-threatening at some point for most people, ebb and flow, and are often replaced by other pathologies. People traverse through difficult times and tend to recover, often without any treatment. I've seen clients with what we can assume are compromised biochemical systems and thereby prone to a host of disorders through their lifespan. It is important not to place a great deal of significance, let alone plot a course of treatment, on these pathologies at the beginning of therapy. By so doing, we treat the problem, not the person, and the person has much more of importance going on in their lives than pathology.

encouraging introjection of the therapist

Moreover, the person will tend to introject the treatment which maybe quite appropriate for dealing with their particular pathology but is not necessarily a good imprint when applied to other life dilemmas. An introject does not distinguish between problems. I've seen this manifested when a client comes to me after successful cognitive therapy for dealing with panic disorder, say, and unsuccessfully attempts to apply the same treatment approach to a marital problem. It is deleterious for a client to introject the treatment for a particular pathology. We should strive for the client to introject a healthy approach to living, in general.

I am also sensitive to the fact that there is a prime imprinting period that occurs in therapy and seek to take advantage of the timing for maximum carry-over effect on change to client's lives. With regard to particular pathologies, I prefer to have the client functioning at a higher level of motivation so that their dealing with the pathology can emanate from a greater sense of self-esteem. In this way, their approach to the *pathology* approaches an optimized medical-model approach. In other words, the client goes on to seek treatment, either with me or some other expert, program, or group, to deal with their phobia, depression, or eating disorder in a very matter-of-fact way, much as a person with an injured knee would seek surgery or physical rehabilitation. The motivated client will tend to take charge of treatment, seek out experts, make informed choices, follow treatment regimens and recommendations, be resilient to treatment difficulties and side effects, and is less sensitive to transference distortions. Underlying all this will be a sense of entitlement: I deserve to be or feel *normal*. The resolution of psychopathology is the removal of the pathology, or normalcy, that is, to be and act similarly to others. Resolution of motivational difficulties, on the other hand, is the replacement of self-hate with self-love and self-esteem. In other words, there is a creation of what is optimal. This is an important distinction which suggests that motivational work is revolutionary and transformative whereas psychopathology work alone may only modify dysfunctional operations. If a person feels this sense of deservedness, they can, theoretically, resolve any psychopathology that may occur because their motivation and resiliency will be high. As I stated earlier, this potential resolution is supported by sound scientific evidence, as good, and in some cases, excellent treatments exist for most disorders.

Perhaps the most important, even stunning, implication is that in the primitive phase of motivation in which most clients arrive in or relapse into within a short period of time in therapy, we cannot do any significant or long-lasting work on the client's psychopathology or diagnosable difficulty. Even if we could be sure of an accurate diagnosis and of successfully treating the pathology without addressing the larger motivational question, I have little faith in the staying power of that work.

I am not making a case for symptom substitution in the classic sense but merely stressing that the primitively motivated person will be at risk, depending upon their biochemical weaknesses, for a host of problems. By focusing on motivation, I choose to have an effect upon intra- and interpersonal resiliency. Rather than helping them to return to normalcy, I'd rather give them an opportunity to attain optimality, via the introjection of the therapist as a container for their positive wishes and expectations alongside a new value-based approach to living. Part of that value-system is a message that the client doesn't have to live with debilitating or even simply limiting pathologies or problems, whether a social phobia, dysthymia, or an obsessive-compulsive disorder. It is more important for the client to introject that message, not the particular therapeutic approach. Moreover, that introject will promote independence and further growth. If I offer cognitive therapy for depression to a client in the primitive phase then that is what they'll introject. In the best of circumstances, their depression will abate but s/he will leave therapy with an introject of limited usefulness. Of course in real-life psychotherapy, the client does not introject only the cognitive approach itself, since the approach is proffered by a person, the therapist, who ends up executing a set of operations that may have little to do with cognitive therapy per se.

In fact, what the client may introject is the confrontation which the cognitive therapist delivered in session-four after the client failed to attend session-three. Perhaps the therapist has confronted the client about an uncaring attitude about himself and his problem in a way no one had previously. The client may have cried and this became a corrective transactional experience (of reparenting, if you will). The client may have realized that the therapist stretched the boundaries of his role by being confrontational and hence experienced the confrontation as caring or loving.

The client may then have been better able to accept the cognitive treatment. The cognitive therapist who relates in this manner may be, inadvertently or consciously, working on motivational issues. These kinds of interactions go on every day in consultation rooms across the world, and we need to recognize the rightful place of these therapy events.[1] They are not inert ancillary by-products but rather essential elements of successful psychotherapy. As such, each of our models must account and plan out these events. We tend not to do this because this kind of work generally requires imposing values where therapeutic technique and method become secondary.

In the primitive phase. the imposition of values and introjection of the therapist is figure and the therapeutic method isground. This conceptualization can serve to increase the required commitment and patience on the part of the therapist, while decreasing unnecessary frustration on the part of the clinician and client.

For similar reasons, I tend not to refer clients to adjunctive treatments while they are in the primitive phase. This includes twelve-step programs, group therapies, and the like. During the potential-imprinting stage, I do not want my clients introjecting theories, ideas, and notions associated with a particular target problem. This is not because what goes on in a self-help group like Alcoholics Anonymous is negative; I simply do not trust the primitively motivated client to make sound decisions for themselves about which aspects of the experiences are helpful and what they can discard. Clients in the primitive phase will tend to swallow introjects whole (dependency) or reject them whole (counterdependency). The counterdependent client will tend to say things like, "AA's fucked up—just a bunch of know-nothing ex-drunks." The more dependent client may come back into a session full of excitement, telling me he's decided to drop out of therapy since he needs "to work the program and his sponsor said that therapy could get in the way of that." The

---

1. There has been recent attention on such events in the process-oriented-psychotherapy literature. This is consonant with reports I get from clients and others about their therapy experiences. Ex-clients of therapy will be much more likely to tell us about these events than the technical aspects of their treatment.

dependent primitively motivated client, we must remember, would not be attending AA to deal with their drinking problem, per se, but more broadly to find out how to live, how to relate, and how to make sense of their complicated world. While I have faith in the twelve-step approach in dealing with the target behaviors, I question the twelve-steps themselves as a good philosophy of living for each and every person (see Humphreys, 1993 for a discussion of the limitations of integrating psychotherapy and a twelve-step approach).[2]

By the later stages of the external phase of motivation, clients can make better distinctions, but in the early stages of externalized motivation they may become easily confused by what sound like conflicting messages. Adjunctive programs tend to have a one-size-fits-all approach which is problematic for susceptible clients. It is best for the therapist to maintain control over their involvement in adjunctive therapies wherever possible. This may not be possible, of course, in situations where a client comes to therapy already involved in an adjunctive program. Also, clients who are at severe risk should be directed into appropriate adjunctive programs according to the therapeutic dictum of assuring safety-from-harm first.

I should point out though that here we are talking about the phenomenon of primitive-phase clients who have briefly but not yet substantially entered the external phase, and who are in a state of imprint-readiness. Imprint-readiness occurs directly after initial penetration. While a client is in a default regression and remains unpenetrated, there is a kind of treatment-immunity; nothing will be effective. They may go to therapy, twelve-step programs, and the like, but nothing of substance will occur in the absence of therapeutic penetration.

The default regression is a curious state of imprint-immunity; yet the possibility for transformation remains but a leap of faith away. How this occurs will be different for each subgroup of primitively motivated clients. The default regression is a state of imbalance for B clients, and hence this occurrence is intermittent. For A clients, the default regression is a latent phenomenon, because the false self of the client provides a kind of insulation against object loss. For highly schizoidal AA clients, the false self and its attendant lack of emotional connection provides the greatest insulation against object loss. AA-type clients do not manifest default regressions. If they do, they are precipitated by

---

2. I recognize that each program's particular one-size approach may be clearly appropriate for a specific client.

major personal traumas (e.g., divorce) and even then are usually temporary. The BB client (the classic borderline) on the other hand, is in an almost chronic default regression. With the exception of the BB client, the default regression creates both a crisis and an opportunity for the therapist to penetrate the person. The despair and hopelessness the client is experiencing is a regressive experience that provides a window for the therapist to enter into the client's psyche. While the task can be a difficult one, and often requires a series of attempts, the potential for transformation remains.

A person need not be penetrated by a therapist; indeed, any reparental figure will suffice. Once penetrated, the person is in a state of imprint-readiness. To be penetrated, a person simply needs to have an experience of being understood, known deeply and empathically. The more schizoidal A and AA clients can even be penetrated by a self-help book since a book does not threaten their guarded relational boundaries the way a person might. A book can be accepted more easily. The book may become a kind of Bible—a new map for healthy living. The problem, of course, is that a book, no matter how great its ideas, is one-dimensional and cannot address the specific and unique needs of the person. Most self-help books unfortunately offer a one-size-fits-all approach that can also be problematic, and I am very careful about what books I recommend to clients who are in states susceptible to penetration.[3]

A person in such a state may be vulnerable to the influence of group seminars and encounter-type weekends, like Forum or Insight. I have nothing against these experiences per se but clients who are susceptible to penetration tend to "convert" to the new program and methodology. As in psychotherapy, this can be good or bad; it depends upon the values inherent in the program. There is a process of influence that leads the person to a new way of experiencing themselves and their life and in seminar-like experiences the person is led to believe that the new map and methodology that is being offered will help or heal them. While that may ultimately be true I am skeptical of influence not exercised by a change agent with whom the client has an

---

3. I am, in general, careful about what books I recommend to clients. Bibliotherapy has a nice "help-the-client-help-themselves" value-set behind it but fails to take into account the transferential power of recommending a particular "authority." When I do recommend a book, I tend to choose authors who espouse a more complex view of life and are not so easily digested such as *The Road Less Traveled* (Peck, 1978) or *Intimate Worlds* (Scarf, 1995).

ongoing and direct one-to-one relationship with. Cathexis is always to the *person* delivering the message. Cathexis to the message may be critical but is secondary to the relational vicissitudes of object-loss. In seminar situations the person tends to become cathected to someone (seminar leader, healer, guru) they do not have a real one-on-one relationship with. Without a constant rapprochement-figure to deal with the unique and expected complexities of a person's situation, mid- or long-term failures are likely (see also Cushman, 1989).

People who attend these seminars and get penetrated may become excited when the message they swallow whole is spiritual in nature, as often happens in religious groups. These people will become pseudospiritual. They appear to be in the ultimate, spiritual phase to which I refer in my model, but are really primitives in disguise. The way to determine the truth is to examine other aspects of the person's life. Many spiritually enlightened gurus, for example, engage in questionable activities (e.g., various abuses of members or financial indiscretions) or lead contradictory lives (they may be beloved by their followers as "the great father" but abandon their biological children).

The excitement the person experiences in these seminars occurs because they are provisionally lifted out of their default regression. They are infused with hope and belief that there is something or someone out there that will work for them. A similar experience often occurs in residential or inpatient drug and alcohol settings. The hopelessness of the default regression is impinged upon by the hospital staff, other residents, and twelve-step programs. The patient has an excited experience of rebirth: there's another way, a way out from the despair, another life. But when the person leaves the facility, s/he will typically and significantly relapse within a short period of time. This happens because the healing object is no longer available to them. It is too diffuse, embodied in too many places (AA, the other now ex-residents, their primary inpatient therapist, etc.). Interestingly, aftercare therapists have to actually compete against these objects as the client may have no room for new reparental figures.

It is best if there is *one consistent healing object*, so when the person reexperiences the default regression, as they always will, there is one person to seek out. This person need not be a therapist, but frankly, I know of no better structure for finding a consistent healing object. It can certainly be modified and improved, but Freud's little invention of one client, one therapist, one hour, and one frame is almost inexplicably brilliant. For all the revision of Freud's theories and the many paradigm-shifts after the high point of psychoanalysis, it is both curious and significant that no matter what our orientation, the frame remains essentially the same. While this may be in part simply explained by convention and therapists' reliance on what is familiar, surprisingly few theoreticians have challenged that basic framework.

A person may be penetrated by virtually anyone. One arena where default regressions are impinged upon regularly (particularly with B and BB-types, and occasionally with A-types) occurs in romantic relationships. People meet an appealing other with whom they fall in love. Falling in love itself may be considered a penetration of the default regression. Here, too, there is attraction to the healing aspects of a new person. There is excitement, renewed hope and faith in the world, and, we might say complete object fulfillment. In actuality, such people are temporarily in the spiritual phase of motivation. People who are in love become very open, giving, generous, and quite resilient to normal upsets. There is a willingness to overlook the negative (faults, problems, issues), replaced by an attitude that anything can be worked out.

Infatuation is commonly suspect. The common wisdom is usually correct if the person in love remains primarily in the primitive phase. All attachments, no matter how productively they begin, will develop problems. The initial excitement is partially based on a fantasy: the other person is all-wonderful and would never intentionally hurt me. After the infatuation and discovery phases, familiarity invariably develops and the newness of the experience wears off. As this occurs, older familiar patterns of behavior, relating, and thinking, initially submerged, rise to the surface again. This may lead to transferential distortions (e.g. "Oh, shit, you're just like my mother") when the other repeats familiar ways of relating or behavior. The less primitively motivated the client, the greater the ability to tolerate and put into perspective negative aspects of the other.

One implication for general psychotherapeutic practice is that therapists should be discouraging of a client's entering into this kind of romantic attachment. It is preferable that the practitioner be the primary penetrator of the default regression, since we do not know the intentions or capabilities of the romantic other. Clients, of course, will be drawn to such attachments and will typically ignore therapeutic warnings. In these situations, it is best for the therapist not to place

much importance on the inevitable trials and tribulations of the relationship. Most typically, these clients will enter into an infatuation that
ends up being short-lived. The person will become very excited, full of
hope and passion for life through the penetration of the default regression and temporary entrance into the spiritual phase. As the relationship continues and the client's familiarity with the other increases, fears
of engulfment surface. Without successful prior experiences of trust and
working-through, disillusionment occurs. The less mature the client the
more it is likely the relationship will falter and eventually dissipate.[4]

Of greater significance, though, is that couples work should be
avoided, inthe primitive phase since the client's fear of abandonment is
so predominant. When fear of losing the romantic other is central,
transformative growth in the relationship is virtually impossible since
decisions are made on the basis of keeping an attachment to the person,
even at the cost of one's own self-esteem. Couples therapy may be successful at stabilizing a primitive dysfunctional couple or modifying particularly harmful interactions (e.g., abuse) and creating a new, albeit
only slightly higher, state of homeostasis. Quelling a crisis state in a relationship via couples therapy may have the unwanted effect of reducing
opportunities for growth and transformation.

Growth based on emerging self-esteem is transformative; growth
based on increased understanding and improved communication is
only modifying, although the latter may set the stage for the former in
some cases. We favor interventions that take into account fear-of-loss
dynamics in the couple, as where loss is utilized as a potent motivator
to change. For example, we may encourage an abused spouse to take a
stand designed to activate the abusive spouse's fear of losing their partner, in order that contingencies for abusive behaviors be removed. This
is called the fear-of-loss maneuver and lies at the heart of marital therapy work where the power imbalance based on fear-of-loss is upended
and the pattern enacting the healthier behaviors (e.g., nonabusive
"Let's go to therapy together" or "I want a better marriage") emerges
(Kirschner and Kirschner, 1986, 1989, 1990b; Kirschner, Kirschner and
Rappaport, 1993). We will discuss fear-of-loss technique in Chapter 10.

---

4. Typically our B-type clients will be the ones who are left/abandoned, and our A
clients will be the one abandoning the other.

encouraging appropriate relationships for primitive and externally-phased clients: a paradigm of progressive expectations

For single adults who present for treatment in the primitive or external phase we tend to introduce what we call the "program of three." (Kirschner and Kirschner, 1986; Kirschner, Kirschner and Rappaport, 1993) This program is a suggested dating pattern where a client is encouraged to date several people at once. We thus help the client not to get precipitously involved with only one person, since clients who are organized by the fear-of-loss will tend to attach to one person at a time based on a fear of losing the other rather than true feelings of like or love. Dating a few people at the same time provides a kind of natural inoculation against precipitous romantic involvements whose excessive drama (e.g., family-of-origin replays) may waste time and energy. Other benefits include the client's getting to know more about themselves and their own likes and interests. Self-esteem tends to increase since the person may be pursued (or at least be spurning interest) by more than one person (e.g., "I am a desirable romantic partner" internalization).

Like mastery of fear-of-loss in the committed partner, instituting the "program of three" is a prime example of a progressive goal or expectation in the external phase of therapy work. It becomes something the therapist seeds for in the early primitive phase, plans for in the late primitive phase, and helps the client achieve through the external phase. In the early external phase we seed for the client ultimately choosing one romantic partner for a monogamous intimate relationship. We help the single client achieve this goal toward the end of the external phase. In the internal phase, we plan for the client's focus to be on that primary love relationship; couples therapy at that point may be indicated, since the fear-of-loss is, at least hypothetically, no longer the central operating dynamic in the relationship. Most forms of couples therapy work on the various fears of *intimacy* through focusing on improved communication, more satisfying sexual experience, and more fulfilling and deeper patterns of interaction. Each partner's fear of abandonment can circumvent therapy work on the fear of engulfment. It is only when fear of losing the other abates that intimacy fears can be addressed in any substantial way.

No meaningful love commitment to another is possible in the primitive phase because loyalty remains to the introjected family-of-origin and its contemporary representations. For commitment to another to take place, loyalty must first shift to oneself. When this occurs, free choice is finally possible. *Freely* making the commitment to a primary love relationship is paramount. One may make a constricted or legislated commitment (e.g., choosing to get married in the primitive phase) but ultimately commitment is a state of being that must be established on a daily, interaction-by-interaction basis. This requires a prior working-through of abandonment issues.

Couples therapy work that is predicated on a primitive client's spoken commitment to a particular number of sessions may be strategically wise in the short run but hazardous in the long run since this commitment is essentially false. Commitment must be a goal of the therapy, not a precondition. We must expect and plan for clients not being committed to therapy. Since therapy represents a projection of the healthy self, why would we expect primitive clients to commit to be self-loving and other-loving, if that means losing their connection to the familiar but largely negative patterns of interacting in relationships?

The abovementioned is a hypothetical model of health and optimal functioning but in real-life and real-life psychotherapy, few clients come prepared to accept such a healthy program, no matter how brilliantly offered or presented by the therapist. The few exceptions present in what I've referred to as a state of imprint-readiness. These clients are lacking less in object skill than in having a good-enough object willing to provide support, guidance, and confrontation. The latter is often what is missing in most real-life therapeutic relationships. When presented with a progressive goal like the "program of 3," we fully expect clients to resist, since any progression involves a stretching of one's self-esteem boundaries. The expectation of progress is a kind of psychological leap for the client, a challenge to what is known and familiar. Of course, clients may resist the progressive expectation for various reasons, depending upon their unique intellectual or emotional armor. When I *strategically* and *empathically* offer the "program of 3," a typical client reacts, "Yeah, right, I can't even get one person to go out with me and you want me to find three!"

We see the range of possible responses as normal regressions in the face of a positive self-affirming extroject, the therapist's saying, "You *can* do this, you *can* have this and (importantly) here's how . . ." The client enacts or "becomes" the self-hating introject from their past which says, "You *cannot* do this; you *cannot* have this." This dynamic is at the heart of resistance. The therapist is essentially saying, "You are worthy," and the client says, "No, I am not." This conversation may take place in a multitude of forms.

While the particular substance and form of each client's "story" is important, the client's resistance typically remains rooted in this fear of the unknown. Even though many clients intellectually understand that this unknown is probably good and emotionally realize that their present state of hopelessness is a result of fear of positive change, this fear is predominant. Therapists typically attempt to work through this fear with the client by asking responses such as "What are you afraid of?," "Let's talk about this fear," or "What does this fear remind you of from your past?" This kind of work will sometimes result in successful abreaction of the regressive material and this in turn may lead to engagement with the progressive tasks at hand. Unfortunately, usually it does not. Insight, even emotional insight, does *not* produce or lead to change when a client is in the primitive and early- and mid-external phases, which applies to the vast majority of therapy clients. I cannot state this more strongly. A change in the client's *organic* operations occurs where the fear-of-loss of the familiar is supplanted by a greater fear—the fear of losing the love, respect, admiration, and caring—of the therapist if one does not change.[5] Again, the therapist is a part-construction by the client, and a container for the client's true wishes and positive goals, so the love s/he fears losing is essentially a concentrated product of the client's own positive projections.

In the real-life primitive and external-phase work of psychotherapy, though, these projections are experienced as the therapist's love, which the client fears losing. The therapist may respond in various ways to the client who chooses not to undertake the progressive tasks; s/he may challenge, confront, or withdraw from the client. Whatever the therapist's response, the client will likely sense *some* reaction if the therapist has successfully penetrated the client. Clients who remain unpenetrated by the therapist or therapeutic other will not be attuned to the real movements toward or away from them; to fear losing an attachment, one must first *have* an attachment. We first attempt to bond and penetrate in the primitive phase, in order to create the healthily dependent attachment necessary for progressive work in the external phase.

---

5. I prefer the term "operations" to "behavior," which is more limited. One can change behavior without a concomitant change in attitude or point of view. By "organic" I mean naturally occurring operational changes as opposed to therapist- or model-imposed structural changes.

The therapist may suggest but should not push any particular agenda until this penetration has occurred. For example, I might recommend the "program of three" to primitively motivated clients but if they fail to implement it, I will not make an issue of it.

avoiding premature progressive expectations

Similarly, therapists who require client's abstinence from abusive substances or relationships prior to therapeutic penetration are dooming the therapy relationship to failure. We do not "push the P" as I call it, until there is an empathic and secure therapeutic relationship. Otherwise, the client will simply not engage in the progressive operation and the therapist will diminish in importance and power. Occasionally, doing so can help create or contribute to the external phase of the therapeutic relationship, but in most cases "pushing the P" too early will at best be ignored by the client, or worse, lead to default regressions, since the default regression process is often a deflation triggered by the unempathic inputs of a significant other. It may even lead to premature termination, with exit lines like "I guess I'm not ready to do this (therapy)." The therapist who unwittingly "pushed the P" may remain befuddled, perhaps not even remembering having advocated a particular agenda. Sometimes the client's awareness of "what s/he needs to do" is far ahead of their ability to engage in the object relations and behavioral skills necessary for the healthy operations.

The *attached* client, *appropriately* challenged, may also attempt to terminate treatment. The therapist must remain firm and insist on the progressive movement. We may view the client's attempt at termination as testing, much as a child does to see how much s/he can get away with. Therapeutic toughness is an underrated and underutilized quality since our emphasis has largely been on healing clients who have been abused and misunderstood. We must remember that while abusiveness may be defended as discipline gone awry or inappropriately delivered, healthy discipline and abusiveness are not the same, or even related, phenomena. Healthy confrontation and toughness are lacking in many parental and therapeutic relationships.

The intricacies of assessment, diagnosis, and history-taking tend to dominate early therapy work for many practitioners. By the time the therapist has figured out what's going on, the client has become discouraged and may have terminated, or be close to terminating, treatment. Therefore, I suggest that standard therapeutic practices like note-taking, assessment questionnaires, genograms, diagnostic testing, assessment sessions, and intake interviews are problematic for two major reasons. First, it is preferable for data to emerge organically in the course of therapy. Otherwise, a good assessment tool may give us accurate information that the client is unprepared to deal with. Frankly, I do not want to know something that the client has not independently selected to tell me. Finding out that they drink three glasses of wine each night or that on weekends they engage in anonymous sex, although important data, is useless information in the absence of the client's willingness to face such issues. I am not saying that as therapists we shouldn't ask questions; we always do and will. But the informal process of data gathering organic to the therapy process will provide us with more usable information. Unusable information tends to obstruct the naturally evolving therapy relationship, since we may base our interventions and relational posture on the data and not the person.

Second, more formalized assessment procedures tend to distance therapist and client. If our initial goal is to bond and penetrate the psychological space of the client, it is best to interact in a more naturalistic conversational manner. The usual critique of formal note-taking and such is that it is rooted in the medical model and poses the therapist as an expert. In my view, there is nothing inherently wrong with the therapist-as-expert position (although, as I always point out, this may be inappropriate for some clients and some situations). However, the therapist needs to be an expert more in relating and less, particularly early in treatment, in psychopathology.

An expert in relating can provide what the other needs to grow. S/he must be able to be empathic, to be nurturing, to direct, as well as be confrontational. In relationship-central models of psychotherapy, there is emphasis on the nondirective aspects of therapeutic relating. Other models hold the technical aspects of the therapy to be central. Our model attempts to bridge these two paradigms by maintaining that more directive and confrontational relational approaches can be empathic and compatible with nondirective relational approaches.

Of course, in the primitive phase it is often necessary to engage in non-relationship-oriented psychotherapy work. The client does not come to therapy looking for a relationship as such. They are looking for help with a particular problem. But to get this help, a good-enough relationship must be formed to help the client engage in the PAR-oriented tasks of the external phase and to plug the default regression process with corrective transactional experiences. This will further assist therapeutic work in the external phase by providing a distortion-free rapproachement relationship. In the meantime the therapist must begin to work on the problems presented. This can be awkward since the therapist may be quite aware of the client's lack of readiness to effectively handle their problems. In the primitive phase, the therapist must make this work secondary to the relationship, yet do so in a way that the client does not feel their real-life concerns diminished.

We may reanalyze the so-called failures of therapy. A client may come to therapy with a problem of feeling uncomfortable in social situations or having difficulty in forming lasting intimate relationships. They may be quite resistant to engaging in the necessary tasks of the preferred therapeutic treatment for social phobias and social anxiety, systematic desensitization, cognitive restructuring, or some integration of cognitive and behavioral therapy.[6] We may assign incremental behavioral/social tasks that we suggest the client engage in. The client may refuse. The client may have difficulty doing *in vivo* relaxation or role-playing exercises. I tend not to even label this difficulty or even outright refusal as resistance, because I don't believe that clients come to therapy to work on a particular problem. Clients first come to therapy to get something *relational* from the therapist so that they can work on their problems.

synergism in the external phase: therapy along the edges

While our model is predicated on the notion that therapy work in any arena can occur at virtually any point in the treatment process, we should also stress the synergistic relationship amongst the various targeted transactions. Successful work in one particular transaction may translate into successful work in another area as core issues may be similar. Here, resolving fear of abandonment remains central as this will lead to increasing levels of empowerment, such as in any of the transactional areas career, marriage, family-of-origin, and child-rearing as the client introjects the therapist's attitudes, values, and goals. Synergistic growth is a function of the PAR-process in the external phase of motivation, while in the primitive phase, building the therapeutic relationship remains the central focus.

---

6. Of course, this is all assuming that we could truly boil down the client's presenting difficulty to a simple treatable diagnosis at the beginning of therapy, a questionable endeavor in light of the usual complexity of human beings.

Not all clients enter treatment in the primitive phase and automatically accept the practitioner distortion-free as a penetrating good-object. In some cases, the synergistic external phased work begins immediately but the therapist must be aware of potential relapses into the primitive phase sparked by a negative growth (PAR) experience or an accompanying negative transaction between client and therapist. Since the therapeutic relationship lacks strength from the buildup of positive experiences over time, the client may be inclined to terminate treatment or at best, lapse into a default regression while remaining in treatment.

But negative or potentially negative interactions between therapist and client often prove to be excellent fodder for resolution of core or foundational issues that propel synergistic growth. I have called these interactions "therapy along the edges" (Rappaport, 1995b) where the edge is represented by the boundary of the safe therapeutic frame. When we "push the P" in the absence of overt "go" signals from the client, the therapist is activating the process of therapy along the edges. The client's experience of safety is temporarily removed. On one level we may consider this the therapist's deliberately raising the anxiety level of the client (i.e., as in Gestalt therapy). This is certainly true, but the crux of the phenomena is relational. The therapist who provided a safe atmosphere in the earlier phases of therapy is now pushing a particular agenda that the client is actively or passively resisting. The client indeed may overtly say, "I don't want (this)," but the therapist may not respect this overt resistance, since in our model, the therapist remains the container for the positive goals, wishes, and values of the client even, and especially if, the client cannot or will not.[7]

Strategically, the therapist must remain highly flexible but with steadfast regard to the ultimate goals of the treatment. The lower the self-esteem level of the client, the more the therapist must actively be the container for his or her positive goals and wishes. Thus, it is not unusual for the therapy to become an ongoing oscillation between the therapist's "pushing the P," the client's returning to a state of default regression, therapeutic penetration around the edges, the client's par-

---

7. The philosophical question of when the therapist ceases to be the container for the client's positive wishes is an important one. In practical terms this occurs when the client terminates treatment. My position is that as long as the client remains engaged relationally with me, it is my almost contractual obligation to hold the positive goals and values for them until proven unnecessary. I take the position of letting the client prove to me that they do not want to reach the goal by not remaining in growthful therapy.

tial or complete resolution of the foundational fear of abandonment, and the client's propulsion forward into synergistic growth. Before discussing an example of such phenomenon, let us examine the theoretical precepts of therapy on the edges.

The classic conceptualization of the various aspects of the therapeutic relationship has been offered by Gelso and Carter (1985) and others, who posit three main aspects to the therapy relationship. These include what are referred to as the working alliance, the transference relationship, and the real relationship. The first two have received the bulk of the attention in the literature, while the real relationship has received minimal analysis. This is unfortunate since the real relationship offers the most potential for direct healing although it is difficult to separate the interactive effects of all three.

The premise of our model is precisely that there is no neutrality in therapy; the therapist is always doing something no matter what posture s/he takes at any given time. There is always transference of one sort or another no matter what the therapist is doing or not doing. Transference is not determined by the type of therapy, an analytic stance, or the length of the relationship. I've had clients "love" or "hate" me on the basis of their first phone call, or even before their first phone call, just from hearing about me. Some transference reactions are more intense than others. Clients who are strongly penetrated by the therapist will be susceptible to strong transferential reactions. Clients who are unpenetrated or with therapists who discourage dependency will tend to have more tepid transferential reactions.

power triggers and the real relationship

There are two major transference reactions in generic psychotherapy. First, the therapist may take a stance that engenders a reaction to power stimuli. In other words, the therapist may act in a way that is more powerful, such as being more directive, active, or omnipotent. Whatever the client's historical imprint regarding power stimuli (e.g., "When someone in authority acted powerfully, my feelings were not always considered"), s/he will tend to get activated. This imprint may be projected onto the therapist (e.g., "my therapist is not considering my feelings"). Through projective identification, the therapist may actually *enact* this projected imprint (e.g., by being, in fact, dismissive of the client's feelings). We consider this enactment, should it occur, a therapeutic error. If the projected imprint is not enacted we simply refer to the phenomenon as negative transference, which is an unwanted event. We do not want our client to experience us negatively since the therapist cannot be the container of the client's positive wishes while being experienced so negatively. It is only at, or near the end, of the external phase, when the therapist no longer serves this function, that negative transference is a more desired outcome. We recognize that negative transference is unavoidable but assume it will occur organically, without overt manipulation.

We are emphasizing negative transference but each client also has a positive historical imprint that may be triggered by power stimuli offered by the therapist (e.g., "My therapist may have the answers I've been searching for since I was little"). This imprint may be projected onto the therapist in the form of positive transference (e.g., "My therapist is a great healer"). Again, through projective identification, the therapist may enact this projection, for example, by encouraging unproductive dependency. This, too, would be considered a therapeutic error.

However, since our model is a reparental one, we are inclined to encourage, or at least not discourage, positive transference since positive transference assists in the development of the working alliance for doing the actual inside- and outside-of-therapy work. Most significantly, though, the positive transference reaction promotes the therapist's serving as the container of the client's positive hopes and wishes. Indeed, the therapist cannot become the positive container in the absence of positive transference. The presence of a healing agent is a necessary precondition for the emergence of positive goals, hopes, and wishes. Therefore, the therapist must be open to greeting and holding onto virtually all but the most unrealistic positive transference reactions.[8]

In cases where positive transference is not developing easily, the therapist must make every attempt to create it through adjustments in therapeutic posture and continued attempts at penetration. Clients who are in default regressions have an immensely difficult time viewing the therapist positively. A-(schizoidal) type clients who are in default regressions are particularly difficult to penetrate since they do not necessarily present as having a negative, or even not positive, view of the therapist. Therapist and client seem to get along well and appear to have a positive working alliance. These are clients who after long periods of time in therapy make no significant gains, seemingly with-

---

8. There are therapeutic situations when we discourage the development of such positive transference, as with BB clients.

out explanation, since on the surface, they appear cooperative and willing. Below the surface however, may be a host of negative transference reactions rooted in the unseen default regression. Usually the negative reaction is of the sort, "S/he does not know me or understand me just like everyone else in my life" even though the client may not have offered the practitioner any opening to do so.[9]

While positive transference is critical, it has no healing properties in and of itself. The client must reclaim the projected positive wishes, values, and goals for themselves, perhaps discarding or altering some, or many, of them. The client cannot achieve this if there is only positive transference. The client may make positive gains, that is, acting powerfully in some aspects of their lives, but only as long as they maintain proximity to the practitioner. This may be sufficient for a time but their growth will be too entangled with their therapist.

Curiously, the only transportable commodity the therapist has to offer is love. When the client receives the therapist's love, in whatever emotional form, the client has a corrective transactional experience that changes the ending of their fruitless repetition compulsion. A new relational imprint is created that says, "You are deserving of love," which forms the basis of self-esteem. When the client experiences the loving input they are in the first stages of leaving the therapist and the therapy. The imprint "I am deserving of love" is the first step in the client's spiritual quest. They may be open now to receiving love from their current partner, from their parents, by seeking a new love relationship, and may be more giving of love to their children and the world in general.

As I said, however, this is only the first step of the journey. Many religious and psychological cults, even very conventional ones, lead their adherents to believe that they can be spiritually awakened and capable of loving others and doing anything they set their minds or hearts on. These are the pseudospiritual people I spoke of previously. Therapy or therapeutic interaction is by no means over at this point; in fact, the hard work has just begun. Interestingly, now the client or seeker no longer has adequate excuses not to face the fears that inhibit growth, since s/he is now capable of independently overcoming those fears, with therapeutic assistance, if necessary.

---

9. Positive thinking and constructivist schemata and spiritual/religious paradigms become attractive to clients who are susceptible to interpreting simplistic messages, like "Changes in your thinking change everything," or "love/empathy conquers all." As Peck (1978) put it so elegantly, life is difficult and requires tremendous discipline.

Love, of course, is not only transportable, but must be real. By real we mean based on the true feelings and intentions of the giver, in this case, the therapist. This is why the real relationship is therapy's most important healing aspect. The real relationship occurs as the client experiences the therapist's actions as rooted in loving feelings and intent. Again, the client internalizes the powerful imprint "I am lovable."

As one might imagine, this kind of interaction is "edgy," much like a love relationship outside-of-therapy. I use the term "edgy" to suggest that the therapist is on the edge of what the client considers safe or appropriate. This is not to say the operations of the therapist are in fact unsafe or inappropriate; just that the client may experience them as such. As in other spiritual endeavors, we could refer to the client's experience of letting go of these relational fears as a leap of faith. The client enters into unknown territory unsure of the process but hopeful of the outcome and lets go of a priori negative expectations. Perhaps, more simply put, it is a process of trusting the good intentions of another and the resulting corrective transactional experience.

a case example

Ellen, 25, presented for therapy with diffuse complaints about her life, mostly centering about her upcoming marriage to her fiancee, Joe. She had fantasized about having an affair with her married, and sometimes abusive, boss. Joe was, as she described him, "the sweetest man I've ever been with" but Ellen was unsure whether she could remain faithful to him. She was extremely reluctant and highly resistant to involving Joe in the therapy for fear he would leave her if he knew of her ambivalence.

I allowed Ellen a period of several months to develop a trusting relationship with me before I began pushing her to bring Joe to a session where the progressive movements forward (P) was to confront her issues directly. I pushed particularly hard as their wedding date approached and it was clear, barring potentially destructive last-minute dramas (a definite possibility), that she was going ahead with the marriage.

We engaged in a yes-no-maybe dance for a period of weeks. In one session, Ellen remained particularly defensive in a not-unfamiliar, immature, and bratty manner. I decided to use a paradoxical technique. I told her she "was destined to live a life of marital mediocrity. But that was okay; not everyone can have a strong marriage." She had told me she wanted this to be a strong marriage, since her first marriage to a rather abusive man had ended in divorce. As is often the case, she reacted negatively to the paradox. "Well, why bother being in therapy," she ultimately replied. I simply agreed. Ellen left the session without making an appointment.

Based on her prior experience of familiar others, and of myself, up to that point, she expected me to pursue her. I had done that a few times previously when we had particularly difficult sessions. This time I did nothing, knowing she had to truly face the direction she wanted to go in. Ellen left a message on my answering machine the next day saying she couldn't sleep all night and that she knew she had to face the issues with Joe and herself and that she knew she needed my help in doing so. In fact, she had already talked to Joe about coming to a therapy session. Joe, as it turned out, was quite open and willing to deal with problems in their relationship.[10] The subsequent transcript is the individual session following her phone call. I confronted Ellen throughout the session on her commitment to herself, her impending marriage, and to her therapy.

CLIENT: [Crying] You know, no one knows how it feels. . . No one knows what it's like to be me.

THERAPIST: Right.

CLIENT: You know, if you were me, you'd give up, too.

THERAPIST: Not if I had me to help me.

[The client is in an easily penetrable default regression (punctuated by the plain remark, "You'd give up, too.") The therapist offers a corrective transactional experience ("Not if I had me to help me"). My reply is empathic in that I am validating her experience of deflation in the absence of a therapeutic other.]

CLIENT: You know not having (anyone) . . . and then you get someone who can help you . . . Sometimes you think that person will put up with anything.

[Her comment "and then you get someone who can help you" indicates successful penetration. Her assumption that I would put up with anything is based on her prior experiences in close relationships— either you are abused or *become* abusive.]

THERAPIST: I'm not going to stand for that.

CLIENT: It's easier to do that . . . It's what I've always done.

---

10. I strongly emphasize that Ellen's fear of losing me (my respect, her projected wishes) was what led to the positive result, not the paradoxical technique.

[Silence]

THERAPIST: This is hard, really hard—but you're fortunate. This time you got a break.

CLIENT: By having you?

THERAPIST: Yeah. Now you can either be smart, take advantage, or be stupid and keep drowning in your shit. What I'm telling you now is that there are no more in-betweens. Trying to do a little of both—being here, being there—those days are over . . .

[The therapist is challenging her, despite her fear, to remain in the external phase and to take a more complete leap of faith by separating from her dysfunctional but familiar patterns of relating from the primitive phase.]

CLIENT: [Looking up with a half-smile] People do what you let them get away with.

[The client's statement is a request for therapeutic discipline.]

THERAPIST: Well, I'm not letting you get away with it, and no more week-by-week quitting.

[The therapist responds to her request.]

CLIENT: I didn't do it that much, did I?

[The client signals the therapist to pull back from continued confrontation.]

THERAPIST: You did it enough.

[Silence]

What are you thinking?

CLIENT: I was just wondering how you felt about me?

THERAPIST: I love you.

[The client is struggling with the notion that confrontation does not have to mean loss of the relationship. The therapist provides a simple reply ("I love you") that indicates his love is unconditional.][11]

CLIENT: How come I feel like you really don't sometimes.

THERAPIST: You're not used to someone who loves you and doesn't put up with your shit, and in fact that's why they don't put up with your shit. Everyone else in your life has put up with your shit.

CLIENT: Actually because they don't really love me . . . [smiles]. I'm using a lot of tissues tonight.

---

11. I am not suggesting that saying "I love you" to a client is paradigmatic. There are many ways to display caring and love. I am suggesting that saying those words are appropriate, even necessary, with certain clients in particular situations. This transcript represents one such situation. Unfortunately, "I love you" may connote romantic intent. I held no such intention, nor did the client misinterpret one.

THERAPIST: Good.

Of course, some clients take this leap while others do not. While this "leap" is in a sense a misnomer (a series of incremental leaps is more accurate), referring to this step as a leap, particularly directly to the client, is not only dramatically enlightening but holds a spiritual accuracy. The truest translation of the leap into practical terms is the person's willingness to do whatever it takes to heal, including, most significantly, trusting the good intentions of their therapist.

The real relationship is the hypothesized point at which the positive transference and potentialized negative transference merge. Positive transference opens the way for the real relationship to occur, as penetration is not possible in its absence. As the real relationship occurs, the potential for misunderstandings, mistakes, and the like increases exponentially. Negative transference easily emerges in a real atmosphere, where negative events and outcomes can occur. Real relationships, of course, hold the potential for old hurts to be triggered. The negative historical imprint is tapped into and negative transference occurs.

The therapist is offering a reparental input that is real and which the client may experience in the framework of the negative transference ("My therapist is dismissive of my feelings *just like* my father"). Remember, there is no neutrality, no alternative. If the therapist is acting in a way experienced as unpenetrating and not powerful, there may be negative transference in the opposite direction. That is, if the therapist is too nondirective or passive, the client will have a negative reaction based on historical imprint triggered when significant others act in ways experienced as nonpowerful ("Here's another person who will disappoint me because they're afraid of having an impact on me"). This negative transference reaction tends to be quieter, although not always so, and may be what is happening when a client complains to the therapist, "Nothing's happening here."

A real transaction is rooted in the intent of the therapist to engage in operations, even edgy ones, in order to help the client grow. The therapist who avoids the nonpowerful set of postures and enacts the powerful set for a particular client, even if it has the potential for triggering negative transference, will in the end be viewed as loving and relationally courageous. The client will internalize this introject and hence, self-esteem will increase. Of course, self-esteem may be achieved in many ways, such as through the mastery of progressively more difficult and challenging tasks. But we must remember that clients will not tend to engage in attempts at mastery in the absence of a penetrating good-enough reparental agent, the PAR-figure. Once the loving intro-ject begins to be internalized, then the client will be more inclined to launch into the hard work of therapy occurring outside the therapy hour in the progressive areas of marriage, child-rearing, family- of-ori-gin, and independent transactions.

For example, a female client I was working with whose husband had been emotionally abusive and who, in time, came to feel loved by me and therefore lovable herself, was able to stand up to her husband as never before. The experience of not-love or abuse was consonant with her experience while growing up, in which her father physically abused her mother and sexually abused her. Not coincidentally, at the same time she first experienced the love from me and herself as lovable, she came to a therapy session furious with her father for mistreating her over the telephone.[12] She was now ready, with help and coaching, to confront her father for the first time in her life. Her anger at her moth-er for not protecting her rose to the surface, triggered by her mother's long-standing and continual requests for help. "I'm doing this because I'm tired of being my mother's caretaker and doing everything my father doesn't do for her," she told me in the same session. Over the next few months, she spoke of wanting to open her own business, as she was tired of "making money for everyone else . . . Hell, I have the same relationship with my boss that I had with my mother . . . On the sur-face, it looks so wonderful and supportive, but the real truth is I give and don't get back."

This interaction represents the synergistic change of the exter-nalized phase of motivation. Change in one area spurs change in another. The acceptance of the therapist as a reparental agent who is both real and good, creates the potential for growth in a host of areas because of the resolution of the fear of abandonment, which has inhib-ited empowerment of the self. The fear-of-loss that my client experi-enced, however covertly, in interpersonal situations kept her truest self from emerging with her parents, her husband, and her boss. "If I express myself as I am (especially anger and acting powerfully), then I will be left" was her guiding self-principle.

Of course, the same principle emerged in her interactions with me, and if not positively resolved, may result in a positive transference

---

12. Previously she talked as if she was angry with her father, not experiencing her truest feelings. Experiencing those feelings of anger meant she would have to face "los-ing" her father and perhaps even her mother, a possibility intolerable to her in the ab-sence of a PAR-figure to quell her fears of abandonment.

cure, where the client must hold onto the therapist wholly and fully, either in actuality or psychologically, to maintain the gains of therapy. Ideally, we want the client to go through a process of introjecting real, good, and helpful inputs while rejectiing the others.

Still, a client's ability to be powerful with their therapist is *secondary* to being powerful with others. Many therapists commit the error of prematurely applauding a client's attempts at empowerment vis-à-vis them. Except in situations where there has been a true error, this kind of intervention will tend to diminish the potential impact of the therapist. Therefore, we tend to discourage the client from acting powerfully with us too early in treatment, because the client's early attempts at empowerment are generally resistance to growth maneuvers, an act of "killing the messenger," the holder of positive but frightful wishes. The client must first form an attachment and dependency before a breaking of that attachment and dependency can take on any meaning or import; one does not fear losing something they never had. Resolution of the fear of abandonment must occur first with parental objects, both historical and contemporary, and secondarily with reparental objects. If the reverse occurs, growth will be incomplete.

intimacy triggers and the real relationship

Besides therapeutic postures that trigger fears associated with power, there are a set of therapeutic postures that can trigger fears associated with intimacy. This cluster of operations includes therapist's expressions of nurturance, emotional closeness, congruency, and warmth. As the clinician engages in these operations, fears of engulfment tend to rise to the surface except for clients with more severe borderline (BB) traits.[13] The therapist cannot easily avoid such an occurrence since reducing such decreased expressions in ways that do not trigger fears of engulfment may trigger fears of abandonment in the already attached client, or be nonpenetrating in the not-yet-attached client. If our therapeutic aim is to create a strong attachment and penetrate the emotional space of the client, engaging in operations that potentially trigger negative historic

---

13. With the classically borderline BB-clients, it is virtually impossible for the therapist to be conceived of by the client as too nurturing or too intimate. In other words, there is no negative transference in that direction. These clients will react negatively to perceived withdrawal of these kinds of inputs, however. With those clients, the more conventional therapeutic role (i.e., neutral-like) will be healing as it provides a safe frame for them to confront their need for separateness.

events associated with closeness and intimacy is virtually unavoidable. Moreover, if we are attempting to communicate love to the client, the expression of warm and genuine feelings is highly indicated.

The specific cluster of behaviors that may trigger such negative reactions include increasing physical proximity and contact with the client, contact between sessions and outside the consulting room, and therapist self-disclosure. These are all operations that stretch the boundaries of traditional psychotherapy. While the boundaries of therapy need not be stretched with every client, they must be transcended with every client. Humanistic therapists have spoken eloquently of the I-Thou relationship where there is a merging of two real selves.

This may occur quite naturally in psychotherapy if the therapist adopts the nonjudgmental, accepting attitude that Rogers and others have spoken of. The problem though, is that many clients reject, or simply do not respond to, such a posture because of their prior relational experience. By the internal phase, a Rogerian posture is quite appropriate, healing, and helpful to virtually all clients. If the boundaries of therapy cannot be transcended naturally, then the therapist must engage in operations that communicate love, commitment, and genuine interest in other ways.

Although clients come to therapy searching for this missing input, albeit covertly and unconsciously, acts of genuine interest, commitment, and love by the therapist are often dismissed. We often hear phrases like: "I pay you to care about me," "You only care because I pay you," and "Of course you care, that's your job. You're my therapist."

This rejection of loving inputs and a real relationship may be understood from the perspective of negative object-expectancy or transference. The love the client is experiencing is incongruent with their internal view of self, unfamiliar and unknown, and therefore suspect and quickly rejected. The old comedic line, "I wouldn't want to belong to any club that would have me as a member" is relevant here.

Only new experience can change such introjects and their concomitant relational patterns. We can provide such new experience by stretching the boundaries of therapy and pushing past the defensive structure of the client. We need to help the client experience, "S/he wouldn't have done this if s/he didn't really care about me." Simply remaining within the traditional frame of psychotherapy is often inadequate to provide such corrective experience. While I have a host of verbal responses to clients who are certain I could not possibly care about them or that I only care because that is my role or because I get paid to, these verbalizations do nothing to produce actual change.[14] The practitioner needs to *do* or display something different.

I was once working with a man who felt very empty at the loss of his father's love. His father, an alcoholic, rarely initiated contact with my client and never claimed him as his son or as a man. My attempts to get closer to Jeff were typically rejected, not overtly, but by his being skittish and somewhat distancing. Over the course of six months in therapy, Jeff became teary at a couple points specifically around his unmet needs for physical closeness with his father. Whenever I attempted to bridge the physical distance, however, between us, he would emotionally recoil. Physically, he remained stiff and apparently frightened.

Since we both had an interest in basketball, I began to joke with him (to warm him up to the idea) about how "I'd have to get him on the court." I soon bridged the joke into a reality and talked with Jeff about our playing ball together. He was somewhat dismissive at first, but he could not completely contain his eagerness. We made plans to meet at a local athletic club I belonged to. The actual experience, while fun for both of us, was fairly uneventful. Jeff was somewhat looser than usual and there was a father-son-like physical closeness experienced, that Jeff later reported felt very good to him.

However, the basketball experience represented a turning point for our relationship. Following the event, Jeff was more open and communicative with me. While the event itself was not significant, my *willingness* to engage in the event was. I made the relational stretch that his father could not. I was willing to give up a Sunday afternoon. I was inviting Jeff into my world. I took a risk for him and that is what mattered. It felt healing and loving, and was a corrective experience. As the therapy was approaching its end, Jeff reported to me that that Saturday was indeed the turning point in his treatment. Most heartening was Jeff's comment:

> I grew up watching shows like *Leave It to Beaver* . . . wondering why my family wasn't more like that . . . knowing that it could be different when I am a father. I always thought, "Shit, when I'm a father, my son and I

---

14. A good example of such a therapeutic response might be "You can pay for my time and expertise but you cannot pay me to care." Clients pay for the frame of therapy. What goes into the frame is determined by the therapist's intention.

are going to do things together." So I've had this picture in my head of what it could be like. I've always had that picture in my head. But now (after therapy) I can feel it (*smiles*) . . . It's weird, you know, now I know I can do it, I can be the father I want to be (because) now I know what it feels like. It's in my heart, too, now.

Jeff was talking about the limitations of insight and the value of the corrective transactional experience. Interestingly, and not surprisingly, this corrective experience gave Jeff a new perspective on his father.

You know what else is strange? I realized just the other night I just thought about this—that I would've been just like my father with my kid. I didn't have a clue, really. I'm sure I would've tried to be different but I would've been like those dads who try to be different, try to be like Ward Cleaver or something, and get pissed off at their kid for not being cute like Beaver. And I realized my father was raised by . . . I mean his father was a bastard, really cruel. Shit, he was physically abused. I always knew that. In fact, that's what I always used to say when you'd try to get me to be angry with my Dad . . . He didn't have it easy; it wasn't his fault . . . blah . . . blah . . . blah. . .

Now I get it. I'm sure he did what he could do. I'm not excusing him. I mean there were a lot of things he didn't do (right). But he didn't really *know*. I thought I knew (before) but I guess what I'm saying is I know what it was like to be him. I was him . . . I don't have to be like him anymore. Now I can be different. Now I have choices. He's still in me, I know that, boy, do I know that. But I have the power to do things differently. I can make choices. Like just the other night with Jennifer [his new girlfriend]. She was talking to me about something that happened at work and I was spacing out and she just kind of gave me this look like, "are you listening to me?" And I realized, I am my fucking father. That's exactly what my father did with my mother all the time. Just spaced out, entirely. And I knew at that moment I have a choice. I can be different. I can listen to (Jennifer). It sounds

funny, but I didn't know I could listen. I didn't. It's nice
coming out of a trance, except it happens everyday now .
. . Oh, I'm here, okay.

We see the synergy of growth in the external phase that comes
about as Jeff internalizes a new healthier introject to replace the old
unhealthy introject. The heart of this transformation is provided by the
corrective transactional experience. Interestingly, the *information* may
remain the same: that is, he always knew his father's approach to relating
was inadequate and that he wanted to do things differently, and even
that his father was limited by his own negative experiences growing up.

What changed was Jeff's *perspective* on the information as he got
in touch with his true self after being penetrated by me. He could now
express his anger at his father without guilt. He could now forgive his
father without feeling as though he was shortchanging himself. He was
now free to make other choices in the progressive transactions of his
adult life: independence, marriage, and child-rearing.

Moreover, he was now also free to express his true self with me.
Two weeks after the session from which the above transcript was culled,
Jeff came to session angry. He had called me during the week and I had
failed to return his call. I had apparently forgotten.[15] I apologized but
treated it lightly. Jeff remained angry and brought up several other occasions in the past when he felt I had been uncaring (e.g., not remembering his birthday). I explained that, yes, that was true; there are times
when I behave in ways that are uncaring. While I did not offer an explanation as such, I validated his perception of me as sometimes acting as
an unloving person. I did say, "I'm far from perfect; I'm not Ward
Cleaver." Jeff laughed but remained steadfast: "Well, you should work
on that." I agreed but said, "You know, we *are* different."

Jeff looked a bit perplexed but this began a process of individuation from me whereby he could discard his positive projection onto
me and view me as a real person, and not an idealized parent figure. By
doing this, he could claim the parts of me that are useful (i.e., the commitment and love that I showed by taking him out to play basketball)
and reject the useless, extraneous, and superfluous aspects (the person
that forgets his birthday). The true Jeff is not like the "true" me—*he*
would never forget a birthday. Let us not forget, though, that these

---

15. Although I did "forget" to return his call sometimes events like this are unconsciously organized.

transformations in Jeff came about because of the work he did in the external phase.

Below is a compilation of work in each of the four major transactions:

FAMILY-OF-ORIGIN

Goal/Progressive Task	Relational Stance	Technique
To get in touch with feelings about growing-up experience	Disciplined client when he would make excuses for his parents	Letter-writing, journaling Gestalt empty chair Bataka bats
To express more of his true self (rather than family-of-origin role-self) in contemporary interactions.	Disciplined him when he would revert to weak, childlike self with family	Coaching Role playing Behavioral rehearsal

COUPLING

Goal/Progressive Task	Relational Stance	Technique
Date women appropriately	Confronted him when he would get precipitously involved with a woman he was not sure about making a commitment to; also confronted him when he avoided dating and social situations	Place personal ads Coaching Social-phobia desensitization techniques Program of three
Be more of true self in committed relationship Express feelings	Confronted him when he avoided confrontation by distancing	Role playing Coaching Brief communication-oriented couples therapy

INDEPENDENT

Goal/Progressive Task	Relational Stance	Technique
Commit self more to goal of completing Law School	Confronted him when he avoided opportunities because of relational fears or his own ceiling barriers as to what was possible	envisioning mentoring programming encouragement

REARING

Goal/Progressive Task	Relational Stance	Technique
Encouraged him to become a Big Brother or an athletic coach for youth.	Confronted him when he avoided pursuing this for several months.	None

The progressive tasks were achieved, as one can see, through pushing, prodding, encouragement, and confrontation; I also did a great deal of coaching. The particular approach, relational posture, or set of techniques is not of significance here, however. My approach with another client might be entirely different. What is significant is that the progressive tasks are designed so that the client achieves mastery and attains increased levels of maturity. By approaching, engaging, and completing the tasks set forth, Jeff incrementally became more mature, committed, loving, and oriented toward growth. The tasks I have laid out here are not unusual; they could have been a part of another therapist's treatment plan. Many of the techniques I employed are standard ones that other schools of therapy have established. I utilized a lot of Bowen's family-systems work for the family-of-origin arena. I utilized cognitive/behavioral ideas, i.e., role playing, systematic desensitization, behavioral rehearsal, self-talk, and thought stopping. I interspersed Gestalt and experiential techniques throughout the treatment. The possibilities for technical variation in this kind of therapy are infinite, and not specific to this model.

What *is* unique about the model is the therapist's role as a motivator to engage in this work. Jeff would not have engaged in this work without my taking on such an active (directive) role and my being more committed to his growth than he was when he first entered treatment.

other aspects of the real relationship

But what does it mean for the therapist who is accepted as a reparental agent to be real, good, and helpful? By real, we mean that the therapist is an authentic person, that they engage in operations that are rooted in how s/he truly feels about the client, i.e., not playing a role. We are especially avoiding the traditionally conceived role of the therapist as neutral, objective, clinical, and highly bounded. These are not negative therapeutic qualities except for a small minority of clients who might benefit from them. It is simply that the vast majority of clients only require enactment of this traditional role in small doses at specific times. Otherwise, the role may be acceptable but not effective healing in and of itself. Lazarus (1993) has called the adoption of therapeutic realness being an "authentic chameleon." In other words, the therapist acts as a real person, but the kind of real person the specific client before them needs.

By good, we mean that the values of the clinician are utilitarian and in the interest of the client's growth, as outlined in Chapter 7. By helpful we mean that the therapist is knowledgeable, wise, and skilled enough to assist the client in all areas of growth and in dealing with psychopathological barriers. The therapist must be able to call on a multitude of resources outside of his or her areas of expertise that might be helpful to the client. As explained earlier, the appropriate time for referring clients to these resources is usually in the late external or internal phases of growth.

Above all, we need to add specificity to our understanding of the real relationship. In most conceptualizations, the real relationship is described with words not unlike those I have used here: "helpful," "good," "wise," etc. How this translates into clinical practice is a more pertinent but complex question. Very few will disagree with the generic benefits of therapeutic "wisdom" for instance (see Hanna and Ottens, 1995 for a cogent review of the role of wisdom in psychotherapy). In our model, the translation of the real relationship into clinical practice involves specific mechanisms. I hesitate to call them interventions, since that would imply some sort of technique, which is antithetical to our notion of the real relationship. There is, however, a set of mechanisms designed to communicate love, commitment, and caring within the confines of the therapeutic relationship. As stated previously, these mechanisms are "edgy" and tend to stretch and transcend traditional therapeutic boundaries. To illustrate this complexity, the following is a transcript of the fifth session of Jeff's therapy, which occurred after we discussed family-of-origin issues in session and was followed by a cancellation due to a "scheduling difficulty."

JEFF: So I was thinking this would be my last session for a while.
THERAPIST: Huh?
JEFF: Well, I'm feeling better about things. So I'm figuring I'd go it alone for a while . . . I've got a lot to think about.

THERAPIST: You've been thinking your whole life. And I've got news for you—it hasn't gotten you anywhere.

JEFF: (*Surprised*) Maybe.

THERAPIST: Not maybe. Definitely. Look, you're free to go, but I have to tell you I think it's a bad move. And I think you're doing it because you're scared; there's a bunch of shit you don't want to look at or deal with. And furthermore—and I don't know how you're going to take this—I think you're wimping out.

JEFF: What do you mean, wimping out?

THERAPIST: I just think you're letting fear run you. And that's wimping out. And I expected more from you. I didn't think you'd wimp out like this.

JEFF: I'm not saying I'm not gonna deal with any of this stuff . . . It's just not here. I talked to my mother, my sister over the holidays . . . I don't think I'm wimping out. Plus this is expensive, man. I told you when I started I wasn't sure I could afford this.

THERAPIST: This is all bullshit, Jeff. If this was about money, you'd come to me, you'd come to me and say, "Rick, I want to contin- ue my therapy but money is a problem, is there anything we could do? I really want to continue." But you didn't. You're not coming to me like that; instead you're just bailing out . . . on yourself.

JEFF: What do you mean?

THERAPIST: I mean, you're not gonna work on this "on your own." You're gonna do what you always do—avoid, procrastinate—all those things you told me you do in the first session: "Rick, I need help with procrastination. I don't follow through on anything . . ." You're doing the same thing now! And that's fucked up. Is that the kind of person you want to be?

JEFF: No.

THERAPIST: Well, stop kidding yourself. This stuff is hard, really hard, and it's gonna take a lot of work, but most of all commit- ment, to fix (it) . . . to get things right.

JEFF: A lot?

THERAPIST: Yeah, a lot.

JEFF: Of time?

THERAPIST: Fuck time. For five sessions that's all you've been talking about: "how long, how much money is this gonna cost me— when?" I don't know! That's not the point. The point is what's your commitment to this, to yourself, to changing, to be different, to being the kind of person you told me you wanted to be more like.

JEFF: I am committed to that.

THERAPIST: Then show it. Then prove it.

JEFF: How?

THERAPIST: By saying to me, and meaning it, "Rick, I'll do whatever it takes to make these changes."

JEFF: I am willing to do whatever it takes.

THERAPIST: Then show it.

JEFF: (*Silent*).

THERAPIST: Jeff, you in there?

JEFF: (More silence) Okay, I guess I didn't realize what it takes exactly.

THERAPIST: I know you don't. That's fine. That's why you're here. I know. I know. And when you don't know something, ask—don't assume.

JEFF: (*Relaxes*) Okay.

Here we see therapeutic penetration occur via confrontation, but it may also happen through nurturance or supportive postures. The specific relational posture is important in penetration, but once the client is penetrated, it is the real relationship that makes the most difference. What Jeff felt was that he was cared about, specifically, cared about enough for his therapist to show how invested he is in Jeff's progress and development as a person. Jeff realized I was going to the edge, perhaps a dangerous one in that we could easily see him reacting negatively to my input. Readers of this transcript identified with Jeff may also have internally responded in some negative fashion: "Who do you think you are, telling me what's best for me?" for example, or even, "Stop cursing at me." This is, of course, a reaction which in this model may represent a therapeutic error or negative transference. But Jeff did not react this way; in fact, he experienced the input as both loving and necessary at the time. One person's negative transference is another person's loving real input. With another client, I might never utter an expletive in their presence, let alone direct it at them, as they might experience that as abusive. I am arguing for the therapeutic flexibility to engage in either operation.

The question for therapists, I believe, becomes a simple one: at what point do I show love, caring, and commitment to this client? This is the essence of the real relationship. I have said anything from "I love you" to "Fuck you" to clients, depending upon circumstance and appropriateness. Both are edgy, of course, and require instantaneous monitoring of the client's reaction, positive or negative. If timed properly with a client who is penetrated by the therapist, such real displays of love are accepted with relative ease, and such input feels empathic, congruent, and "right" to the client.

the importance of distinguishing between the real relationship and the transference relationship

We must remember that as therapists, we're often trained and acculturated to be more aloof, professional, and clinical. Clients are not, unless they've had prior therapy experiences. Therapists, on the other hand, may be more troubled. I've had several therapeutic situations where clients say "I love you" and "Fuck you" to me in an attempt to get me to be more real with them. I repeat, though, there are situations where a client's saying "I love you" or "Fuck you" to their therapist has no meaning with regards to the real relationship, but rather represents positive or negative transference. Therefore, the therapist must handle the situation differently. To say "I love you" in response to such a client, for example, would unnecessarily fuel a positive transference and enact their inappropriate positive projection. This could be harmful, since it would *inhibit* the real relationship from developing. A real relationship is predicated on the merging of two separate beings, not the fusing of two part-objects. If the client's narcissistic wishes are fueled by the therapist, the real self will not emerge.

Whether the client is attempting to narcissistically fuse with the therapist or expressing their true self must be largely determined with the intuition of the clinician: "Does this *feel* real to me?" This is possible, of course, only for a mature, individuated, and real practitioner. The therapist will not be able to accurately read or relay true expressions of love unless s/he has attained a certain degree of health or growth through relationships, whether parental, spousal, child, or therapeutic. Since most therapists are indeed wounded healers, a great deal of personal, couples, or family therapy is a necessary requirement. The therapy may be of any orientation, but must be based on the importance of real connections, and not just detached analysis or intellectual insight. Still, a gut-feeling response is the barometer by which the therapist measures degree of real connection. Although I am dissatisfied with such an oblique measurement, which in and of itself is an inadequate instrument for the scientific or clinical enterprise that psychotherapy is, I know of no better determinant of the real relationship at this time.[16]

The real relationship may be viewed as the crux of any treatment as the internalization of the loving, caring, and committed introject begins to occur. Therapeutic love translates into "I am loveable," "I deserve love," "I am loved," or "Since someone is committed to and invested in me, I am therefore committed to and invested in myself." The client who feels loved becomes a more fulfilled person capable of expressing love to others. Clients will in fact very quickly, even instantly, wish to express this love to others, although   perhaps clumsily at first but with positive intentions. The now-loving client is open to receiving love from others and is more likely to receive love. From a simply behavioral perspective of contingencies, we know that being open and having positive expectations of others, will lead to more positive outcomes. This cycle continues in a kind of positive morphogenesis, becoming the essence of personal and spiritual growth. It is at this point that true commitment to another is possible.

between-session contact

The penetrating real relationship may be expressed in a variety of ways. Between-session contact is helpful for many clients in the external phase of motivation. In the primitive phase, the therapist may use between-session contact as an extroject to fulfill the object-loss of the default-regression process. By the external phase, this process is interfered with enough for the client to engage in the progressive movements needed to effect true change. The client cannot, and generally will not, engage in the PAR-process alone because, as they approach their self-esteem ceiling barriers as to what is possible for them, there will be a tendency to self-sabotage in some particular way. The role of the therapist is to keep the client on track and moving forward to work through recapitulated issues as necessary.

Generally speaking, it is not possible to accomplish this in the once-a-week therapy format, because the regressive pulls and issues emerge frequently outside the treatment hour. This is not even an unconscious manipulation on the client's part, as it may be during the

---

16. Obviously, investigation into the real relationship ultimately becomes spiritual in nature. The construct of "energies" is one such possibility that "New Age" theorists have been exploring. I am, however, unimpressed with the lack of specificity in such constructs.

primitive phase when the client shuts-down emotionally and may express their need for connectedness between sessions in an emergency like phone call. In the external phase, issues may arise in reality that literally cannot wait for the next scheduled session, or an opportunity for growth will be lost. In these cases, it is not only necessary and appropriate, but extremely beneficial, for the therapist to encourage between-session phone calls. Normal therapeutic strictures against excessive between-session contact must here be suspended.

The benefit of between-session contact in the external phase is twofold. First, the client will simply be more likely to engage in the desired behavior. For example, if therapist and client agree that the client should end a destructive love relationship, the client may encounter a PAR-crisis on Saturday evening when the lover calls. If therapist and client are able to speak *then* about the desired behavior, the chances are increased that the client will enact the healthier behavior. We must distinguish between a PAR-crisis and a standard emergency phone call. No therapist would object per se to the need to return emergency phone calls or be available to clients over weekends, although having colleagues accepting such calls is contraindicated in this model. I am discussing situations where the client requires the therapist's assistance, monitoring, and support.

Secondly, introjection of the therapist's love is increased since the boundaries of therapy may be clearly stretched. Many clients correctly experience the therapist's interest and investment in them as false if it is framed *only* within the treatment hour. Encouraging between-session contact is a stretching and transcendence of therapeutic boundaries which may be experienced as corrective and healing.

However, this does not apply to the negative occurrences typical of the borderline (BB) type. It is not unusual for a client to express a sentiment familiar in destructive love relationships: "If you loved me you would . . . (want to have contact with me outside the hour)." This client's wish will never be satiated no matter what the therapist's behavior and no matter how many boundaries are stretched. This is so because it is based on a primary distortion, the belief that the therapist actually does not care about him or her and needs to prove that s/he does want the client to feel loveable. However, this distortion is unaffected by proofs of caring because they will always be interpreted through the same distorted lens. This negative transference reaction can only be corrected by the therapist's confrontation of the distortion and/or steadfast refusal to act on the client's skewed reality by trying to prove his or her caring. Such dynamics are typical of the primitive phase.

In the external phase, the client's need for extra-session help is genuine. Most clients are actually quite reticent to call the therapist, largely out of a fear of rejection. This goes against the myth of the over-needy and insatiable therapy client and the practitioner who must respond by setting firm boundaries. The client's reticence to call must be challenged by the therapist. I convey to clients that to call is the norm and treat it matter-of-factly. In the external phase, I might say, "Of course, you should call when you're in a jam or unsure about how to handle an important situation. How else are we going to accomplish what we're try-ing to do? Your life doesn't suspend itself when you leave this office. Things come up and it is important that our work continue throughout the week."

We should recognize that if the client does not call the therapist to discuss a key situation or in the midst of a PAR-crisis, then there will be a strong tendency to seek out an alternative rapprochement figure. This figure may be their presumably unhelpful familial introject or more likely, a contemporary representative of that introject. Since PAR-growth involves a fear-of-loss which is frightening to most people, contemporary rapprochement figures will tend to discourage progres-sive movements that lead the person toward potential abandonment. Generally, these negative rapprochement figures will either subtly encourage a pulling back from the progressive movement or overtly dis-courage that forward movement.

I recently was working with a client (Jennifer) on family-of-ori-gin issues, encouraging her to express her anger with her often abusive and dismissive father. In a phone call where her father called her stupid and questioned her ability to make a decision about a job, Jennifer, fol-lowing the role-plays we had done and her own intuitive reaction, told her father to apologize. When he didn't, she hung up on him. Jennifer got particularly anxious when her sister called and told her she was being "too sensitive" and she should do what everyone else in the fam-ily does with her father, simply ignore such comments. My client was not sure how to handle the situation. She felt she was taking an impor-tant stand but then began to question herself ("Maybe I *am* being too sensitive") despite her familiar experience of upset.

She discussed the situation with a friend who seemed very rea-sonable in her advice: "Why don't you call your father and tell him how you feel, and that you don't want things to continue like this?" her friend offered. Negative rapprochement figures tend to find apparently rational compromises that may temporarily resolve the situation, but by extinguishing the fear-of-loss possibilities, they also extinguish opportunities for growth. Because of the father's history of abusiveness, the phone call would be interpreted by him as conciliatory and not at all powerful. Anything short of a temporary cut-off would be disempowering for the client. Moreover, she had had similar conversations with her father previously, to no avail. She would report feeling compromised and ill at ease after such conversations since it was she who had opened her heart and become vulnerable, while her father remained defensive and unwilling to take any responsibility for the problem.

My client followed her friend's advice, and it resulted in just such an interaction. The conflict blew over quickly, but three weeks later, her father similarly criticized her again and hung up on her after she challenged him. This time my client called me and we discussed how and why it was important for her to just let it be and not call him back. Of course, this served to escalate the crisis since the holidays were approaching and she was expected to go home no matter what the status of her relationship with her father. She made it clear to other members of the family that she would not be going home for the holidays unless this was worked out with her father and that she expected him to make the first move.

In a subsequent phone call, she told me she was going to give in and go home because it would not be fair to the rest of her family. I confronted her strongly about how important it was for her to stand up for herself. "But I want to go home myself and see the rest of my family," Jennifer protested. "That's bullshit, Jen. You're just scared of the implications of all this. Of course, you want to see everyone, but that's not the real issue here. The real issue is that you've taken a stand and now everyone's freaking out—and now *you're* scared." Because our relationship was solid enough, she accepted the confrontation as real and on target, eventually saying, "I know you're right. I am scared."

"Then let's talk about that," I responded. We went through her biggest fears and fantasies and played out the reality of their occurring. This assuaged her fears of abandonment. Jennifer held her ground and on the day of the family gathering, it became obvious that Jennifer was not going to show up. For the first time in her life, her mother, who had never stood up for any of the daughters against her husband, put pressure on him to call Jennifer and apologize, which he did.

I should point out that this was likely prompted by an intervention several months earlier where I encouraged Jennifer to ask for her mother's support.[17] Jennifer had told her mother how disappointed she always felt when her mother was silent in these conflicts. Her mother argued defensively, "I learned a long time ago, Jennifer, that's between you girls and your father and I'm not getting involved . . ." In some ways, Jennifer was more upset about her mother's abandonment of her than her father's abusiveness, although most of her life she had focused on her father negatively, sparing her mother responsibility. As her relationship with me grew deeper, she could tolerate the potential fear-of-loss of mother by dealing with her negative feelings toward her, as well as with her anger at her father. Her father's apology represented a victorious empowerment for Jennifer. In the next session, Jennifer reported:

> After that phone call, Rick, I knew things would never the same again, I felt so different; it was weird. Like in that moment I knew, I knew that I wasn't gonna take shit from anybody. Not just my father—anybody. Like I've stopped being afraid. . .

Jennifer was resolving her fear of abandonment, resulting in her empowerment. She individuated from the introject, "To maintain proximity with (loved) objects you have to take a certain degree of abuse and dismissal." Her real self emerged:

> I can be myself without worrying what he's gonna say, how she's gonna react. When I went home that night I felt like a different person, only it was me. It's the me I am with people who I know care about me, like Sara and Eddie. I can just say whatever and it's okay.

It is important to note that Jennifer's actions altered the family system, as change in one part of the system necessarily alters others. However, this is not always the case. Sometimes the family reconstitutes and scapegoats the part of the system that is disrupting homeostasis. Jennifer could have actually been cut off from the family. I refer to *her* being cut off by them rather than vice-versa, because an individuated, health-seeking Jennifer has no real choice herself. To grow (that is, to become her empowered real self) and remain a part of the

---

17. This is a good illustration of how seemingly dramatic and transformative change in therapy is the result of incremental movements that build upon each other.

system requires her to take a stand. Her father essentially responded, "No, Jennifer, you cannot be that real and empowered with me." This is unacceptable and therefore not a true choice for Jennifer.

If Jennifer is cut off in some way, her abandonment fears are realized. This result is not significantly different from the positive outcome that actually resulted.[18] Empowerment and the emergence of the real self, no matter what the real-life consequences, are the goals of this work, not change in the family system. The latter is outside of Jennifer's control. She can only control her own behavior. Withstanding the possibility of being rejected and abandoned is sufficient for fueling individuation, empowerment, and emergence of the real self.

Another form of between-session contact involves client check-ins to the therapist during the week. If therapist and client are working together on a particular goal or project, the therapist may request or strongly encourage (depending upon appropriate relational posture) that the client call-in on a daily basis, say, to chart progress.

For example, I was working with a client (Mary) who voiced a desire to detach from an abusive love relationship. It is critical to note that Mary presented as ambivalent: verbally indicating that she wanted to end the relationship but behaviorally remaining firmly entrenched in it. I chose to not see Mary's relationship with Ken as ambivalence; rather, she wanted something different but had difficulty separating from what was familiar, commensurate with her low self-esteem. If we were interested in labeling her problem (which I am not), we would say she was in an addictive relationship. I make this point about ambivalence because the role of the therapist in our model is to enact the client's healthy wish. What was healthy, in this case, was Mary's verbalizations. In a similar vein, if working with a couple, I tend to affirm, although strategic considerations might dictate otherwise, the partner voicing the healthier point of view. This "health" is admittedly subjective and therapeutically constructed.

Thus, I did not spend time working with Mary to figure out what she *really* wanted. I assumed she wanted out of the relationship and helped her do this.[19] If we explored the issue, I'm certain we would

18. Further positive gains came from several family-of-origin sessions with Jennifer and her parents.

19. If it had been clear to me that Mary and Ken had the characteristics of a couple, like a home together, financial entanglements, a longer history, and children, I would handle the case differently by inviting Ken to be a part of the therapy. This dyad had none of these characteristics. Moreover, Ken expressed no interest in couples therapy at several points when Mary had suggested it.

have gotten nowhere since Mary was incapable of discovering the wishes of her real self without individuating from Ken (i.e., exiting the primitive phase, however temporarily).

As therapy progressed, Mary became more frustrated. She would leave a session clearer than ever that Ken was abusive and withdrawn, just like her father, and that she wanted to set firm limits with him. However, setting these limits meant enacting the fear-of-loss, since Ken would nonverbally (and at times, verbally) give her the message, "If you don't like it, leave." Mary was controlled by her fear of abandonment. Whenever she'd sense Ken pulling away, she would reengage despite the fact that Ken did not respect her demands.

After an enlightening session, Mary would stay strong for anywhere from one hour to one day, perhaps two, but ultimately she would emotionally collapse and give in to Ken. At several points, she contemplated ending therapy because as she said, "I'm getting nowhere. I'm no better off than when I came in." Whenever she voiced this concern, I'd agree with her. Sometimes the therapist prefers to challenge such protestations by pointing out increasing levels of insight and the like. I generally do not, since on the level that matters most, their behavior, the client is right, nothing has changed. Growth does not occur until behavior changes. Insight only serves to solidify behavioral changes.

I realized that Mary was like many clients, unable to sustain the loving introject "I do deserve better than this" no matter how successfully I penetrated her during the therapy hour. I also realized that like many clients, Mary was likely to drop out of treatment before the new introject could solidify, because of her frustration. Thus, after a particularly good session, I told Mary that I was afraid she would not be able to hold onto what we talked about. She readily agreed since by this point she herself was well aware of her internal process. I told Mary that to keep the work and the session alive I wanted her to call my answering machine every day after dinner and report on how she doing with what we were working on. If she was having trouble keeping her focus, she was to say so, and we would touch base later that night. Mary agreed. The call-ins would ensure that May had to seriously consider the loving introject and the therapeutic goal at least once daily. Again, we see the dual purpose of behavioral compliance and introject-solidification.

Of course, Mary complied, and for two days, quite strongly. As soon as she weakened her position with Ken, she would stop the check-ins. When I confronted her in the next session, Mary said she felt silly calling in. After further challenge, Mary admitted that she was too embarrassed to admit she had been so weak with Ken. I told Mary that she had broken an important agreement. The purpose of the call-in was not to be "good" or be "perfect" but to report difficulties and request help if necessary. It was to be a tool for her.

After similar interactions over a period of two weeks, Mary began complying regularly, using the call-ins to help her maintain focus. She became very interested in the process of using the tool to her advantage. Within a couple months, she had weaned herself from Ken and begun dating other men who treated her with more respect and interest. As it turned out, she got to appreciate calling-in and used it to give updates on other treatment goals like dating more appropriately, family-of-origin issues, and work-related concerns. On one particular Friday I had not heard from Mary, so I called her, leaving a message wondering what had happened to her. She called back later to say how much it meant to her that I had remembered and cared enough about her to call. Such an experience is both edgy and corrective.

I have utilized call-ins for a multitude of therapeutic goals. Addictive behaviors are difficult to monitor in weekly outpatient psychotherapy so call-ins are an important tool. Procrastination on career issues is another problem (e.g. completing a job resume).

Another example of utilizing call-ins to monitor client functioning is when a client is having difficulty structuring themselves to reach progressive goals. For a client to develop self-discipline, they must have the experience of being disciplined by the therapist, so they can internalize these key elements. Rarely is once-a-week psychotherapy, even with therapeutic tasks and homework assignments, sufficient. The therapist may require the client to call in between sessions to report progress or to discuss these issues directly.

The important factor is that the client must be in the external phase of PAR-readiness to benefit from call-ins. If the client is not sufficiently motivated, utilizing this intervention conveys the message that the therapist is expecting behavioral change. This will tend to lead to disappointment and premature termination

In the next chapter, we will more fully explore the issues of positive and negative terminations in the context of motivational phase of treatment. Figure 6 broadly summarizes our motivational phases correlated with therapy relationship prescriptions.

FIGURE 7: MOTIVATIONAL DEVELOPMENT AND THERAPY-RELATIONSHIP CORRELATES

	Therapy Relationship Posture	Therapist Values Posture	Therapist Progressive/ Regression Posture	Client Regression/ Progression	Adjunctive Treatments
Primitive	Bonding phase of treatment. Need for therapeutic penetration, to get "in there" with client. Intensive relationship the goal. Stepping into the reparental role and the development of positive transference exclusively the goal. Therapist may be seen as god-like. Passive reparental agent.	Unconditional positive regard, accurate empathy via a carefully constructed and formulated therapist posture adapted for each client. Therapist's values or goals are less important. Client's introjected values take precedence. Therapist is inspirational, hopeful, and powerful. Therapy is therapist-centered.	Regressive posture. Client is in regressed position. Client is not expected to progress behaviorially. Emphasis is on allowing and encouraging the client to connect deeply with the practitioner.	Client may exist in a default regression. Client tends to act out default regression and fear-of-loss through addictions to substances and dysfunctional relationships. Client is regressed often in the absence of an obvious "P" or progressive expectation.	12-step programs to control acting out and stabilization; hospitalization a last resort. More intensive therapeutic interventions (e.g., requiring client to call- in to therapist daily) to keep connection present. Guiding therapeutic philosophy: whatever it takes to maintain therapist-client connection.
External	Active re-parental agent as therapist is accepted "new" parent figure. Therapist is much more active and directive, using a wide variety of technical interventions. Some negative transference may develop, but this is now seen as positive, as client is bonded sufficiently to stay and work it through. The "guts" phase of therapy.	Therapist's values take precedence over client's. Therapist "pushes" the healthier inputs and viewpoints via confrontation and direct guidance. At times client is open and appreciative; at other times, hostile. Values-central therapy. Client introjects therapist values.	A PAR-relational posture. Therapist pushes progressive movements forward into new areas of growth. Client may resist as old ways and programs from the family-of-origin reemerge. Therapist serves as rapprochement figure to process old fears and feelings while guiding client through the un-known territory.	Client has PAR-regressions which may include very strong bouts of anxiety and depression and/or negative transference reactions. If the clinician is not tuned into the "R" reactions, a default regression may set in. Lots of in-between session phone contact may be necessary to work through these reactions, which are the heart of this work, i.e., corrective transactional experiences occurring around the edges of the therapy frame.	Avoid adjunctive treatments at all costs because this is how "therapeutic others" tend to inappropriately react to PAR-regressions. The client may engage these others in a triangular activity out of negative transference which has no possibility for being worked through. Emphasis is on containment within the therapy frame.

FIGURE 7: MOTIVATIONAL DEVELOPMENT AND THERAPY-RELATIONSHIP CORRELATES

	Therapy Relationship Posture	Therapist Values Posture	Therapist Progressive/ Regression Posture	Client Regression/ Progression	Adjunctive Treatments
Internal	More distant therapeutic relationship. Final working through of negative transference. Beyond a certain point if there is more negativity, there is no working through it; therapist just accepts it. Therapist is more reflective and active listener. End Phase of Treatment.	Client's values reemerge as central. Emphasis is on individuation, the differences between the therapist and the client. Client-centered therapy.	No client regression at all encouraged. Therapist regresses more; i.e., is more self-disclosing, talks about his or her negative attributes, becomes a more fully real person.	Defined by the absence of default regressions. Some PAR-regressions still occur but they tend to be brief, albeit intense. There are mechanisms in place to deal with PAR-regressions. Client moves from "What would my therapist say/do in this situation," to becoming their own rapprochement figure (or organizing spouse into that position when necessary).	Other mentors encouraged. Spouse is organized to fill in any left-over gaps or deficiencies to handle particular knotty problem spots.
Spiritual	Post-treatment. Therapist may, but tends not to, serve client in a consultant role. If needed, at this point, therapist is superfluous to client.	Not Applicable.	Not Applicable.	No regression at all.	No mentors needed. Here the person becomes a mentor to others. Communal orientation.

motivating clients in the endphase of therapy

In the external phase of motivation the therapist empowers the client so that the therapeutic input may be internalized. Ultimately, the client must detach from the therapist which means reclaiming his or her projected positive wishes, goals, and values; in other words, the client's projected healthy aspects. The client who does not accomplish this will remain in a growth-stifling positive-transference relationship with the practitioner and be dependent upon continued proximity and contact with either the real-life or *wholly* introjected therapist. The client who does not claim his or her own authority will continue to see the practitioner in an unnecessarily positive light; the therapist's exalted status will prevent the client from discarding aspects of the therapist or the therapist's communications that are superfluous, redundant, irrelevant, inadequate, or incorrect.

There are dependent clients who will not detach from the therapist without overt or covert permission or encouragement from the therapist, except via an assertion of power predicated on the client's willingness to end the relationship. In the external phase, there is a consistent struggle to remain in psychological proximity to the therapist, who plays a dominant role in the life of the client. The beginning of the external phase is particularly intense. Through successful PAR-experiences, the client's self-esteem improves dramatically, although quite fragilely and tentatively at first, because the client realizes, albeit unconsciously, their increased feeling of well-being is directly proportional to their proximity to the practitioner. "I feel better because of my therapist, because s/he understands me best, is so smart or has the right answers," is the client's internal experience, whether dialogic or not, in the early external phase; the therapist is viewed as all-knowing, all-powerful, and all-healing. The client believes they will not change without the therapist, and this is probably true. The replication of such a powerful connection is unlikely since opportunities for psychological penetration are not frequent. This is not a fantasized attachment in our model, since the therapist clearly owns and enacts the client's bestowed wishes and power. Analysts may consider this an inappropriate acting out of the client's fantasy for fusion with the parental object, but we consider this reenactment the most fertile soil for corrective transactional experiences, the proverbial second chance at being more effectively parented and loved.

Of course, reenactment may end in the very same way as in the original parent-child relationship, the repetition of which we consider a therapeutic rupture. Ruptures that occur in the early external phase are especially problematic as the relationship still has insufficient historical power to bear such ruptures, as there is little real trust based on actual experience with the therapist. We must do all we can to avoid mistakes, the development of negative transference, and a rewounding of the client in this phase.

when termination occurs in the primitive phase

Of course, we also make every attempt to avoid ruptures in the primitive phase. However, ruptures that occur then will tend to result in quiet terminations, because the client is not particularly attached to the therapist, but rather to the negative introjects and extrojects of the family-of-origin. Hence, they will be less affected by mistakes, negative transference, and rewounding since these require a certain degree of vulnerability and trust. We are rarely clear on exactly when the client enters the external phase, so it is sometimes and unfortunately *only* through a therapeutic rupture that it becomes clear the client was more attached to the therapist than the clinician believed. Clients who exit therapy in the primitive phase will generally do so without having introjected the therapist. The relationship is muted and ending therapy is relatively easy, often through a phone call (sometimes not even that) canceling a session or treatment.[1] It is the therapist who may be more upset, since s/he is usually more attached to and invested in the client than vice-versa.

Dealing with such clients rests on the critical assumption that the therapist has not penetrated the primitive client, so s/he should not assume otherwise. The goal is to do everything possible to create the desired attachment. Usually it is too late for this since leaving therapy provides the client with an opportunity to detach from the physical object of the therapist. The hallmark of the primitive phase is out of

---

1. I am struck by the number of clients who come to me with prior psychotherapy experience but who cannot remember the name of the therapist, despite having had anywhere from three months to three years of treatment.

sight, out of mind; physical proximity is as necessary as psychological proximity in the primitive phase.

Here the frame, regular attendance, and rhythm of therapy are critical whereas in the external phase, they are not important factors, particularly in its later stages. A client may retain more from a five-minute telephone consultation than several one-hour sessions in the external phase. The need for therapeutic connection is activated in the post-penetration states of PAR-readiness. In the external phase, a client may "leave" therapy for a period of time, taking with them a whole therapeutic introject to consult. A client who leaves therapy in the primitive phase carries no such introject; they continue to transport their original family-of-origin introject.

To get the prematurely terminating primitive-phase client back into treatment the therapist must attempt to connect with and penetrate the client. The usual therapeutic protocol of calling and requesting the client to attend a termination session is a good one, but only if the therapist is sufficiently powerful enough in that "last" session to penetrate the client. Generally speaking, discussing the client's unresolved issues and the like is inadequate since intellectually convincing the client of the need to remain in treatment does not address the central problem that created the termination, which is that the *therapist* failed to penetrate the client. The primitive-phase client should not be held responsible for inadequately bonding and attaching to the therapist any more than we would blame an infant for not attaching to its caretakers. The natural inclination of the infant and primitively motivated client is to bond and attach if given the needed inputs. So if the therapist succeeds in getting the client to attend a "last" session, the therapist must take responsibility for reaching the client relationally. At that time I may often express quite frankly my personal feelings, as the therapist has little to lose here.

The primitively motivated client may be leaving therapy because of one of two therapeutic mistakes. The client whose manifest fear is engulfment may be backing away from a therapist approaching them too strongly or directly. The client whose manifest fear is abandonment may be backing away from a therapist displaying insufficient care and interest. These are *pre*-dependency mistakes. In the post-attachment or external phase, these foundational fears may easily reverse. For example, the client whose primary fear was engulfment now becomes afraid of being rejected or abandoned by the therapist.

But in the primitive phase the client who manifests fear of engulf-ment must be penetrated indirectly. Therefore, I may choose *not* to respond to the termination call of this client. Sometimes, this complete absence of interaction spurs the client to conjure the therapist sufficient-ly to at least call again, from a more needy position. Depending upon the situation, I may wait to return the call to give the client an experience of absence which may further harden the image of the therapist.

Sometimes one of the life crises that dominate the lives of these clients will intervene in the interim and regenerate the original desire to see the therapist (or some other practitioner). When this occurs I engage in a process of "upping the ante." I may say, in the session and not on the telephone, that I will see them only under certain condi-tions, which translate into increased investment, commitment, and motivation for treatment. Fees that had been negotiated downward may be renegotiated upward. For the client with a manifest fear of engulf-ment, the practitioner pulls away relationally to create attachment.

A temporary foray into needing the practitioner will most assuredly be followed by renewed engulfment fear. If the clinician is clear on this at the outset of therapy, vividly predicting that (and how) this client will lose their motivation, may be powerful enough to pre-vent just this kind of premature termination. The client will likely remember the therapist's warning and be ready to introject the practi-tioner at the appropriate time, if the therapist reinforces the message.

The client who is prematurely terminating because of fear of abandonment requires another strategy, one that is much more direct. The therapist should feel free to call the client and attempt to pene-trate saying, "I want you to come in," or some other strong inviting message. Therapists sometimes shy away from these transactions for fear of badgering the client. However, such attempts at penetration will either go unfelt by the client, who will remain unmoved, or experi-enced as penetrating, however slightly. I've had many clients return to therapy on the basis of one or several phone calls, sometimes over a period of weeks. The therapist must be careful to do this without becoming disempowered and keeping the client's needs primary.

Many clients oscillate between engulfment and abandonment; this requires an admixture of direct and indirect relational strategies. Clients who do terminate in the primitive phase will tend not to con-sider their therapy experience as either negative or positive and hence may later seek out another practitioner with relative ease at some future stress point. The therapist will be *experienced* as ineffectual, even though the terminated client may talk as if the experience was negative or positive. No matter how the client speaks of their experience, if therapy ends here we consider it to be a failure, since the client's motivation remains primitive or predependent.

when termination occurs in the early external phase

In contrast, if there is a rupture in the early external phase, the client will experience the therapist as negative and this will not change with time, as the introject is hardened and set at the imprint-readiness point in treatment. Every attempt must be made to heal therapeutic ruptures that occur here since the client may become generally negative about the possibilities of change and growth. Moreover, the practitioner is at risk for having his or her clinical reputation tarnished by an actively unhappy client. This type of client is in a borderline-like fusion with the therapist which may be highly positive or highly negative but never in-between.

If the client terminates treatment on the basis of this rupture, it is as a result of having been rewounded. We do everything we can to prevent such rewounding, but it is sometimes, unpreventable. First, the rewounding may be inadvertent, or if in any way intended, was so unconscious that the therapist may be unable to identify its origins. Second, the rewounding may occur due to unresolved countertransference the therapist has not acknowledged. Third, the therapist may have committed a genuine but unavoidable error. For example, the therapist may have not returned a telephone call because of illness or a family problem. In all cases, the therapist must be willing to take responsibility for that error, however inadvertent or unavoidable, just as a parent would feel bad upon finding out that their toddler had been crying for five minutes without being heard. The error may have not truly have been the fault of the parent (or therapist), but it is their responsibility to heal the wound. Just as the parent may now decide to check in more often while the toddler is in another room, the therapist may, at this point in the therapy, decide to call this client back promptly, regardless of personal circumstances.

We recognize that the therapist is triggering an historical wound in the client, but it may be virtually impossible for the client who is in the early external phase to adequately comprehend this. Even a bright or therapy-wise client in the early external phase may cognitively understand this, but also be unable to assimilate this knowledge emotionally. The intellectual insight may help the client to remain engaged with the therapist, but this may be only on a very limited basis (e.g., a session or two).

This triggering provides an opportunity to heal the wound with the therapist by offering a corrective transactional experience, taking complete responsibility for the working-through process. It is only later, toward the internal phase of motivation, that we can count on the client's ability and willingness to emotionally understand the rewounding process as a triggering of older wounds that must be worked through in *that* context. In the meantime, this rewounding is experienced as a real contemporary event, and the context for the healing of the rupture must be equally real and contemporary. The historical correlate is not relevant to the client, except perhaps as information.

A parallel to marital rewounding and reparenting may be apparent here. The primary healing for married partners in the early-and mid-phases of treatment must be corrective experiences that do not occur in the context of childhood genesis or its correlates ("I only triggered the wound that was placed by your abusive father"). In most cases, direct reparenting by the therapist rather than spousal reparenting is required, because the occurrence of rewounding is too ubiquitous in such marriages for spousal repair. By the internal phase, however, the client is motivated by the integrity of self to act responsibly. It is easier for the internally motivated client to see the intentions of their partner in a more benign fashion, and hence, see the rewounding in the larger context of family-of-origin genesis correlates.

We believe this occurs because prior corrective transactional experiences tend to create an organic inwardness in the person. This internally motivated person sees ruptures or negative events as their personal responsibility. They may see that some other has a role in the transaction, but they are interested only in their own role. They fully expect the other to take responsibility for his or her own part in the transaction; if not, they may be inclined to disengage from that other. Moreover, prior corrective transactional experiences lead to internalized responsibility-taking because the person has internalized the therapist who has taken 100 percent responsibility which becomes the template for dealing with ruptures and problems. If the therapist takes less than 100 percent responsibility for the rupture, the client could be mimicking their family-of-origin experience and introjecting a re-parental agent who took less than 100 percent responsibility for problems and ruptures. This would be an even more significant reenact-ment of the original rewounding since this enactment also represents the introject of healing and repair.

This suggests that the therapist only take his or her behavior, attitudes, and feelings into account when analyzing the rupture. Subsequent changes should be made on the basis of this analysis. While it is tempting to hold the client at least partially responsible for the event, this will result in the client not trusting the intentions of the therapist. This is because the client is being asked to take responsibili-ty, and relationally progress beyond what reasonably can be expected. The client may be able to play the *role* of responsibility-taker but this is essentially an enactment of what is expected, a pseudomaturity or parentification. I referred to this process when discussing the childhood antecedents of object loss and the default-regression in later childhood and adulthood. The falsely progressed self encases and protects the wounded and regressed real self.

Thus, the regressed real self, submerged prior to therapeutic pen-etration, is now manifest. Of course, this manifestation has gone from largely positive to largely negative. While this may be highly problem-atic, we do not want the regressed or real self of the client to resub-merge, thus requiring subsequent penetration, an unlikely scenario. Woundedness tends to lead to anger which may last anywhere from a minute to 20 years and then retreat. Once back in the familiar, despair-ing confines of the default regression from the early external-phase the client is rather immune to penetration by the same practitioner, and even by others until a new life crisis develops. For A-type clients, whose reactivity to crisis tends to be muted and diffuse, their adapta-tional functioning may be adequate, but opportunities for penetration, and thus transformation, remain low. For B-type clients, the reverse is true, as functioning tends to be more inadequate, but opportunities for penetration and transformative growth remain high.

To reiterate, the goal after a therapeutic rupture in the early external phase is to maintain client regression and recreate the positive connection. The likelihood of this is good, if the therapist implements a model of 100 percent responsibility-taking, but is not easy, since it requires the clinician to withstand and tolerate a good deal of project-ed anger, hate, and disappointment. The practitioner must accept responsibility for the client's anger and hate and disappointment with-out personally enacting it in the form of self- or other-hate (especially client-hate).

We do not want the client to continue viewing the therapist from a such a regressed position. The old analytic dictum of regression in the service of the ego is useful here. We utilize the client's dependency on the therapist as healer, expert, guru, and the like to directly and indirectly encourage progressive movement which stretches the client psychologically, as *a priori* ceiling barriers to growth are broken.

When the client initially enters active PAR-growth, dependency on the practitioner is particularly strong because of the newness of the contemporary experience, and the triggering of positive expectations (transference) in the historical sense. The client's desire to please the therapist must be accepted in the early external phase; expecting the client to engage in difficult progressive tasks to please him or herself is simply not realistic. The independent act of setting a progressive goal and engaging in progressive tasks initiated by self-love, self-esteem, and self-integrity is the hallmark of the *internal* phase.

For example, the adult client may now be more assertive with parents when mistreated. This emanates from having enough sense of self-esteem to realize that maltreatment by another is incongruent with one's belief in being worthy of respect. But we know that this assertiveness will only arise out of a willingness to face the fear of losing the significant (even if only symbolically) other. Surviving this fear-of-loss, even thriving through it, will have the effect of creating self-esteem in the client who lacks it.

The early, external-phase PAR-process requires the therapist to be the caretaker of the client's absented self-lovingness, and takes the form of reparental therapist-client love. The client's continued engagement in the PAR-process is driven by the desire to not lose this projected self-love by disappointing the therapist. As the client achieves the progressive goals, self-esteem builds organically. S/he realizes that it is not the therapist's critical inputs but themself who makes attaining these goals possible. Their environment will tend to support this and provide positive contingencies, particularly if the therapist retains an appropriate back-seat posture when outcomes are positive. If others in the client's life have a stake in his or her remaining weak or ill, they may react, "Is that what your therapist told you to do or say?" when the client begins to enact new self-empowering behavior or attitudes. In the early external phase, of course, this may be precisely the case. The client may be indeed saying or doing what the therapist has recommended, suggested, or role-played. But it is ultimately the client, not the therapist, who must enact the healthy behavior. The therapist may begin to step back from the reparental relational posture, if only subtly and slightly at first, and intense forms of dependency begin to dissipate as telephone calls, check-ins, etc. become less important.

when termination occurs in the mid-external phase

Another form of dependency emerges in the mid-external phase, where the therapist becomes more of a *tool* for achieving progressive goals. The clinician may be an essential hard-to-replace tool, and maintaining proximity may still be an important consideration to the client, but s/he is a tool nonetheless. After the shift from the early to the mid-external phase, the therapist is now seen as dispensable. The early-external-phase client believes a kind of psychological death will occur if they lose contact with the therapist.

The mid-external phase client would be highly upset by the loss but would believe in his or her ability to withstand the loss, to go on psychologically through the process of PAR-growth. There have been enough affirming PAR experiences to produce sufficient self-esteem for the client to seek out another rapprochement figure to complete therapeutic work. Clients who arrive in therapy at this point, either from other therapeutic experiences or from outside-of-therapy growth are usually quite motivated to change. They realize that perhaps they have outgrown prior reparental and rapprochement figures, whether their actual parents, mentors, spouses, or therapists.

Ruptures that occur in the mid-external phase are potentially growth-enhancing as the client is able to take more responsibility for negative projections and hence, behavior and attitudes. The therapist comes to be seen in a less stereotyped and more real light. In the mid-external phase the primary goal is for the relationship not simply to continue, but to continue more productively, with less positive and negative distortion.

The following is an example. Joan had come to therapy seeming depressed and with great difficulties in functioning, maintaining healthy, non-abusive social relationships, individuating from a highly abusive contemporary family-of-origin, and managing (that is, not sabotaging) work-related relationships. Within ten months of treatment, I had managed to penetrate Joan psychologically and keep her out of the default regressions which spurred much of the self-hating negative behavior and depression that had brought her into treatment. Joan successfully engaged in several progressive tasks, like asserting herself in various relationships. Each time she did so, she felt increasingly better about herself, as attested by her now bringing the correct material into therapy. Instead of my having to track the default regression to some rejection in her personal life and pointing this out to her, Joan herself said things, "My mother called me yesterday. I got off the phone feeling like shit and I realized what happened. I didn't say what I needed to say—I swallowed it."

I could see that Joan was becoming less dependent upon me. Previously, she had needed and expected me to decipher what was wrong with her. To the extent that I could do this, I was viewed by her as a kind of savior. At times, she would say to me, mystified, "You know you're right about X . . . How did you know that?," as if I was unearthing the secrets of the universe. To Joan, of course, I was helping her unearth the secrets of *her* universe. At first, this help was somewhat unilateral, but it gradually became a more mutual process. Joan became less dependent and more appreciative of herself; thus I realized that my posture needed to change.

I began to "push the P" more, tentatively at first, but increasing my expectations for growth. The period of dependency for its own sake where the work consists of penetrating and impinging upon the default regression, was largely over. I would now utilize her dependency upon me to service her own growth in co-created progressive areas. One of these areas was procrastination in her work. This procrastination, we determined, was an acting out of her internalized self-hate, a form of self-sabotage to ensure that she did not achieve the success and satisfaction she wanted from her career, but did not believe she deserved.[2]

After a particularly destructive self-sabotaging event where she allowed a critical deadline to pass in her work and her employer put her on probation, at Joan's request I intervened. I decided to place her on a schedule of accomplishing work tasks. Although reticent at first, she agreed to the schedule, and I told her to construct a reasonable work schedule and bring it to the next session. I was very specific about what needed to be included in the schedule: things like dates, contingencies, rewards and punishments, etc. She complied and brought me a copy of her schedule. However, the schedule was incomplete and very rough, and included little of what I had asked for. From her response I discov-

---

2. I point out though that Joan did not *say* these things nor did my saying them provide any kind of direct change. She was behaving *as if* these feelings were true.

ered that she did this quite unconsciously; likely another, albeit more sophisticated, form of self-sabotage.

In contradiction to other therapy models, I did not take this event as an opportunity to explore with Joan "what she really wanted," nor did I concern myself with the idea that I was pushing her in a direction she was not willing to go, at least at this time. Instead, I confronted her.

THERAPIST: (*Looking over the sheet*) This isn't what I asked for . . . Where are the dates? The rewards?

CLIENT: (*starting to cry*): Look, I gave you what you wanted— why can't you just leave it at that. It's never enough. It's never enough. (*Now sobbing uncontrollably*).

I was genuinely surprised by Joan's reaction. I did not expect her to react so negatively to what seemed a mild confrontation. I had unintentionally and inadvertently rewounded her. Had this occurred in the early-external phase, I would have willingly explored my inappropriate and careless confrontation and would have taken complete responsibility for not being attentive enough to realize how difficult this task would be for her. If I took a similar posture with her now, I would only be reinforcing her belief that she could not accept healthily intended confrontation. Her negative reaction was based on the distorted notion that she could *never* fulfill my expectations. The truth was that *this* time she had failed to fulfill my expectations. Nor did I think any less of her because of that, although later she said she assumed I did.

Moreover, this was a reenactment from childhood that was played out consistently enough at work to lead to her being placed on probation. I recalled that she had told me that her boss's expectations were unfulfillable. Previous therapeutic discussions around the reality of that assumption and how that mimicked her childhood experience did little to help her alter her operations. Indeed, her major interpersonal problem was difficulty in dealing with criticism and authority. She would either dismiss it entirely, becoming counterdependent and self-sabotaging, by procrastinating, for example, or would become deflated and exit the situation feeling victimized.

[*Later in the session*]

THERAPIST: What are you thinking?

CLIENT: I'm thinking about leaving. I keep looking at the door, I could just leave . . . I'm wondering why I haven't yet.

THERAPIST: Maybe because you know you need to stay and work this out with me. Just because you're angry doesn't mean you just walk.

CLIENT: Maybe.

THERAPIST: I'm done protecting you, really over-protecting you. You've had too much of that in your life, too, you know. We've talked a lot about how much shit you've taken from people, all the abuse, and it's true. But it's not the only truth. You've also had a bunch of people in your life who say, "Poor Joan." You say, "Poor Joan," and you go in the corner and lick your wounds. I criticized you. Take it for what it is—a simple criticism. And go on from there. And know that I don't think any less of you . . . that I want to help you.

CLIENT: I know you do.

I had said many similar things to Joan by this point. What seemed to stick with her the most was the part about others in her life having overprotected her, seeing her as a victim. At such points in treatment, the therapist may make many statements, not knowing which ones will reach the client. Joan became curious about what I had said, asking me several questions about what I thought of her very supportive circle of friends. Because of their own limitations and fears they had almost never confronted her, particularly if she became upset and cried. This led to a discussion about how even her previous therapists, whom she liked a lot, tended to reinforce the notion of Joan-as-victim.

Joan called later that night to thank me. When I asked her what for, she replied, "For not being scared of confronting me, for realizing I'm not so fragile. I realized today how much I hate that. I'm not that fragile." Joan said she also called to tell me that she was working on a new schedule of tasks. I laughed when I realized that I had almost forgotten the original trigger of the rupture.

Ruptures in the mid-external phase will tend to arise out of "pushing the P," but as we can see, it is the corrective transactional experience that enables the working-through of negative transference distortions ("It's never enough") that disrupt interpersonal relationships and may lead to a default regression. This rupture propelled Joan forward, and I could be more confrontational with less concern that I was triggering a rewounding. In other words, I could be increasingly real, more myself, and less in a role. Specifically, I could abandon the role from our early relationship, that of overprotective and nurturing mother figure.[3] To the extent that I became more real, Joan had the opportunity to see me in a more real, less distorted (either positively or negatively) light. This allows the therapist to move from the exalted status of reparental agent in the early-external phase to the status of highly useful tool in the mid-external phase. It also greatly helps the client separate from the therapist.

It is obviously much easier to let go of a useful tool than a guru. Indeed, it is almost impossible to individuate from someone of such exalted status. But if the therapeutic other is so exalted, it is also because the client is projecting his or her own power onto the therapist. By the same token, however, if the therapist is *never* exalted, power may remain projected elsewhere, onto the family-of-origin, the spousal representation of the family-of-origin, or fundamentalist-like religious or spiritual systems. Such systems do not call for individuation and therefore, the projected power can never be reclaimed.

when termination occurs in the late-external phase

Individuating from a highly useful tool is difficult but manageable. Therapeutic ruptures that end in a negative termination, while not indicative of true individuation, are recoverable if the client continues along the growth process. If the client remains in treatment and PAR-growth can continue through the mid-external phase, the client's self-esteem rises as fears abate and mastery increases proportionately. The therapist's centrality to the client's life fades as the client reaches the late-external phase.

In its place, the self emerges as the central motivating force. While in the mid-external phase, the therapist functions as a useful tool, by the later stages of the external-phase, the therapist begins to become more of a *consultant* to the client. The client needs the therapist less to traverse through progressive movements to achieve PAR-growth.

The therapist is no longer the tool, but has given the client the tool. If the tool is not working properly and is in need of repair, the therapist may offer ideas or suggestions. The client may realize that a tool for handling one particular area of growth may be inappropriate for another, and the therapist can begin to consult with the client on these

---

3. I believe this familiar object was a representation of the only positive figure in Joan's childhood, her paternal grandmother, who was loving but ineffectual in helping her deal with her abusive mother.

matters. This occurs organically because both positive and negative distortions are diminished. The therapist's advice is more clearly heard and discussed, and can be accepted or dismissed, partially or completely. Perhaps not surprisingly, the working alliance is at its strongest here.

It is this relatively distortion- and projection-free dialogue that the client can assert their own needs, desires, and viewpoint and therapeutic interventions may be altered accordingly. The therapist may serve as a kind of mentor, offering advice or suggestions and then getting out of the way. Therapeutic systems that utilize therapist-as-consultant relational paradigms are particularly effective at this point.

therapy approaching the internal phase

As self-esteem improves and the default regression abates the client's level of motivation begins to peak. The organic emergence of difficulties associated with more traditionally defined psychopathology, an important phenomenon foreshadowed in Chapter 6, occurs for two reasons. First, the aspects of these difficulties that are a function of low self-esteem and inadequate motivation have abated. For example, the client may now feel basically good about him or herself, but still experience bouts of depression or chronic low-level dysthymia. Prior to the late-external phase it would have been difficult to determine how much the "dysthymia" was related to a dysfunctional relationship or unhappiness in their careers: a lack of fulfillment in various life transactions.[4] Quite often, depression and anxiety in the primitive phase is more a function of low self-esteem, inadequate motivation, and the client's default regression. Secondary dysfunctions like addictions and eating disorders emanating from depression, anxiety, and inadequate coping mechanisms may abate as a result of impingement upon internal emotional cues from the default regression process.

Second, a client with higher self-esteem will finally take more serious note of a difficulty that may have been present for some time. Prior to this point, their depressed mood may have felt congruent with their depressed *spirit*. When the client begins to feel better about their beingness, they feel themselves deserving of being problem-free in other ways. Moreover, because their object-relations skills have improved and

---

4. Some might suggest that we determine whether the client's lack of fulfillment is a more recent phenomenon, but it is usual for clients to have experienced a string of dysfunctional relationships and be generally dissatisfied in their work life.

there is less distortion in their relationship with the practitioner, the client may now be quite willing to follow more standardized treatments that require stricter adherence to be effective. Particularly effective toward the end of the external phase are treatments of choice like anti-depressant medication; systematic desensitization and behavior therapy for phobias and anxiety disorders; sex therapy for premature ejaculation and disorders of sexual desire and cognitive therapy for obsessive-compulsive disorders.

These are treatments that follow fairly standardized treatment protocols and the relevant research literature reports high rates of success among compliant populations. With some disorders, relapses and recurrence rates may be high but the client approaching the internal phase is typically quite resilient and resourceful, willing to try alternative approaches. These treatments may, of course, be utilized in the primitive phase, but relapses and side-effects tend to demoralize the already despairing client. If, for example, the client is prescribed SSRI antidepressant medication with an unwanted sexual side-effect like retarded ejaculation, the client may refuse to try another medication even if it does not have the same side-effect profile. An internal-phase client tends to be more resilient and more willing to at least temporarily accept an unpleasant side-effect.

This viewpoint is in opposition to standard treatment practices that proscribe assessment and treatment as early as possible. We suggest the therapist delay treating psychopathology until motivational issues have been addressed. Sometimes this is not possible, as when symptomatic distress is creating problems or inhibiting the development of the therapeutic relationship. In such cases, directing the client to the appropriate treatment takes precedence. However, successful treatment of the particular pathology should be viewed as *stabilizing*, and not an end in itself. For the primitive client, the treatment is associated, even synonymous, with the therapist, who becomes an expert in whatever treatment is prescribed. If the treatment "fails," the therapist, too, will be viewed as a failure.

As the client approaches the internal phase, s/he is open to a host of therapeutic suggestions and outside-of-therapy paradigms. At this point I may refer the client fearful of public speaking to seminars like Dale Carnegie or Toastmasters. I may recommend large group seminars like the Forum to clients who may benefit from having their ways of thinking and methods of perception challenged, group therapy for socially reluctant clients or drama therapy for a client who has difficulty letting go physically. I often encourage couples approaching the internal phase to participate in Imago Relationship Therapy.

By the late-external phase I am no longer worried about the client introjecting other therapeutic agents or finding rapprochement figures. The issue of "too many cooks," is not relevant here. The client is free to pick and choose whatever best fits them. They may reject or ignore aspects of the therapist and accept aspects of some other therapeutic agent. We can trust their ability to do so without engaging in triangulation or acting out negative transference. These referrals aid the client in separating from the practitioner in two ways. First, the therapist clearly conveys to the client that it's okay to seek appropriate assistance elsewhere; that there are lots of good tools out there. Second, the client will experience other therapeutic agents as potentially helpful and useful. This will tend to diminish positive transference toward the practitioner.

By the end of the external phase or the beginning of the internal phase the therapist can terminate intensive treatment. For the great majority of therapeutic situations this will transpire organically as the client recognizes that the therapy is no longer needed or redundant. The client may reach this decision independently and propose it to the therapist. They may first suggest cutting back on the number of sessions per month, and the therapist should respond positively to the client's lead in this regard.

The key determinant here is the client's relationship to the therapist. Does the client view the clinician in an *appropriately* positive manner? If there is positive transference that remains, the clinician must work to create a more realistic view of him- or herself. Dismantling the transference is greatly assisted by appropriate self-disclosure at this point.

If the client terminates treatment prior to the positive transference being dismantled, then they have failed to separate and will not enter the internal phase. This phase is marked by clients' coming to own their changes, to the point that they often cannot distinguish their ideas about growth from those of the therapist. These ideas about growth seem to the client to have been their own all along, and in the truest sense, they were.

A failure to individuate from the therapist means the client must rely on the externalized figure to continue growing. This gives rise to two major problems. First, even if the client terminates treatment they will still retain a sense of need or object-loss because of the physical absence of the therapist. Letting go of the external therapeutic agent, that is, experiencing and ultimately thriving through the fear-of- loss, comes at the end of the default regression. The introject of the therapist is swallowed in the external phase and discarded in the internal phase. It is through discarding the therapeutic introject that the client fills the remaining pockets of object-loss with positive aspects of the self. We may call the end of this process the act of self-fulfillment. The client is now interested in pleasing oneself, not the family-of-origin (as in the primitive phase) or the therapist or spouse (in the external phase).

The second problem with terminating treatment without successfully individuating from the practitioner is that the client relies on a hardened and unmovable introject. In times of PAR-regression the client will consult with an inner object that may be an exact replica of the therapist's inputs. The client may internally hear what the therapist said several years earlier in times of distress, which is undesirable, as the therapist's viewpoint *then* might not represent a good fit for the current situation. Moreover, the client may be reluctant to replace the introject of the therapist when it becomes necessary to accept the healthy viewpoint of another for fear of losing connection with the still-needed object.

If the client has individuated from the therapist, they will be consulting with an ever-fluid, always developing "therapeutic object," the self of the person. S/he will continually be asking themselves questions like "Is this right for me?," "Can I live with myself if I do this?," and "Does this represent the kind of person I am or aspire to be?" The unindividuated but terminated client would ask, "What would my therapist say about this?" The "therapist" here may be the therapist from 1988 or whenever they were in treatment. The client of today is different and the healthy introject of 1988 may no longer be appropriate.

Thus, I strongly encourage clients who have terminated treatment prior to individuation, to return in times of stress and PAR-growth. They do return, typically, and dismantling the transference can resume. Time and distance assist in the individuation process but as in an unresolved familial rupture, growth tends to be stifled. If the client wishes to terminate in the external phase and the negative transference still has not been worked-through, the therapist must strongly encourage the client to stay in treatment long enough to work through these feelings. Otherwise, s/he will leave therapy with unchecked distortions that will create intra- and interpersonal distress, particularly when confronted with situations involving power or intimacy. They are likely to continue operating in a dependent or counterdependent manner.

The working through of negative transference can be aided by analytic interpretation, experiential and Gestalt techniques, role-playing (e.g., switching therapeutic roles) and anger-releasing techniques (e.g., bataka bats). If therapist and client remain entangled in a largely negative dance, referring the client to another practitioner may be useful, particularly if the therapist's countertransference is part of the problem. Occasionally, a third person in the form of the new therapist can help the client formulate negative experiences via a healthy triangulation process. Some clients require a therapist of a particular gender to work through some experience. With particularly dependent or counterdependent clients, it is often helpful to set a specific date for termination and carefully outline its structure so that the client will not feel the need to deny the loss of the therapist. With clients who have bonded deeply with the practitioner, termination is difficult and the therapist must be sensitive to the particularities of the ending. Giving the client a gift or celebrating the end of therapy with a restaurant meal may be excellent markers and remembrances for the client.

The client may ask about contact with the practitioner after therapy ends. In this model, it may be appropriate for the therapist to attend a graduation ceremony, a wedding, or visit a newborn, particularly if the therapist has been involved in working on these aspects of the client's life. The therapist should choose *not* to attend such events if s/he determines that the client is attempting to connect with the practitioner from a regressed position, as opposed to a desire to share the event with the practitioner.

Still, the idea of "once a therapist always a therapist" remains valid. We can expect some level of regression no matter how much the individuated client has grown. The therapist must, therefore, remain clearly a "therapist" or "ex-therapist" with regard to the real life of the client. Attempts on the part of the client to befriend the practitioner must be resisted as the client may wish to return to therapy in the future, at a time of extreme stress (e.g., death of a spouse). The therapist must maintain an adequate boundary so this is possible.

In the internal phase, the client becomes his or her own expert on him or herself. The client is encouraged by the end of this phase to trust their own intuition rather than rely on the therapist's direct assistance. Nondirective relational paradigms that emphasize active listening and reflection are particularly effective in the late-external and early internal-phases. The client begins to realize that the answers they need are within themselves. However, I cannot emphasize more strongly that if Rogerian approaches are applied too early in treatment, the client will likely not discover *healthy* answers. Because of their fears-of-loss, they will cling to dysfunctional or homeostatic ways, behaviors, or programs that inhibit growth.

When a client who terminated in the internal phase returns for a session or two, the therapist should listen and reflect empathically. One exception to this rule is when the client is engaged in unhealthy operations, which is an indication that the client still has some unresolved issues and should return for a course of more directed treatment. Their foray into the internal phase was temporary and they have returned to the external phase of growth. This is not unusual if termination occurred too quickly, before certain psychological issues emerged and were resolved. This may also be due to life-cycle issues, such as the uncoupled client who returns to treatment with a new partner and new problems. Certainly, if a client returns to treatment in a default regression of some kind, i.e., a sense of hopelessness, emptiness, or despair, then repenetration is necessary. This is not difficult if the therapist can achieve this without the client's feeling ashamed of having regressed or failed in some way.

As with most stage theories, some fluidity between phases may be apparent to the reader. The common therapeutic credo "two steps forward, one step back" may be relevant here. Growth rarely occurs in a straight line. For example, the synergistic excitement of PAR-growth in the external phase may lead to transformative, albeit fragile, gains in self-esteem and self-trustingness (in the internal phase) and transcendence of the self through offering love to others and diminished self-interest (in the spiritual phase). That same client may at the breakup of a love relationship experience a brief default regression (easily penetrable by the therapist because they are truly in the external phase) before they move forward again. The therapist must read the phase-related cues and respond appropriately.

finding therapeutic others and love

As the late-external phase approaches, clients begin to sense that therapy is ending and that termination is inevitable. Loss of the practitioner for the penetrated client is a significant event. One natural consequence is that the client searches the environment for therapeutic others, people who will support the continued growth process. For single adult clients, there is often an organic urgency to find a life partner. This need is a healthy one, assuming, as we do, that it does not arise out of a default regression. The clinician should work to assist the client in finding and maintaining a love relationship through this period.

Earlier we discussed the program of three as an important conceptual guide. This work is progressive and typically includes encouraging clients to expand their social networks, join organizations where they may meet like others, place and answer personal ads, etc. Clients are usually reluctant and may benefit from the three P's of mid-or late-external work—pushing, poking, and prodding. Once the client is activated, the natural positive contingencies become self-rewarding and the client can easily continue. The therapist may help the client in analyzing and evaluating prospective partners on their appropriateness. Choices that are homeostatic and primitive are discouraged while choices that are growth oriented and reparental are encouraged. If an appropriate partner is found, the therapist may coach the client through the early phases of the relationship.

Clients whose primary manifest fear is abandonment are taught how to maintain and withstand distance from the partner. Commitment-phobic clients whose primary manifest fear is engulfment are challenged to proceed forward while processing their fears of being swallowed or taken advantage of by the partner. The practitioner must be alert to switches where the latent fear manifests itself differently as conditions, resulting from the movements of the partner, change. The client who once feared abandonment by the partner may become commitment-phobic when the partner suggests marriage. As the love relationship deepens though, the practitioner's role should become less intensive. If the therapist is too intrusive, the bond with the partner may become problematic for the client as loyalty issues come to the fore.

The lone exception here is when a primitive or early-externally phased client gets involved in a love relationship prematurely, or even perhaps against the advice of the therapist. In such a case, we should simply invite the partner to become involved in treatment and seed for mutual growth. An intensive psychotherapeutic relationship may develop with both partners. Some therapists recommend that the partner be referred to another practitioner. In our model the aims of the partners are viewed as similar, that is, continued personal development. Just as with married partners, intensive individual growth with the same therapist is possible for both.

If one partner is adverse to growth or inhibits the growth process of the other, the growth-oriented partner should be encouraged toward empowerment, even if that means moving away from the other. Such aversion may manifest itself in any number of ways, including abusive or abandoning behaviors and attitudes which justify such a fear-of-loss strategy.

Late-external phase clients who are in primary love relationships will be naturally inclined to expect, even demand, more from their partners, since their self-esteem increases so dramatically. Harmful behaviors and attitudes that were once ignored or tolerated become intolerable with this new-found sense of entitlement. Such a client will often come to sessions with this kind of material, and may therefore be quite open to the therapist's views on how to get more out of their relationship. If the partner is also invested in the growth of the relationship we tend to emphasize conjoint couples work and reduce individual work with the more "identified" or originally penetrated client, while increasing it with the partner.

But what if the spouse or lover refuses to participate in treatment for any number of reasons, or if that participation in sessions is simply perfunctory? Here, too, we institute a fear-of-loss strategy, where the therapist encourages the growth-oriented spouse to decathect their growth-averse partner (Kirschner and Kirschner, 1986; Kirschner and Kirschner, 1989; Kirschner, Kirschner and Rappaport, 1993). From a systemic perspective, the fear-of-loss strategy is designed to increase the motivation level of the noncompliant spouse. From an individual perspective and that of our model, the fear-of-loss strategy allows the growth-oriented spouse to individuate from the last of the negative introjects of the family-of-origin manifest in the contemporary family-of-creation.

For example, Ann, a married female client, recently said to me, "I spent my childhood alone with parents who were more interested in themselves and their friends and their traveling. I spent so much of my time with babysitters. I'll be damned if I'm going to have my kids grow up with a father who's more interested in going out with his buddies. I want a real husband, a real family, a real father for our kids. And if he's not interested in that, he can spend *all* his time with his friends. I feel like a single parent anyway."

Ken, a married male client, complained about his wife's long-standing lack of interest in sex. His wife, Debbie's response was largely one of inaction, marked by an unwillingness to examine the issue either for herself or within the couple. She would instead attribute their problematic sexual life to "a very low libido" or make semi-serious negative comments like "Men are pigs—they want sex all the time." After a great deal of frustration and attempts at change, Ken came to a session saying, "I've had it. We have a sexual problem and I'm the one dealing with it. I'm the only one concerned about it. I deserve to have a good sex life. You know, I was thinking the other day, in two weeks I'll be 35 years old. I don't want to be 35 coming in here saying the same things. If Debbie can't do this or doesn't want to do this, then I want to find someone who can. I'm tired of complaining, I'm tired of wanting and not having."[5]

In both cases, I encouraged the client's organic movements away from the negative introjects in the other, especially the primary one that asserts, "You are undeserving of having your needs met or being fulfilled." The practitioner should not engage in this fear-of-loss maneuver is if the client is in the primitive phase, where such statements by the client are not growthfully organic, but rather expressions of object loss and the default regression. Moreover, if the therapist suggests a fear-of-loss maneuver, the client will not even attempt to carry it through. The focus in the primitive phase should be on therapeutic penetrating while pointing out the source of the negative introjects, the family-of-origin and not the spouse.

The fear-of-loss in the aforementioned cases involved graduated decathexis from the partner. The client is encouraged to take small steps toward exiting the relationship. For example, the client may be guided to pull away from normal social activities or types of conversation that maintain the illusion that nothing is wrong. At each step, client and therapist analyze the movements for effectiveness. If the growth-adverse partner does not respond, further distancing is recommended. This may sound quite structured and manipulative but in practice, the client naturally intuits such steps because of increased

---

5. We could certainly make the case that through the process of projective identification and symptomatic functionality, Ken is covertly or unconsciously supporting Debbie's lack of interest in sex. This may be a "correct" or "useful" theoretical explanation, and we may derive a host of clinical interventions to support it ranging from insight to paradox (none of which I would be opposed to). However, the organic motivating force in individual or couple change here is Ken's sense of deservedness. Accepting projective identification and systems theory as good theoretical precepts, I am open to the possibility that when Ken gets what he wants, i.e., Debbie is more interested in sex, he may attempt to sabotage the positive gain (e.g., "It's too little too late," he might offer). Consistent with the DWF principle, I would confront Ken directly. If such sabotage occurs, it may be an indicator that the client's assertion was not a true assertion of power, but rather homeostatic in nature. It is important in this model that the clinician distinguish between the two.

self-esteem. The practitioner simply gets out of the way, or provides the necessary "go" signals as part of the PAR-process. This presumes, of course, that direct approaches with the couple have failed.

It is also necessary to keep clients from making extreme reactive movements like initiating divorce proceedings. This may happen if the practitioner does not provide adequate hope for change in the relationship by utilizing fear-of-loss dynamics. Such precipitous movements may be destructive to a marriage if the growth-oriented partner, too, becomes hopeless about change. The idea is for the growth-oriented partner to make movements in the direction of individuation, while offering the partner an opportunity to recognize the problem and show his or her willingness and motivation to change.

In both these cases, the fear-of-loss rather quickly led to the partner becoming more interested and invested in improving themselves and the relationship. This happens because the growth-averse partner experiences the spouse as being *different*, that is, empowered. This is why earlier attempts in the primitive and early-external phase to change the attitude and behavior of the growth-averse partner did not work. There were no organic consequences to not changing. Why would a spouse face the tremendous fears involved in acknowledging their problems? For Ann's husband to enact the healthier behavior of becoming a more involved husband and father meant he had to confront his own childhood issues, which included processing his relationship with a very critical and abusive father. After the successful fear-of-loss, he cried in one session admitting he was detached from the family because he was "afraid of turning into (my) father . . . I thought they'd be better off without me."

Ken's wife, Debbie, who avoided dealing with the couple's sexual problems had to face the issues of sexual abuse by an older cousin and the possibility that her parents knew of the abuse but did nothing to stop it.[6] She had to face her anger at her parents, an unacceptable emotion in a family-of-origin that prided itself on a principle of conflict-free interaction. Although I point out the technical aspects of fear-of-loss maneuvers, it is crucial to remember that this *will* occur organically. The growth-averse spouse will experience the empowerment of their growth-oriented partner, and are likely to alter their problematic or

---

6. Debbie had divulged this before when the sexual issue would heat up, but in a way that indicated she had no interest in exploring it and no motivation to examine its effects on her or the relationship.

noxious behavior as, at the very least, an accommodation of the other's new expectations or requirements.

Sometimes, however, the more growth-oriented spouse comes to the brink, deciding whether to leave the growth-averse spouse. Sometimes these clients cite financial and child-rearing considerations. The role of the therapist here is to provide an opportunity for the client to confront abandonment issues by challenging the veracity of their reasoning, which often consists of reasonably constructed but less than valid excuses by a frightened client.

Increased self-esteem is a highly potent and resilient natural element. The client who has recovered self-esteem will choose to cope with these financial and child-rearing difficulties because of the motivation to find a better solution. The client who chooses *not* to individuate from a partner enacting negative introjects is lacking in adequate self-esteem, and such a choice is a barrier to future growth. The client may attempt to convince the therapist (and themselves) that the choice is made for them (e.g., "I *can't* leave because all our money is tied up in his business and the house"). It is necessary in these cases to help the client see that, no matter what circumstances exist, there is *always* a choice to be made.

If the client does make a choice to remain in an unsatisfying relationship or to "make the best of a bad situation," that is a choice they should be honest about making. Therapeutic emphasis on this movement as a *choice* concentrates the client's painful awareness and may lead to a reinitiation of leaving the spouse. But it is also important to remember that engaging this fear-of-loss, whether successful or not in outcome, will lead to increased self-esteem. In a morphogenic feedback loop, increased self-esteem leads to increased empowerment measures, and these measures lead to increased self-esteem, and so on. Again, the only time such maneuvers do not lead to increased self-esteem is the pseudo-fear-of-loss situation of the primitive phase. People may act as if they are engaging in a fear-of-loss maneuver (e.g., "I'm leaving because he treats me like shit"), but leaving prior to attachment, the hallmark of the primitive phase, is meaningless. These persons will typically find another to enact the negative introject or perhaps its flip side, by switching roles: (e.g., "I'll treat my new lover poorly so I don't get hurt again").

If the client chooses not to proceed further with empowerment work, the practitioner should realistically discuss the ramifications of that decision and, if no other significant issues remain, begin the termination process. A short termination process (approximately two-to-four sessions) is preferable, since the therapist would be encouraging dependency for its own sake by allowing continued treatment without a strong commitment toward independence on the part of the client. Conditions for returning to treatment may also be discussed. With clients whose experience of abandonment is profound, the therapist may need to provide extra time and support throughout termination. There are occasions when the fear-of-loss of the therapist may provide the motivation to reengage in the empowerment work. Sometimes the client would rather face the intense fear of abandonment by a negatively-acting spouse than lose the growth-enhancing potential and positive projections of the therapist.

Again, this sounds more conscious and manipulative than it is in actuality. In practice, clients sense these movements by the therapist toward and away from them, and will quite naturally base their decisions to increase or decrease motivation accordingly. If the client does end treatment at this point it is with a certain degree of ambivalence. Moreover, the aspects of health that were projected onto the therapist in the external phase cannot be reclaimed, and end with the termination of therapy. While great gains may have been made, the growth process is still incomplete.

The client who successfully engages in the empowerment work will naturally move away from the therapist, since the fear of losing the therapist is lessened by the abatement of their fundamental fear of abandonment. The client may feel fondly toward the therapist and sad about, but not fearful, of leaving. In these cases, termination formats may be more flexible.

when clients present for treatment in the internal phase

Some clients, albeit a very small percentage, arrive for treatment already in the internal phase. They do not require therapeutic penetration, dependency, or reparenting as such. They may come to therapy with a psychopathological condition requiring treatment, but more likely come for a course of self-improvement, often with regard to interpersonal relationships. These clients usually signal the practitioner specifically what it is they need, unlike the diffuse complaints of clients who enter treatment in the primitive phase. Their motivation level is, and remains, high. Unlike clients who enter treatment in the external phase, they do not revert to the primitive phase after a period of time.

Clients clearly in the internal phase of motivation do not require intensive psychotherapy of any kind. In the following chapter we will explore the internal and spiritual phases of motivation as essentially post-therapy phenomena.

chapter 11

post-therapy motivation

key aspects of the internal phase of motivation

Clients in the internal phase are no longer in need of intensive treatment of any kind but may wish to avail themselves of the expertise of the practitioner or another therapeutic agent in dealing with their specific issues.

But how do we determine when a client has reached the internal phase? The following are characteristics of people in this phase of motivation:

(1) Clients in the internal phase are impervious to the opinions of others regarding them, but recognize and accept that others may think and feel differently about them than they do themselves. They are not particularly troubled if someone does not like them; the impact of others on their sense of self-esteem is minimal. We may contrast this healthy narcissism with the narcissism of the primitive phase, where the views of others are so highly influential that the person may strongly comply (dependency) or strenuously object (counterdependency).

(2) Their motivation to behave in a particular way arises from within the self, in their values and principles, and they act in ways consistent with them. This occurs largely without struggle, as if acting on their values is assumed. In the external phase, operating in a value-consistent manner is generally a struggle.

(3) These values and principles tend to be rather stable; there will be evolution and metamorphosis over time, but no drastic changes or revelations. Specific ideas and views are, on the other hand, subject to great alteration and change.

(4) These clients tend to be pragmatic as well. Ends and goals tend to be more important than the means of reaching them. In contrast, people in the primitive phase tend to be highly invested in a particular way of doing things, even when it does not help them reach a stated goal. People in the internal phase tend to be goal-oriented, having learned to appreciate the process of getting there, whatever that process may be.

(5) They have a difficult time compromising on values but an easy time compromising on methods and techniques, things that do not matter much. Primitives, on the other hand, may be unnecessarily uncompromising about even the smallest of details.

(6) There is full individuation from the family-of-origin (including, very significantly, separation from their anger and disappointment). They no longer play out old family roles and scripts or regress in the presence of their family-of-origin. Therefore, their choice to interact with their family-of-origin is freer, but primary loyalty is to the family-of-creation: spouse and children.

(7) There is a tolerance of separation from significant others, i.e., an appreciation of aloneness, as opposed to the dystonic experience of aloneness in the primitive phase and in the default regression.

(8) They tend to be unconventional in their thoughts, actions, and feelings, not as a reaction to something as in the primitive phase, but rather a true expression of the self. They may also act in conventional ways but do so only when there is a desired goal to be achieved.

(9) With regard to career and work, they tend to value freedom and independence more than anything, since compromise on values is so difficult for them. Therefore, they have a difficult time functioning in organizations that are operationally not value-based, and more specifically, consonant with *their* values.

(10) With regard to children and child-rearing, decisions are based on values and principles as opposed to cultural norms (if their values and cultural norms happen to match, so much the better), unlike the counterdependency of the primitive phase where unconventionality may be cultivated for its own sake. The children of internally motivated parents may also be offbeat, out-of-step, or have unique sensibilities.

Marriages in the internal phase are marked by:

(1) Extreme bondedness to the partner: they may even function, when necessary, as one interlocking organism. This may be considered healthy enmeshment.

(2) Mature and unfailing loyalty to the growth of the other.

(3) A lack of long-standing unresolved conflicts.

(4) Fear-of-loss is built into the infrastructure of the relationship. Neither partner has to threaten to leave the relationship to get their needs met. There is simply a mature assumption and expectation that the other will be motivated to meet one's stated needs.

(5) An assumed trust and belief in the positive intentions of the spouse.

(6) Intimacy is quickly and powerfully achieved. Partners do not require great quantities of time together to feel intimate.

(7) There exists a strong, positive romantic and sexual energy between spouses.

(8) There exists a strong collaborative win-win mind-set established between partners.

(9) There exists sharing and teamwork in the rearing of children, a result of strongly congruent superimposing values.

(10) There is consistent mirroring of the positive qualities of one to the other, both overtly and covertly. Negative qualities and events are seen as minor aberrations and are not emphasized.

key aspects of the spiritual phase of motivation

The spiritual phase involves further expansion of the internal phase, but with an important twist. The internally-phased person may individuate from the self. What does this mean? The self is an organism that functions on the basis of need, primarily the need for fulfillment. The internally-phased person continues to search for fulfillment. While this fulfillment is value-based, that is, "I am fulfilled to the extent that I follow my principles," there still remains a kind of involvement with self that ultimately becomes stifling to growth. Healthy narcissism is, after all, *still* narcissism, albeit a more evolved form.

In the spiritual phase, one individuates from self-involvement and self-interest. There is a freeing of the self that emerges from an existential awareness that one is small and insignificant in a grander scheme of things, and that there is something bigger or greater than the self. The significance of what this something is, is irrelevant; there is awareness that there are forces greater than the self. Moreover, with this acute awareness of life and death the person is no longer preoccupied with psychological survival. Narcissism of all kinds abate and the person is at peace with their smallness and insignificance of the self. There arises a possibility of giving oneself to children, a larger cause, or the betterment of the world, in general. This stands in stark contrast to the self- and other-destructiveness of the primitive phase. I hasten to point out though that the culture is replete with pseudospiritual people who are truly primitives in disguise, yet acting as if they are spiritual, or according to a script of what is spiritual. This is not what I am referring to here.

The model I propose may be outlined as follows:
Stage 1 Be loved by others
Stage 2 Love self
Stage 3 Love significant others
Stage 4 Love (potentially all) others.

Love may be seen as an evolution, where loving significant others arises out of love of self and concomitant identification with others. Further, one may, in the spiritual phase, identify with many (theoretically, all) others and hence, love (all) others. In the primitive phase, shame, self-consciousness, and narcissism predominate because the self is experienced as inordinately huge, which is a defense, of course, against the perceived and true reality of one's smallness. In the spiritual phase, this reality is accepted, and ultimately embraced. In the primitive phase, the default regression is marked by hopelessness, faithlessness, pessimism, and trust-lessness. In the spiritual phase, we have bliss states marked by hopefulness, faithfulness, optimism, and trustfulness—in a word, transcendence.

How does this transcendence occur? Let's return to our under-standing of the default regression. In the default regression, there is a breakdown in the organic PAR-rapprochement process. Object-loss is experienced because the progressive expectation outweighs what is truly possible for that particular child. In the external phase, the therapist and therapeutic others fill the object-loss and the healthy PAR-process is restored. In the internal phase, the PAR-process is internalized, so that the self of the person becomes one's own rapprochement figure. The outcome is self-fulfillment, the psychological opposite of object-loss or the default regression. In this state of self-fulfillment the PAR-process is optimized. Regressions are minimized, energy-consuming abreaction becomes unnecessary, and progressive movements become easier.

In this state of self-fulfillment, the person is not inappropriately demanding nor dependent upon others. Rather s/he is self-directed and self-driven. If one no longer needs to search for fulfillment, there is an organic tendency, even a need, to fulfill others. We may call this need, desire, or *motivation* to give to others, love.

To return to our model of psychological evolution, we may then join stages 1 and 4:

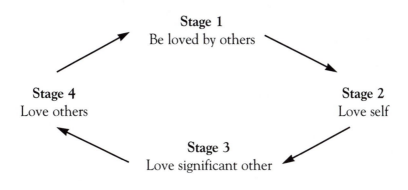

The persons who reach stage 4 are fulfilled in such a way that they love and help others in stage 1. This is the basic nature of the therapeutic enterprise.

With regard to personal growth and psychological development, our culture is in a process of evolution. With each succeeding generation our parenting becomes increasingly better. But evolution is rarely straightforward and there are many negative trends, such as our high divorce rates and the preponderance of single-parent families.

We must never forget, though, that child abuse, whether physical, sexual, or emotional, was until a short time ago more the accepted norm than the aberration it is today. Pedagogic practices that emphasized shame and suppression of emotional experiences are being replaced by more child-focused and child-sensitive approaches. Romantic idealization of the past and the underestimating of the difficulties inherent in our rapidly changing economic and social climate aside, we continue to evolve to a better place.

While the incidence of child abuse and just about every known psychological disorder is higher than ever before, this is so because only now do we live in a culture that suppresses the truth about the human experience so much less. Only now do we allow for the emergence of personal problems and issues as a basis for our construction of the self. Still, we have a long way to go from the perspective of personal growth and good mental health.

Psychotherapy is also a recent invention. At its best, psychotherapy represents a personal, familial, and ultimately, cultural revolution. As in all revolutions, the existing social order is upended by change, sometimes radical change. Order may resume only when power has changed hands.

For each client, psychotherapy is a personal revolution, a rejection of old ways from the past and the embrace of something new and different. As in any revolution, some opt to go forward and others do not. This is a decision, or more accurately, a series of decisions, that only the client can make. The model presented here is a guide for helping each client advance their own personal revolution, one map among others. We need more such maps.

Psychotherapy is in its infancy. Our knowledge base, our understanding of why people do what they do, and our ability to integrate seemingly competing paradigms is disturbingly inadequate. Succeeding generations of therapists will have the benefit of our ignorance and mistakes.

If this model proves a useful guide for you in assisting your client's personal revolution, I am grateful. If not, use your wisdom to create a better one.

references

Abroms, G. M. (1978). The place of values in psychotherapy. *Journal of Marriage and Family Counseling, 42*, 3–17.

Addis, E., Truax, P., and Jacobson, N.S. (1995). Why do people think they are depressed?: The reasons for depression questionnaire. *Psychotherapy 32*(3), 476–483.

Allen, D. M. (1991). *Deciphering motivation in psychotherapy*. New York: Plenum.

Anderson, C. M. and Stewart, S. (1983). *Mastering resistance*. New York: Guilford.

Andrews, G. and Harvey, R. (1981). Does psychotherapy benefit neurotic patients? A re-analysis of the Smith, Glass, and Miller data. *Archives of General Psychiatry, 38*, 1203–1508.

Antonuccio, D. (1995). Psychotherapy for depression: No stronger medicine. *American Psychologist, 50*(6), 450–452.

Aponte, H. J. (1986). The negotiation of values in therapy. *Family Process, 24*, 323–337.

Arkowitz, H. (1993). Introduction to the special issue, What can the field of psychopathology offer psychotherapy integration. *Journal of Psychotherapy Integration, 3*(4), 295–296.

Arnkoff, D. B. (1995). Theoretical orientation and psychotherapy integration: Comment on Poznanski and McLennan (1995). *Journal of Counseling Psychology, 42*(4), 423–425.

Ascher, M. L. (1989). *Therapeutic paradox*. New York: Guilford.

Baekeland, F. and Lundwall, L. (1975). Dropping out of treatment: A critical review. *Psychological Bulletin, 82*, 738–783.

Balint, M. (1968). *The basic fault: Therapeutic aspects of regression*. London: Tavistock.

Barlow, D. M. (1993). *Clinical handbook of psychological disorders* (2nd ed.). New York: Guilford.

Barlow, D. M. and Waddell, M. T. (1985). Agoraphobia. In D. M. Barlow (ed.), *Clinical handbook of psychological disorders: A step-by-step treatment manual* (pp. 1–68). New York: Guilford.

Basic Behavioral Science Task Force of the National Advisory Mental Health Council (1996). Basic behavioral science research for mental health: Family processes and social networks. *American Psychologist, 51*(6), 622–63.

Beck, W. G., Lambert, J., Gamachei, M., Lake, E. A., Fraps, C. L., McReynolds, W. T., Reaven, N., Heisler, G. H., and Dunn, J. (1987). Situational factors and behavioral self-predictors in the identification of clients at high risk to drop out of psychotherapy. *Journal of Clinical Psychology, 43*, 511–520.

Beckman, L. J. (1980) An attributional analysis of Alcoholics Anonymous. *Journal of Studies on Alcohol, 41*, 714–726.

Bellack, A. S. and Henson, M. (1993). Clinical behavior therapy with adults. *Handbook of behavior therapy in the psychiatric setting.* New York: Plenum.

Benjamin, L. S. (1993). Every psychopathology as a gift of love. *Psychotherapy Research, 3* (1), 1–24.

Beutler, L. E. (1979). Values, beliefs, religions, and the persuasive influence of psychotherapy. *Psychotherapy, 16,* 432-440.

Beutler, L. E. (1986). Systematic eclectic psychotherapy: A systematic approach. In J. C. Norcross (Ed.), *Handbook of eclectic psychotherapy.* (pp. 94–131). New York: Brunner/Mazel.

Beutler, L. E. (1989). Differential treatment selection: The role of diagnosis in psychotherapy. *Psychotherapy, 26,* 271–281.

Beutler, L. E. and Clarkson, J. F. (1990). *Systematic treatment selection: Toward targeted therapeutic interventions.* New York: Brunner/Mazel.

Beutler, L. E. and Consoli, A. J. (1993). Systematic eclectic psychotherapy. In J. C. Norcross and M. R. Goldfried (Eds.), *Handbook of Psychotherapy Integration.* New York: Basic Books.

Binder, J. L. (1993). Observations on the training of therapists in time-limited dynamic psychotherapy. *Psychotherapy, 30*(4), 592–598.

Blatt, S. J. and Felsen, I. (1993). Different kinds of folks may need different kinds of strokes: The effect of patients' characteristics on therapeutic process and outcome. *Psychotherapy Research, 3*(4), 245–259.

Boszormenyi-Nagy, I. and Spark, G. M. (1973). *Invisible loyalties: Reciprocity in international family therapy.* New York: Harper & Row.

Bowen, M. (1978). *Family therapy in clinical practice.* New York: Jason Aronson.

Bradshaw, J. (1989). *Healing the shame that binds you.* Deerfield Beach: Health Communications.

Bray, J. H. and Heatherington, M. E. (1993). Families in transition: Introduction and overview. *Journal of Family Psychology, 7*(1), 3–8.

Buckley, P., Karasu, T. B., Charles, E., and Stein, S. P. (1979). Theory and practice in psychotherapy: Some contradictions in expressed belief and reported practice. *Journal of Nervous and Mental Disease, 167*(4), 218–223.

Bugental, J. (1988). What is failure in psychotherapy? *Psychotherapy, 25,*(4), 532–535.

Buss, D. M. (1995). Evolutionary psychology: A new paradigm for psychological science. *Psychology Inquiry, 6,* 1–30.

Cecchin, G. (1987). Hypothesizing, circularity and neutrality revisited: An invitation to curiosity. *Family Process, 26*(4), 405–413.

Chathman, P. M. (1996). *Treatment of the borderline personality.* Northvale, N.J.: Jason Aronson.

Cherry, E. F. and Gold, S. W. (1989). The therapeutic frame revisited: A contemporary perspective. *Psychotherapy, 26*(2), 162–168.

Clickauf-Hughes, C. and Chance, S.E. (1995). Answering clients' questions. *Psychotherapy, 32*(3),

Clickauf-Hughes, C. and Mehlman, E. (1995). Narcisstic issues in therapists: Diagnostic and treatment consderations. *Psychotherapy, 32*(2), 213–221.

Coen, S. T. (1996). Love between therapist and patient: A review. *American Journal of Psychotherapy, 50*(1), 14–28.

Colapinto, J. (1984). On model integration and model integrity. *Journal of Strategic and Systemic Therapies, 3,* 31–36.

Cushman, P. (1989). Iron fists/velvet gloves: A study of a mass marathon training program. *Psychotherapy, 26*(1), 23–28.

Danisch, S. J. and Smyer, M. A. (1981). Unintended consequences of requiring a license to help. *American Psychologist, 36*(1), 13–21.

Dewald, P. A. (1992). The "rule" and role of abstinence in pychoanalysis. In A. Sugarman, R. Nemiroff, and D. Greeson (Eds.), *The technique and practice of psychoanalysis: Vol. II: A memorial volume to Ralph R. Greeson.* Madison, Ct: International University Press.

Dicks, H. V. (1967). *Marital tensions.* New York: Basic Books.

Dunn, R. L. and Schwelsel, A. I. (1995). Meta-analytic review of marital therapy outcome research. *Journal of Family Psychology, 9*(1), 58–68.

English, H. B. and English, A. V. (1958). *A comprehensive dictionary of psychological and psychoanalytical terms.* New York: Longmans, Green and Co.

Eysenck, H. J. (1952). The effects of psychotherapy: An evaluation. *Journal of Consulting Psychology, 16,* 319–324.

Fairbairn, W. R. D. (1952). *An object relations theory of the personality.* New York: Basic Books.

Fenster, A., Rachman A., and Wiedemann, C.F. (1990). The investigation of a psychoanalytic pioneer: Empirical data on the clinical work of Sandor Ferenczi, *Psychotherapy, 27*(4), 547–552.

Ferenczi, S. (1921). Further development of the active therapy in psychoanalysis. In *Final contributions.* New York: Basic Books. Reprinted 1955.

Ferenczi, S. (1928). The elasticity of psychoanalytic technique. In *Final contributions.* New York: Basic Books. Reprinted 1955.

Ferenczi, S. (1931). Child analysis in the analysis of adults. In *Final contributions.* New York: Basic Books. Reprinted 1955.

Fiedler, F.A. (1950). A comparison of therapeutic relationships in psychoanalytic, non-directive, and Adlerian therapy. *Journal of Consulting Psychology, 14,* 436–455.

Fischer, J. (1995). Uniformity myths in eclectic and integrative psychotherapy. *Journal of Psychotherapy Integration, 5*(1), 41–56.

Framo, J. L. (1970). Symptoms from a family transactional viewpoint. In N. W. Ackerman (Ed.). *Family therapy in transition* (pp. 125–171). Boston: Little, Brown and Co.

Framo, J. L. (1976). Family of origin as a therapeutic resource for adults in marital and family therapy: You can and should go home again! *Family Process, 15,* 193–210.

Frank, J. (1971). Therapeutic factors in psychotherapy. *American Journal of Psychotherapy, 25,* 350–361.

Frank, J. D. (1973). *Persuasion and healing.* New York: Schocken Books.

Frank, J. D. (1982). Therapeutic components shared by all psychotherapies. In J. H. Harvey and M. M. Parks (Eds.). *The Master Lecture Series, Vol 1: Psychotherapy research and behavior change* (pp. 73–122). Washington, D.C.: American Psychological Association.

Frank, J. D. and Frank, J. B. (1991). *Persuasion and healing* (3rd ed.). Baltimore: Johns Hopkins University Press.

Freedheim, D. K. (1992). *History of psychotherapy: A century of change.* Washington, D.C.: American Psychological Association.

Freud, S. (1914). *Remembering, repeating, and working through.* Standard Edition Vol. XII.

Fromm-Reichman, R. (1950). *Principles of intensive psychotherapy.* Chicago: University of Chicago Press.

Garfield, S. L. (1992a). The outcome problem in psychotherapy: Rebuttal. In W. Dryden and C. Feltham (Eds.), *Psychotherapy and its discontents.* Buckingham, England: Open University Press.

Garfield, S. L. (1992b). Eclectic psychotherapy: A common factors approach. In J. C. Norcross and M. R. Goldfried (Eds.), *Handbook of psychotherapy integration.* (pp. 169–201). New York: Basic Books.

Gelso, C.J. and Carter, J.A. (1985). The relationship in counseling and psychotherapy: Components, consequences, and theoretical antecedents. *The Counseling Psychologist, 2,* 155–243.

Glad, D. D. (1959). *Operational values in psychotherapy.* New York: Oxford University Press.

Glasser, W. (1965). *Reality therapy.* New York: Harper and Row.

Goldfried, M. R. (1995). Toward a common language for case formulation. *Journal of Psychotherapy Integration, 1*(1), 43–54.

Goldstein, W.N. (1995). The borderline patient: Update on the diagnosis, theory, and treatment from a psychodynamic perspective. *American Journal of Psychotherapy, 49*(3), 317–337.

Greben, S. E. and Lesser, S. R. (1983) The question of neutrality in psychotherapy. *American Journal of Psychotherapy, 40,* 623–630.

Greeson, R. J. (1967). *The technique and practice of psychoanalysis* (Vol. I). Madison, CT: International University Press.

Guntrip, H. (1968). *Schizoid phenomena, object relations and the self*. New York: International Universities Press.

Gurman, A. S., Kniskern, D. P., and Pinsoff, W. M. (1986). Research on the process and outcome of marital and family therapy. In S. L. Garfield and A. E. Bergin (Eds.), *Handbook of psychotherapy and behavior changes*. 3rd ed, (pp. 565–624). New York: Wiley.

Hanna, F. J. and Ottens, A. J. (1995). The role of wisdom in psychotherapy. *Journal of Psychotherapy Integration, 5*(3), 195–220.

Hanna, F. J. and Puhakka, J. (1991). When psychotherapy works: Pinpointing elements of change. *Psychotherapy, 28*(4), 552–562.

Heard, H. L. and Linehan, M. M. (1994). Dialectical behavior therapy: An integrative approach to the treatment of borderline personality disorder. *Journal of Psychotherapy Integration, 4*(1), 55–82.

Held, B. S. (1995). *Back to reality: A critique of postmodern theroy in psychotherapy*. New York: W. W. Norton.

Helzer, J. E., Robins, L. N., Taylor, J. R., Carey, K., Miller, R. M., Combs-Orme, T., and Farmer, A. (1985). The extent of long-term moderate drinking among alcoholics discharged from medical and psychiatric treatment facilities. *New England Journal of Medicine, 312*, 1678–1682.

Hendrix, H. (1990). *Getting the love you want: A guide for couples*. New York: Basic Books.

Hillman, J. and Ventura, M. (1992). *We've had 100 years of psychotherapy and the world's getting worse*. San Francisco: Harper and Row.

Hoffman, L. (1981). *Foundations of family therapy*. New York: Basic Books.

Horvath, A. T. (1993). Enhancing motivation for treatment of addictive behavior: Guidelines for the psychotherapist. *Psychotherapy, 30*(3), 473–480.

Humphreys, K. (1993). Psychotherapy and the 12-step approach to substance abuse: The limits of integration. *Psychotherapy, 30*(2), 207–213.

Hurvitz, N. (1967). Marital problems following psychotherapy with one spouse. *Journal of Consulting Psychology, 31*, 38–47.

Hynan, M. (1981). On the advantages of assuming that the techniques of psychotherapy are ineffective. *Psychotherapy, 18*, 11–13.

Institute of Medicine. (1990). *Broadening the base of treatment for alcohol problems*. Washington, D.C.: National Academy Press.

Jones, E. E. (1996). Introduction to the special section on attachment and psychopathology: Part I. *Journal of Consulting and Clinical Psychology, 64*(1), 5-7.

Kaplan, H. S. (1979). *Disorders of sexual desire and other new concepts and techniques in sex therapy*. New York: Brunner/Mazel.

Kaplan, H.S. (1992). *How to overcome premature ejaculation*. New York: Brunner/Mazel.

Karasu, T. B. (1986). The specificity versus nonspecificity dilemma: Toward identifying therapeutic change agents. *American Journal of Psychiatry, 143*(6), 687–695.

Kazdin, A. E., Mazurick, J. L., and Siegel, T. C. (1994). Treatment outcome among children with externalizing disorder who terminate prematurely versus those who complete psychotherapy. *Journal of the American Academy of Child and Adolescent, 33*, 549–557.

Kazdin, A. E., Stolar, M. J., and Marciano, P. L. (1995). Risk factors for dropping out of treatment among white and black families. *Journal of Family Psychology, 9*(4), 402–417.

Kertany, L. and Reviere, J. (1993). The use of touch in psychotherapy: Theoretical and ethical considerations. *Psychotherapy, 30*(1), 32–40.

Kessel, P. and McBrearty, J. F. (1967). Values and psychotherapy: A review of the literature. *Perceptual and Motor Skills, 25*, 669–690.

Kiesler, D. J. (1966). Some myths of psychotherapy research and the search for a paradigm. *Psychological Bulletin, 65*, 110–136.

Kirschner, D. A. and Kirschner, S. (1986). *Comprehensive family therapy: An integration of systemic and psychoanalytic treatment models*. New York: Brunner/Mazel.

Kirschner, S. and Kirschner, D. A. (1989). Love and other difficulties: Goals in couples therapy. *Family Therapy Today, 4*(3), 1–4.

Kirschner, S. A. and Kirschner, D. A. (1990a). Comprehensive family therapy: Integrating individual, marital, and family therapy. In F. W. Kaslow (Ed.). Voices in Family Psychology (Vol. 2). Newbury Pk., Calif.: Sage

Kirschner, D. A. and Kirschner, S. A. (1990b). Couples therapy: A new look. *Journal of Couples Therapy, 1*(1), 91–100.

Kirschner, S. and Kirschner, D. A. (in press). *Comprehensive therapy of couples and families*. New York: Wiley.

Kirschner, S., Kirschner, D. A., and Rappaport, R. L. (1993). *Working with adult incest survivors: The healing journey*. New York: Brunner/Mazel.

Koss, M. P. (1979). Length of psychotherapy for clients in private practice. *Journal of Consulting and Clinical Psychology, 47*, 210–212.

Kramer, P. D. (1993). *Listening to prozac*. New York: Penguin.

Lambert, M. J. (1992). Psychotherapy research: Implications for integrative and eclectic therapists. In J. C. Norcross and M. R. Goldfried (Eds.), *Handbook of Psychotherapy Integration*. New York: Basic Books.

Lambert, M. J., Shapiro, D. A., and Bergin, A. E. (1986). The effectiveness of psychotherapy. In S. L. Garfield and A. E. Bergin (Eds.), *Handbook of psychotherapy and behavior change*. (pp. 157–211). New York: Wiley.

Langs, R. (1981). *Resistances and interventions*. New York: Jason Aronson.

Lazarus, A. A. (1989). *The practice of multimodal therapy*. Baltimore: Johns Hopkins University Press.

Lazarus, A. A. (1993). Tailoring the therapeutic relationship or being an authentic chameleon. *Psychotherapy, 30*, 404–407.

Lazarus, A. A. (1995). Different types of eclecticism and integration: Let's be aware of the dangers. *Journal of Psychotherapy Integration, 5*(1), 27–39.

Lazarus, A. A., Beutler, L. E., and Norcross, J. E. (1992). The future of technical eclecticism. *Psychotherapy, 29*, 11–20.

Lebow, J. L. (1984). On the value of integrating approaches to family therapy. *Journal of Marriage and Family Therapy, 10*(2), 127–138.

Lee, C. M., Picard, M., and Blain, M. D. (1994). A methodological and substantive review of intervention outcome and studies for families undergoing divorce. *Journal of Family Psychology, 8*(1), 3–15.

Liddle, M. A., Dakof, G. A., Parker, K. B., Diamond, G. S., Barrett, K., and Garcia, R. G. (1995). (Submitted for publication) Multidimensional family therapy for treating adolescent substance abuse: A controlled clinical trial.

Linehan, M. M. (1993). *Cognitive-behavioral treatment of borderline personality disorder*. New York: Guilford.

Lipsey, M. W. and Wilson, D.B. (1993). The efficacy of psychological, educational, and behavioral treatment: Confirmation from meta-analysis. *American Psychologist, 48*(12), 1181–1209.

London, P. (1964). *The modes and morals of psychotherapy*. New York: Holt, Rinehart, and Winston.

London, P. (1986). Major issues in psychotherapy integration. *International Journal of Eclectic Psychotherapy, 5*, 211–216.

Luborsky, L. (1995). The same and divergent view of "Fashion and preoccupations in psychotherapy research." *Psychotherapy Research, 5*(2). 118–120.

Luborksy, L., Singer, B., and Luborsky, L. (1975). Comparative studies of psychotherapy: Is it true that "everyone has won and all must have prizes?" *Archives of General Psychiatry, 32*, 995–1008.

Mahler, M. (1980). On the first three subphases of the separation-individuation process. *International Journal of Psycho-Analysis, 53*, 333–338.

Main, M.(1996). Introduction to the special section on attachment and psychopathology: Part II, *Journal of Consulting and Clinical Psychology, 64*(2), 237–243.

Masson, J. M. (1994). *Against therapy*. Monroe, Me.: Common Courage Press.

Masterson, J. F. (1988). *Search for the real self: Unmasking the personality disorders of our age*. New York: The Free Press.

McNeilly, C. L. and Howard, K. I. (1991). The effects of psychotherapy: A re-evaluation based on dosage. *Psychotherapy Research, 1*, 74–78.

Miller, W.R. (1985). Motivation for treatment: A review with special emphasis on alcoholism. *Psychological Bulletin, 98*(1), 84–107.

Minuchin, S. and Fishman, M. C. (1981). *Family therapy techniques*. Cambridge, MA: Harvard University Press.

Neimeyer, R. A. (1993). Constructivism and the problem of psychotherapy integration. *Journal of Psychotherapy Integration*, 3(2), 133–157.

Norcross, J. C. (1993). Tailoring relationship stances to client needs: An introduction. *Psychotherapy*, 30(3), 402–403.

Norcross, J. C. (1995). Dispelling the dodo bird verdict and the exclusivity myth in psychotherapy. *Psychotherapy*, 32(3), 500–504.

Norcross, J. C., Alford, B. A., and DeMichele, J. T. (1992). The future of psychotherapy: Delphi data and counseling observations. *Psychotherapy*, 29, 150–158.

Omer, H. (1990). Enhancing the impact of therapeutic interventions. *American Journal of Psychotherapy*, 44, 218–231.

Omer, H. (1992). Theoretical, empirical, and clinical foundations of the concept of "therapeutic impact", *Journal of Psychotherapy Integration*, 2(3), 193–206.

Omer, H. and Alon, N. (1989). Principles of psychotherapeutic strategy. *Psychotherapy*, 26(3), 282–289.

Omer, H. and London, P. (1988). Metamorphosis in psychotherapy: End of the systems era. *Psychotherapy*, 25, 171–180.

Patterson, C.H. (1989).Values in counseling and psychotherapy. *Counseling and Values*, 33(3), 164–176.

Patterson, C. H. and Hidore, S. C. (1996). *Psychotherapy: A unitary theory*. Northvale, NJ: Jason Aronson.

Paul, G. L. (1967). Strategy of outcome research in psychotherapy. *Journal of Consulting Psychology*, 31, 109–118.

Peck, M. S. (1978). *The road less traveled*. New York: Simon and Schuster.

Phillips, B. N. (1982). Regulation and control in psychology: Implications for certification and licensure. *American Psychologist*, 37(8), 919–926.

Phillips, E. (1988). Length of psychotherapy and outcome: Observations stimulated by Howard, Kopta, Krause, and Orlinsky. *American Psychologist*, 43, 669–670.

Piercy, F. P., and Sprenkle, D. U. (1990). Marriage and family therapy: A decade review. *Journal of Marriage and the Family*, 52, 1116-1126.

Pollack, J., Mordecai, E., and Gumpert, P. (1992). Discontinuation from long-term individual psychodynamic theory. *Psychotherapy Research*, 2(3), 224–233.

Poznanski, J. J. and McLennan, J. (1995). Afterthoughts on counselor theoretical orientation: Reply to Arnkoff (1995) and Gelso (1995). *Journal of Counseling Psychology*, 42(4), 428–430.

Prochaska, J. O. and DiClemente, C. C. (1982). Toward a comprehensive model of change. In W. R. Miller and N. Heather (Eds.). *Treating addictive behaviors: Process of change*. New York: Plenum.

Prochaska, J. O., Diclemente, C. C., and Norcross, J. D. (1992). In search of how people change: Applications to addictive behaviors. *American Psychologist, 47*(9), 1102–1114.

Rappaport, R. L. (1988). Psychotherapist postures: Parents, directors, and facilitators. (Doctoral dissertation, University of Pennsylvania, 1987). *Dissertation Abstracts International, 49*(2), 549–B.

Rappaport, R. L. (1991a). Where system meets psyche in marital therapy. Keynote address, American Association of Pastoral Counselors, Regional Conference, Wintergreen, VA.

Rappaport, R. L. (1991b). When eclecticism is the integration of therapeutic postures, not theories. *Journal of Integrative and Eclectic Psychotherapy, 10*, 164–172.

Rappaport, R. L. (1993a). Beyond very private practice: How demonstration can close the theory-practice gap. Paper presented at the Society for Exploration of Psychotherapy Integration Meeting, New York City.

Rappaport, R. L. (1993b). Therapy with HIV-positive gay men. Paper presented at the American Psychological Association Meeting, Toronto, Canada.

Rappaport, R. L. (1994). Culture, values and therapy. *The Family Psychologist, 10*, 127–138.

Rappaport, R. L. (1995a). Realizing the promise of family psychology. *The family Psychologist, 11*, (3), 5.

Rappaport, R. L. (1995b). Innovations in relational eclecticism. Paper presented at the Society for the Exploration of Psychotherapy Meeting, Bethesda, MD.

Rappaport, R. L. and Delpino, J. (1990). Teaching integrative psychotherapy. Workshop presented at Society for the Exploration of Psychotherapy Integration Meeting, Philadelphia, PA.

Rappaport, R. L. and Kirschner, D.A. (1991). Toward relational eclecticism. Paper presented at the Society for the Exploration of Psychotherapy Integration Meeting, London, England.

Reik, T. (1948). *Listening With the Third Ear.* New York: Ferrar, Straus and Co.

Riebel, L. (1990). Doctor, teacher, and Indian chief: Metaphor and the search for inherent identity. *Journal of Integrative and Eclectic Psychotherapy, 9*(2), 119–135.

Roazen, P. (1995). *How Freud worked: First-hand accounts of patients.* Northvale, NJ: Jason Aronson.

Robins, C. J. (1993). Implications of research in the psychopathology of depression for psychotherapy integration. *Journal of Psychotherapy Integration, 3*(4), 313–330.

Rogers, C. R. (1951). *Client-centered therapy.* Boston: Houghton Mifflin.

Rogers, C. R. (1957). The necessary and sufficient conditions of therapeutic personality change. *Journal of Consulting Psychology, 21*, 95–103.

Rosen, J. N. (1975). *Direct analysis.* Doylestown PA: The Doylestown Foundation.

Rosenbaum, R. (1994). Single-session therapies: Intrinsic integration. *Journal of Psychotherapy Integration, 4*(3), 229–252.

Ryle, A. (1995). Fashions and preoccupations in psychotherapy research. *Psychotherapy Research, 5*(2), 113–117.

Samler, T. (1960). Change in values: A goal in counseling. *Journal of Counseling Psychology, 7*(1), 32–39.

Sartorius, N., deGirolamo, G., Andrews G., German, G.A., and Eisenberg L. (1993). Treatment of mental disorders: A review of effectiveness. Washington, DC: American Psychiatric Press

Saunders, S. M. (1993). Applicant's experience in the process of seeking therapy. *Psychotherapy, 30*(4), 554-564.

Scarf, M. (1995). *Intimate worlds.* New York: Random House.

Scaturo, D.J. (1994). Integrative psychotherapy for panic disorder and agoraphobia in clinical practice. *Journal of Psychotherapy Integration, 4*(3), 253–272.

Schacht, T. E. (1985). DSM-III and the politics of truth. *American Psychologist, 40*(5), 513–521.

Schmidt, F. L. (1992). What do the data really mean?: Research findings, metaanalysis, and cumulative knowledge in psychology. *American Psychologist, 47*(10), 1173–1181.

Schofield, W. (1964). *Psychotherapy: The purchase of friendship.* Englewood Cliffs, N.J.: Prentice-Hall.

Schwartz, B. (1990). The creation and destruction of value. *American Psychologist. 45*(1), 7–15.

Schwartz, R. (1993). Managing closeness in psychotherapy. *Psychotherapy, 30*(4), 601–607.

Seligman, M. (1995). The effectiveness of psychotherapy: The Consumer Reports survey. *American Psychologist, 50*(12), 965–974.

Seligman, M. (1996). Good news for psychotherapy: The Consumer-Reports survey. *The Independent Practitioner, 16*(1), 17–22.

Seltzer, L. F. (1986). *Paradoxical strategies in psychotherapy: A comprehensive overview and guidebook.* New York: Wiley.

Sergant, J., Liebman, R., and Silver, M. (1985). Family therapy for anorexia nervosa. In Gardner, D. M. and Garfinkel, P. E. (Eds.), *Handbook of psychotherapy for anorexia nervosa and bulimia.* (pp. 257-279). New York: Guilford.

Share, I. A. (1994). Borderline personality disorder: A 25-year retrospective and prospective. *The Psychiatric Clinics of North America, 17*(4), 7-10.

Simmerman, R. and Schwartz, K. (1986). Adult development and psychotherapy: Bridging the gap between theory and practice. *Psychotherapy, 23*(3), 405–410.

Simpson, D. D. and Joe, G. W. (1993). Motivation as a predictor of early dropout from drug abuse treatment. *Psychotherapy, 30*(2), 357–368.

Smith, M. L., Glass, G. V., and Miller, T. I. (1980). *The benefits of psychotherapy*. Baltimore: Johns Hopkins University Press.

Speed, B. (1984). How really real is real? *Family Process, 23*, 511–517.

Stein, A. (1980). Comprehensive family therapy. In R. Herink (ed.), *The psychotherapy handbook*. (pp. 204-207). New York: New American Library.

Stiles, W. B., Shapiro, D. A., and Elliot, R. (1986). Are all psychotherapists equivalent? *American Psychologist, 41*, 165–181.

Strean, M. S. (1990). *Resolving resistance in psychotherapy*. New York: Brunner Mazel.

Strean, M. S. (1996). Resistance viewed from different perspectives. *American Journal of Psychotherapy, 50*(1), 29–31.

Stricker, G. (1995). Failures in psychotherapy. *Journal of Psychotherapy Integration, 5*(2), 91–93.

Strupp, H. H. (1969). Psychoanalytic psychotherapy and research. In L. Eron and R. Callahan (eds.), *The relation of theory to practice in psychotherapy*. Chicago: Aldrine Publishing Co.

Strupp, H. H. (1978). The therapist's theoretical orientation: An overrated variable. *Psychotherapy, 15*, 314–317.

Strupp, H. H. and Hadley, S. W. (1979). Specific versus nonspecific factors in psychotherapy: A controlled study of outcome. *Archives of General Psychiatry, 36*, 1125–1136.

Strupp, H. H., Hadley, S. W., and Gomes-Schwartz, B. (1977). *Psychotherapy for better or worse: The problem of negative effects*.New York: Jason Aronson.

Sue, S., McKinney, M. L., and Allen, D. B. (1976). Predictors of the duration of therapy for clients in the community mental-health system. *Community Mental Health Journal, 12*, 365–375.

Sugarman, J. and Martin, J. (1995). The moral dimension: A conceptualization and demonstration of the moral nature of psychotherapeutic conversations. *The Counseling Psychologist, 23*(2), 325–347.

Sundland, D. M. (1977). Theoretical orientations of psychotherapists. In A. S. Gurner and A. M. Razin (Eds.), *Effective psychotherapy, A handbook of research*. Oxford: Pergammon Press.

Sundland, D. M. and Barker, E. N. (1962). The orientations of psychotherapists. *Journal of Consulting Psychology, 26*, 201–212.

Talmon, M. (1990). *Single-session therapy*. San Francisco: Josey-Bass.

Tobin, D.L. (1995). Integrative psychotherapy for bulimic patients with comorbid personality disorders. *Journal of Psychotherapy Integration, 5*(3), 245–264.

Vessey, J. T. and Howard, K. (1993). Who seeks psychotherapy? *Psychotherapy, 30*(4), 546–553.

Tjeltveit, A. C. (1986). The ethics of value conversion in psychotherapy: Appropriate and inappropriate therapist influence. *Clinical Psychology Review, 6*, 515–537.

Vogel, L. Z. (1994). Freud's early clinical work. *American Journal of Psychotherapy*, 48, 94–01.

Wachtel, P. (1977). *Psychoanalysis and behavior therapy*. New York: Basic Books.

Wachtel, P. (1982). *Resistance: Psychodynamic and behavioral approaches*. New York: Plenum.

Wachtel, P. (1991). From eclecticism to synthesis: Toward a more seamless psychotherapeutic integration. *Journal of Psychotherapy*, 1(1), 43–54.

Walsh, R. A. (1995). The study of values in psychotherapy: A critique and call for an alternative method. *Psychotherapy Research.*, 5(4), 313–326.

Watzlawick, P. Weakland, B., and Fisch, B. (1974). *Change*. New York: Norton.

Weinberg, G. (1996). *The heart of psychotherapy*. New York: St. Martin's.

Weinberger, J. (1993). Common factors in psychotherapy. In G. Stricker and J. R. Gold (Eds.), *Comprehensive handbook of psychotherapy integration*. New York: Plenum.

Weiner-Davis, M. (1992). *Divorce busters*. New York: Simon and Shuster.

Weinrach, S. G. (1990). Rogers and Gloria: The controversial film and the enduring relationship. *Psychotherapy*, 27, 282–287.

Weinrach, S. G. (1995). Rogers' encounter with Gloria: What did Rogers know and when? *Psychotherapy*, 28(3), 504–506.

Weiss, J. and Schaie, K. W. (1958). Factors in patient failure to return to clinic. *Diseases of the Nervous System*, 19, 429-430.

Weisskopf-Joleson, E. (1953). Some suggestions concerning weltansgnauung and psychotherapy. *Journal of Abnormal and Social Psychology*, 48, 601–604.

Weisskopf-Joleson, E. (1982). Values: The *enfant terrible* of psychotherapy. *Psychotherapy*, 17, 459–467.

Wierzbicki, M. and Pekarik, G. (1993). A meta-analysis of psychotherapy dropout. *Professional Psychology: Research and Practice*, 24, 190–195.

Wright, R. J. and Medlock, G. (1995). The red herring of epistemological compatibility: Toward discovering the unifying epistemology behind diverse theories of psychology. Unpublished manuscript.

Zieg, J. K. (1987). *The evolution of psychotherapy*. New York: Brunner/Mazel.

name index